Good Housekeeping

Healthy Family Recipes

TRIED, TESTED, TRUSTED ★ GOOD FOR YOU

Good Housekeeping

Healthy Family Recipes

TRIED, TESTED, TRUSTED ★ GOOD FOR YOU

Compiled by Barbara Dixon

COLLINS & BROWN

First published in the United Kingdom in 2011 by
Collins & Brown
10 Southcombe Street
London
W14 0RA

An imprint of Anova Books Company Ltd

The Good Housekeeping website is
www.allaboutyou.com/goodhousekeeping

10 9 8 7 6 5 4 3 2 1

ISBN 978-1-84340-610-5

A catalogue record for this book is available from the British Library.

Repro by Dot Gradations UK Ltd
Printed and bound by Times Offset Malaysia

This book can be ordered direct from the publisher at
www.anovabooks.com

Picture Credits:
Neil Barclay (pages 77, 80, 86, 102, 108 and 184); Steve Baxter (page
265); Martin Brigdale (pages 150, 145, 146, 161, 167, 190 ,204 and 259);
Nicki Dowey (pages 26, 27, 28, 29, 30, 31, 32, 35, 37, 41, 42, 43, 46,
48, 49, 50, 52, 53, 54, 55, 56, 57, 58, 59, 61, 62, 63, 64, 65, 69, 70, 72,
74, 78, 79, 81, 82, 83, 87, 88, 89, 93, 95, 96, 98, 99, 100, 103, 106, 107,
109, 111, 113, 114, 117, 123, 124, 125, 126, 127, 128, 129, 130, 131,
132, 134, 135, 136, 137, 138, 142, 143, 150, 152, 154, 155, 157, 158,
159, 162, 163, 165, 168, 169, 170, 172, 173, 176, 181, 183, 185, 186,
187, 188, 189, 195, 196, 197, 199, 200, 201, 202, 203, 206, 207, 209,
212, 213, 214, 215, 216, 218, 224, 229, 230, 232, 233, 234, 235, 236,
237, 240, 241, 242, 243, 247, 248, 249, 251, 252, 253, 254, 255, 256,
257, 260, 262, 263, 264, 266, 267, 269, 272, 273, 274, 275, 276, 277,
278, 279, 280, 281, 282, 283, 284 and 285); Will Heap (pages 36, 84,
116, 118, 122, 140, 144, 180, 205, 217 and 231); Craig Robertson
(pages 34, 40, 44, 47, 51, 71, 76, 85, 94, 97, 101, 115, 119, 139, 141,
147, 151, 156, 160, 164, 166, 174, 175, 177, 182, 192, 193, 194, 198,
208, 219, 220, 221, 222, 223, 225, 238, 246, 258, 261 and 268); Lucinda
Symons (pages 45, 60, 73, 75, 104, 110, 112, 153, 171 and 228)
Home Economists: Anna Burges-Lumsden, Joanna Farrow, Emma Jane
Frost, Teresa Goldfinch, Alice Hart, Lucy McKelvie, Kim Morphew, Bridget
Sargeson, Sarah Tildesley, Jennifer White and Mari Mererid Williams
Stylists: Wei Tang, Sarah Tildesley, Helen Trent and Fanny Ward

NOTES

- Both metric and imperial measures are given for the recipes.
  Follow either set of measures, not a mixture of both, as
  they are not interchangeable.
- All spoon measures are level.
  1 tsp = 5ml spoon; 1 tbsp = 15ml spoon.
- Ovens and grills must be preheated to the specified
  temperature.
- Medium eggs should be used except where otherwise
  specified.

DIETARY GUIDELINES

- Note that certain recipes contain raw or lightly cooked
  eggs. The young, elderly, pregnant women and anyone with
  immune-deficiency disease should avoid these because of
  the slight risk of salmonella.
- Note that some recipes contain alcohol. Check the
  ingredients list before serving to children.

Contents

Foreword

I know it's an old adage, but we are what we eat, and I feel fortunate that I was taught from an early age that you should feed your body with food that will make it run efficiently. It's similar to filling your car with the wrong fuel, which I imagine would allow it to run smoothly for a couple of miles, then splutter a little and eventually stop in indignation. The same is true of your body, there's only so much processed food it can take before the effects of eating badly become apparent.

With obesity and Type 2 diabetes rates still surging, it's high time that more of us learned how to eat healthily – and this doesn't just mean a diet of brown rice and worthy lentils but rather fuelling your body with food that's full of the right sort of things, rather than salt, sugar, fat and more calories than we need (although a little of these in moderation is a good thing in my books). It comes down to a simple statement: we are eating too much and not moving enough. The virtues of physical activity are undeniable – muscles are strengthened and toned, calories are burnt and appetite is regulated. What's not to like about that?

It's important to realise that healthier cooking for you and your family can be quick, easy and enjoyable. This fantastic book is filled with nutritious recipes that are triple-tested in our dedicated kitchens so they are sure to succeed (and be full of flavour!). There's also plenty of useful information to aid you in munching your way to a happier, healthier you.

So turn the page and allow yourself be inspired to rustle up healthy family meals, which are sure to become firm favourites.

Enjoy!

Meike.

Meike Beck
Cookery Editor

Basics

Eat well, stay well

'We are what we eat' – nutritionists from around the world agree that the food we eat has an important effect on our health and vitality. From the moment of conception and throughout life, diet plays a crucial role in helping us stay fit and healthy. A healthy balanced diet can protect against serious illnesses such heart disease and cancer, increase resistance to colds and other infections, boost energy levels, help combat the stresses of modern living and also improve physical and mental performance. So, eating a diet that is healthy, varied and tasty should be everyone's aim.

Choose wisely

Our body needs over forty different nutrients to function and stay healthy. Some, such as carbohydrates, proteins and fats, are required in relatively large amounts; others, such as vitamins, minerals and trace elements, are required in minute amounts, but are nonetheless essential for health. No single food or food group provides all the nutrients we need, which is why we need to eat a variety of different foods. Making sure your body gets all the nutrients it needs is easy if you focus on foods that are nutrient rich and dump those highly refined and processed foods that provide lots of saturated fat, sugar and calories but not much else.

Nutrition labelling

The five key nutrients are calories, sugar, fat, saturated fat and salt. Two sets of guidelines that claim to help us select a healthy balanced diet are currently in use. The traffic light scheme developed by the Food Standards Agency provides information on fat, saturated fat, sugar and salt and uses a red, amber or green colour coding to indicate whether a food is high, medium or low in these nutrients. The other scheme is based on Guideline Daily Amounts (GDAs) and gives an indication of how many calories, fat, salt, sugar and fibre a food contains and what it contributes to the amount of that nutrient you should eat in a day. GDAs are guidelines for an average person of a healthy weight and average level of activity, and are just that – a guide, not a target. You should try to eat no more than the GDAs for sugars, fat, saturated fat and salt. The GDA values on the front of pack labels are based on the average requirements of an adult woman.

Fruit and vegetables: Five a day

One of the easiest ways to stay healthy is to eat plenty of fruit and vegetables. We can probably all remember being told by our parents to eat our 'greens' because they were good for us, and all the major reports on healthy eating have endorsed this good advice. It's no coincidence that in Mediterranean countries, where people eat almost twice the amount of fruit and vegetables that we do in the UK, they live longer and healthier lives. Fruit and vegetables contain an arsenal of disease-fighting compounds – vitamins, minerals, fibre and phytochemicals, which is why nutrition experts believe that they are the cornerstone of a healthy diet. Eating a diet rich in fruit and vegetables can reduce the risk of a range of medical problems including heart disease, stroke, high blood pressure, certain types of cancer, cataracts and an eye condition called age-related macular degeneration, dementia and Alzheimer's disease.

Variety is key

Wherever we shop, most of us are lucky enough to have a wide range of different fruit and vegetables available to us, but do we really take advantage of the range? It's very easy to get stuck in a rut of buying the same things from one week to the next. Variety may be the spice of life, but it's also the key to a healthy diet and is particularly important when it comes to fruit and vegetables. Different coloured fruit and vegetables contain different vitamins, minerals and phytochemicals that help to keep you healthy in different ways, and so to make sure you get a good selection of all these nutrients you need to eat a variety of different produce. When you're buying fruit and vegetables don't just stick to your same old favourites – be adventurous and try something new. You'll find plenty of recipes to tempt you in this book.

Add colour to your meals

You probably already know that you should be eating at least five servings of fruit and vegetables a day, but did you know you should also be eating a rainbow? When you're planning meals, aim to fill your plate with colour – think of red, orange, yellow, green and purple fruit and vegetables and try to eat at least one serving from each of the colour bands every day.

ASSESSING NUTRIENTS

Another quick and easy way to assess if a food is high or low in a particular nutrient is to use the table below. Look at the amount of a particular nutrient per serving or per 100g (3½oz) for snacks or cooking ingredients and check the table below to find out if it's high or low.

	High	Low
Fat	more than 20g	less than 3g
Saturated fat	more than 5g	less than 1g
Sugar	more than 10g	less than 2g
Fibre	more than 3g	less than 0.5g
Sodium	more than 0.5g	less than 0.1g
Salt	more than 1.3g	less than 0.3g

GDAS

	Women	Men	Children (5–10 years)
Energy (calories)	2,000	2,500	1,800
Protein (g)	45	55	24
Carbohydrate (g)	230	300	220
Fat (g)	70	95	70
Saturated fat (g)	20	30	20
Total sugars (g)	90	120	85
Dietary fibre (g)	24	24	15
Sodium (g)	2.4	2.4	
Salt	6	6	4

Carbohydrates

Carbohydrates provide the body with the most readily accessible form of energy. Carbohydrates in the form of sugars are found in fruit, milk and sugar; starch carbohydrates are familiar in cereals, pasta, rice, potatoes, bread and pulses. In a healthy diet, starch carbohydrates supply a higher proportion of energy than fats or sugar carbohydrates.

With the recent craze for low-carbohydrate diets, you may be forgiven for thinking that carbohydrates are best avoided. In fact, this couldn't be further from the truth. Most nutritionists agree that foods in this group are an important part of a healthy balanced diet. However, not all carbs are equal. Most of the vitamins and protective components in grains are concentrated in the bran and germ layers of the grain, but when grains are refined, as for instance in the production of white flour, the bran and germ are removed and most of the fibre and some of the nutrients are stripped away. This is why it is better to choose wholegrain carbohydrates such as brown rice and wholemeal bread over refined carbohydrates. Studies have shown that diets rich in wholegrain foods can reduce the risk of heart disease, stroke, certain types of cancer and Type 2 diabetes.

THE GLYCAEMIC INDEX

During the digestive process, carbohydrates need to be broken down into glucose – the simplest form of sugar – before they can be absorbed by your body. Recent research suggests the rate at which carbohydrates are broken down can also determine their healthiness. The Glycaemic Index (GI) is a system used for ranking carbohydrates according to how quickly they are broken down. Foods with a low GI (less than 55), such as lentils, apples and pears, are absorbed more slowly and steadily and generate a slow release of sugar into the bloodstream. Foods with a high GI (more than 70), such as cornflakes, bagels and soft drinks, are broken down into sugar quickly, which results in a sudden rush of sugar into the bloodstream. While this can be useful for athletes who need to replenish blood sugar after strenuous exercise, it is not necessary for the rest of us.

Diverse benefits

Although the GI diet was originally developed to help people with diabetes achieve better control of their blood sugar, the benefits are certainly not restricted to diabetics. Studies have shown that following a low-GI diet can help increase levels of 'good' cholesterol and reduce 'bad' cholesterol in the blood, which will help to reduce the risk of heart disease. Recent studies also show that people who ate a low GI diet lost more weight than people who ate a higher GI diet. The GI is only one measurement of what makes a food healthy. Other factors, such as the vitamin content and the amount of fat a food contains, will affect its overall healthiness. Foods that have a low to medium GI and are also low in sugar and fat are the best choice.

LOW-GI SNACKS

Everyone needs to snack sometimes. Resist the temptation to reach for the biscuits or processed snacks and tuck into these healthy low-GI snacks instead.

★ **Fresh fruit, nuts and seeds** are ideal low-GI foods. Make sure you take some of each with you whenever you go out, or travel.

★ **Dried apricots and prunes** are delicious nutrient-packed low-GI snacks, and are the perfect handy snack instead of sweets.

★ **Keep a dip and crudités** in the fridge for emergency snacking. Good dips are mashed avocado (guacamole) and hummus. Mayonnaise blended with a little mustard and natural yogurt is excellent also.

★ **An avocado is a light meal in itself**, highly nutritious – a good source of EFAs (essential fatty acids) and vitamin E – and will keep hunger pangs at bay. Spoon a little extra virgin olive oil or your favourite health oil into the cavity and enjoy.

★ **A couple of squares of dark plain chocolate** (70% cocoa solids) is a permissible treat, and better than a sugary snack.

Bread

✖ White and brown processed breads in all forms have the highest GI ratings.

✔ Wholegrain, Granary, pumpernickel and seed breads, stoneground wholewheat and rye breads, sourdough breads.

Breakfast cereals

✖ Processed breakfast cereals such as Shredded Wheat, Rice Crispies, instant porridge oats, puffed grain cereals, cornflakes and those high in added sugar or honey such as crunchies and cereal bars.

✔ Porridge made with traditional rolled oats or stoneground oatmeal; sugar-free/low-sugar mueslis, All Bran.

Pasta

✖ As long as you eat smaller than normal portions and do not overcook it, pasta is generally OK. Rice noodles are medium-high GI and gluten-free pasta (which is often made from corn) is high GI.

✔ All kinds of durum wheat pasta; fresh pasta made with eggs; cellophane and glass noodles (which are made from pea and bean flours).

Rice

✖ Most varieties of white long-grain rice, including processed American long-grain, jasmine rice, and all short round varieties such as pudding, risotto and sticky glutinous rice.

✔ White and brown basmati, brown, red and wild rice.

Potatoes

✖ All potatoes: boiled, mashed, fried, instant, and so on.

✔ Boiled new potatoes (these are still high-GI, but are significantly lower than maincrop potatoes); sweet potatoes and yams.

Sugar

Though it's sensible to use as little sugar as possible, the only form of sugar that is high GI is glucose. Table sugar (sucrose) and honey are medium GI; the sugar found in fresh fruit (fructose) is low GI. You can now buy low-GI fruit sugar to replace table sugar in tea and coffee and in baking. This is expensive, but you need one-third less. When baking with fruit sugar, reduce the cooking temperature by 25°C.

Chocolate

Generally, chocolates and bars tend to have medium-GI values. Because of their added sugar and fat, however, they are still indulgence foods. Dark plain chocolate, with a minimum of 70% cocoa solids, is low GI. Milk chocolate is also low GI, but is less healthy than dark chocolate because it contains more fat and sugar.

Dried fruits

These are low to medium GI. The one exception is dates, which are very high GI and have a GI value of 100.

Fats, Fibre, Salt and Protein

FATS – THE HEALTHY AND NOT SO HEALTHY

Of all the nutrients in our diet fat must be the most debated and the most misunderstood. Although, in terms of healthy eating, fat is often cast as the villain, it's worth remembering that it also plays a beneficial role. In the body, fat cushions and protects the vital organs, provides energy stores and helps insulate the body. In the diet, it is necessary for the absorption of fat-soluble vitamins (A, D, E and K) and to provide essential fatty acids that the body can't make itself. While some fat is essential, many of us are eating too much of the wrong types of fat and not enough of the right types. A high-fat diet, particularly one that contains a lot of saturated 'animal' fats, is known to increase the risk of problems such as heart disease, stroke and certain types of cancer. There are three types of fat: saturated, monounsaturated and polyunsaturated fatty acids, which occur in different proportions in foods. Saturated fatty acids are linked to higher blood cholesterol, which can lead to heart disease.

Polyunsaturated fats

Omega-6 fats These are mostly found in vegetable oils and margarines such as sunflower oil, safflower oil, corn oil and soya bean oil. Omega-6 fats help lower the LDL 'bad' cholesterol in the blood, but if you eat too much they will also lower the 'good' HDL cholesterol.

Omega-3 fats These are found mainly in oil-rich fish such as salmon, fresh tuna, mackerel and sardines, in linseeds (flax) and rapeseed oil. They help to protect the heart by making the blood less sticky and likely to clot, by lowering blood pressure, and by encouraging the muscles lining the artery walls to relax, thus improving blood flow to the heart. It's important to have a balance of omega-3 and omega-6 fats in the diet. At the moment most of us have too much omega-6 fats and not enough omega-3 fats and recent research suggests that low levels of omega-3s in the blood may contribute to depression, antisocial behaviour and schizophrenia.

Monounsaturated fats

Monounsaturated fats are found mainly in olive oil, walnut oil and rapeseed oil, nuts and avocados. They can help reduce the risk of heart disease by lowering LDL 'bad' cholesterol.

Saturated fats

Saturated 'animal' fats are found in full fat dairy products (cheese, yogurt, milk, cream), lard, fatty cuts of meat and meat products such as sausages and burgers, pastry, cakes, biscuits, and coconut and palm oil. A diet high in saturated fats can raise levels of LDL 'bad' cholesterol in the blood, which will cause narrowing of the arteries and increase the risk of heart attacks and stroke.

Trans fats

Trans fats occur naturally in small amounts in meat and dairy products, but they are also produced during the process of hydrogenation that is used to convert liquid vegetable oils into semi-solid fats in the manufacture of some types of margarine. Trans fats are most commonly found in biscuits, cakes, pastries, meat pies, sausages, crackers and takeaway foods. Although chemically trans fats are still unsaturated fat, studies show that in the body they behave like saturated fat, causing blood cholesterol levels to rise; in fact, some studies suggest that trans fats are worse than saturated fats.

EATING MORE FIBRE

Despite the fact that it passes through the digestive tract largely undigested, fibre plays an important role in helping us stay fit and healthy. It helps keep our digestive tract in good working order and can also help reduce high blood cholesterol and keep blood sugar levels stable. If you start the day with a wholegrain cereal and eat plenty of fresh fruit and vegetables, you will easily have enough fibre in your diet. Fibre can be divided into two groups – insoluble and soluble; both groups help keep the body healthy in a different way.

Insoluble fibre

Insoluble fibre, which is found mainly in wholegrain cereals but also in fruit, vegetables and pulses, helps to prevent constipation and problems such as haemorrhoids (piles) and diverticular disease. It works by absorbing water, making the stools larger, softer and easier to pass. Sometimes referred to as 'nature's broom', insoluble fibre also speeds the passage of waste material through the body. The faster waste materials are excreted, the less time potentially harmful substances have to linger in the bowel.

Soluble fibre

Soluble fibre, found in oats and oat bran, beans and pulses and some fruit and vegetables, helps to lower high blood cholesterol levels, which in turn will help reduce the risk of heart disease. Soluble fibre also helps to slow the absorption of sugar into the bloodstream, which makes foods rich in soluble fibre a good choice for people with diabetes or anyone trying to balance blood sugar levels. The Guideline Daily Amount of fibre is 24g for adults and 15g for children aged between 5 and 10 years (see page 000); to reach this target, most of us need to increase our fibre intake by about 50%.

CUTTING DOWN ON SALT

Reducing the amount of salt in our diet is, say health experts, one of the most important steps we can take to reduce the risk of high blood pressure, a condition that affects one in three adults in the UK. Experts have calculated that reducing our salt intake to 6g a day would reduce the number of people suffering from stroke by 22% and from heart attacks by 16%, saving around 34,000 lives each year.

Hidden salt

You may think the easiest way to cut back on salt is not to sprinkle salt over your food when you're at the table, but unfortunately the answer isn't quite that simple – only around 15% of the salt we eat comes from salt added to our food during cooking and at the table. Three-quarters of all the salt we consume is hidden in processed foods – one small tin of chicken soup, for instance, can contain well over half the recommended daily intake of salt for an adult.

Re-educating our taste buds

Our taste for salt is something we learn to like the more we eat. But just in the same way that we can teach our taste buds to enjoy foods with less sugar, we can train them to enjoy foods with less salt (sodium chloride). If you gradually reduce the amount of salt you eat, the taste receptors on the tongue become more sensitive to salt. This process takes between two and three weeks. Use herbs and spices to enhance the natural flavours of foods and before long you'll be enjoying the real taste of food – not the flavour of salt.

PROTEIN

Protein is made up of smaller units called amino acids, which are an important part of every cell in the body and therefore necessary for healthy skin, teeth, internal organs and other tissues. The body can manufacture some of these amino acids itself, but the 'essential amino acids' must be derived from food. Animal protein and soya protein contain almost all of these and are regarded as 'complete'. The best sources of protein are meat, poultry, fish, eggs, dairy products such as yogurt, milk and cheese, and soya products. Other vegetable proteins are lacking in one or more of the essential amino acids.

Vitamins and Minerals

Vitamins

Vitamins are vital for a variety of body processes and a deficiency will result in illness. Our bodies cannot make all the vitamins we need, so we have to get them from our food and drink They are vital to good health and effective in very small amounts. The fat-soluble vitamins A, D, E and K – as their name suggests – are largely derived from foods that contain fat, though the body acquires most of its vitamin D from the action of sunlight on the skin. These vitamins are stored in the liver. Water-soluble vitamins B and C cannot be stored by the body so a regular intake through the diet is important.

Vitamin A – needed for growth and development, healthy eyesight and good skin. Yellow, orange and green fruit and vegetables are rich in the antioxidant beta-carotene, which the body converts into vitamin A.

Vitamin B complex: B1 (thiamin), B2 (riboflavin), B3 (niacin), B6 (pyridoxine), B12 (cobalamin), biotin, pantothenic acid, folic acid – these vitamins work together to help digestion and aid resistance to infection. Whole grains are rich in these vitamins, as are sprouting seeds, green vegetables and citrus fruits.

Vitamin C – an antioxidant that protects the bones, joints, teeth, gums, nerves, glands and other tissues and aids the absorption of iron. Found in varying amounts in all fresh fruits and vegetables.

Vitamin E – an antioxidant held in cell membranes that is essential for normal metabolism, aids heart function and may protect against heart disease. Found mainly in whole grains, seeds, nuts and green vegetables.

Minerals

These are needed in tiny quantities and are far more readily absorbed by the body than those from supplements. Some of the more important minerals are calcium (for healthy teeth and bones), iron (helps transport oxygen in the blood), magnesium, zinc, potassium, phosphorous, sulphur and selenium. A deficiency of iron will lead to anaemia. Meat and leafy green vegetables are good sources of iron, and the absorption of this mineral is greatly increased if some vitamin C-rich food – even a glass of orange juice – is consumed at the same meal.

Antioxidants

Some vitamins and minerals are antioxidants: they can reduce the risk of many diseases by protecting cells against 'free radicals', which may be harmful.

PRINCIPLES OF HEALTHY EATING

1 Water

Water is the elixir of life, and is nature's prime detoxifier.

- Aim to drink at least 1 litre (1¾ pints) per day, preferably 1–2 litres (1¾–3½ pints).
- Start the day with a glass of hot water and lemon.
- Have a small bottle or a large glass of mineral or filtered water by your side always, and sip regularly.
- Drinking water at room temperature is easier on the digestion than ice–cold water.
- Bored with plain water? Flavour your water with a slice of lemon, lime or some peeled and chopped fresh ginger.

2 Superfoods

For tiptop nutrition and long-term health, incorporate these foods into your regular eating plan:

Avocado	Broccoli
Carrots	Cabbage
Garlic	Ripe tomatoes

Sprouted seeds: for example, alfalfa
Watercress
Winter squash (dense orange-fleshed varieties such as butternut)

Apples	Apricots
Bananas	Berries
Kiwi fruit	Lemons
Pineapple	Live, natural yogurt
Miso	Oats

Sea vegetables (seaweed): for example, nori strips

3 Good fats and oils

Fats are essential to all life processes, including the production of cholesterol, which is vital for nerve communication and an essential component of the brain, nerve fibres and sex hormones. For this reason, a low-fat diet is not a good idea for long-term health. The trick is to substitute bad (processed, hydrogenated and highly saturated) fats for omega-rich good fats and oils, found in oily fish, nuts and seeds, and to eat small amounts of other natural fats such as olive oil and butter.

- Eat 1–2 tbsp extra virgin (cold pressed) oils every day. Olive oil, hemp, linseed and blends of omega oils are especially good. Do not heat. Use them to drizzle over salads, vegetables and fish, and in dips.

4 Sensible eating

Eat plenty of foods rich in carbohydrates and fibre; whenever possible, choose wholegrain cereals. Keep sugary foods and drinks as a treat rather than something you consume every day. Avoid adding salt.

5 Vegetables, salads and fruit

Vegetables, salads and fruit are star performers in all healthy eating plans. Eat at least 5 servings of fruit and/or vegetables each day. Not only do they contain a storehouse of vitamins and minerals, they also help to keep the body at its optimum pH, which is slightly alkaline.

6 Eat regularly

Skipping meals leads to energy dips, stresses your system and is a sure-fire way to put on weight. Eating regularly keeps your body's physical and mental energy levels steady, avoiding hunger pangs and the need to snack.

- Never skip breakfast – it's the most important meal of the day to set you up and it also sustains your energy levels through until lunchtime.
- Eat slowly, and take your time – it takes 20 minutes for your body to register it is full and satiated.

7 Enjoy a variety of food

Enjoy as wide a variety of foods as possible. This way you will ensure your diet contains all the health-giving micronutrients it needs for optimum health. It also helps to avoid developing intolerances to particular foods.

8 Eat the right amount to be a healthy weight

9 If you drink alcohol, drink sensibly and

stay within the safe guidelines, which are no more than 3 units of alcohol a day for women and no more than 4 units of alcohol a day for men, with at least one alcohol-free day a week.

10 Exercise

Regular exercise is vital. It energises you, raises your metabolic rate, helps to maintain your correct weight, is a de-stressor, releases feel-good hormones, and helps you sleep better.

11 Stress less

Stress is a major modern disease and comes in all shapes and sizes, be it pressure at work, from noise and traffic, or the constant barrage of environmental and electronic pollution. The body reacts to stress by going into red alert and your immune system is compromised. Learning to deal with stress, and removing stress from your life wherever you can, is essential for your health.

- Build some form of relaxation into your daily life.
- Learn simple deep breathing techniques.
- Reduce the hours you watch TV or work/play on the computer. Listen to soothing music instead.

12 Sleep

Sleep is Nature's happy pill, the ultimate physical and mental reviver, and the secret to staying young. Take care of your sleep and your body and your immune system will take care of you. Make getting enough sleep a top priority.

- Make your bedroom a peaceful haven.
- Avoid drinking coffee or too much alcohol in the evening.
- Wind down before you go to bed.

13 Positive outlook

How you feel has a critical impact on your health and overall wellbeing. Cultivate an optimistic outlook and do something that makes you happy every day. Laughter is great medicine, and is completely free.

Special diets: Dairy free, Wheat free and Gluten free

In recent years there has been a growing awareness that for some people food allergy or intolerance can cause a range of health problems, including eczema, asthma, skin rashes, migraine and irritable bowel syndrome. Any food can provoke an allergic reaction, although some are more likely than others. Wheat and dairy products are two of the most common causes of food intolerance.

CALCIUM CONCERN

Milk and dairy products are a major source of calcium in our diet. If you can't get enough calcium from your diet you may need to take a supplement. Check with a pharmacist that the supplement you choose does not contain lactose.

Good non-dairy sources of calcium include: canned fish such as pilchards and sardines, dark green leafy vegetables such as spinach and watercress, bread, apricots, canned, fresh and dried beans, including baked beans, and hard water.

DAIRY-FREE DIETS

Foods to avoid on a dairy-free diet:

- Milk
- Cheese
- Yogurt
- Butter
- Most margarines and low-fat spreads
- Milk chocolate
- Cream
- Ice cream
- Fromage frais
- Dairy desserts

Many processed foods contain lactose (milk sugar) or traces of cow's milk protein, and there is also a host of other names for ingredients derived from milk.

Avoid products that list any of the following words in the ingredients:

- Milk protein, milk, milk powder, skimmed milk powder
- Non-fat milk solids
- Animal fat
- Whey
- Casein or caseinate

- Hydrolysed casein or whey
- Lactose
- Lacalbumin
- Lactoglobulin
- Ghee

Non-dairy alternatives

Soya milk and yogurt

If you are allergic to dairy products or lactose-intolerant, drinking milk may cause a variety of symptoms, including skin rashes and eczema, asthma and irritable bowel syndrome. Soya milk and yogurt are useful alternatives – look for calcium-enriched products. Good non-dairy sources of calcium suitable for adding to smoothies include dark green leafy vegetables, such as watercress and spinach, and apricots.

Silken tofu

This protein-rich dairy-free product adds a creamy texture to salad dressings, sauces and desserts.

WHEAT- AND GLUTEN-FREE DIETS

Many people are discovering that their body reacts badly when they eat wheat. Symptoms include bloating, IBS (irritable bowel syndrome), headaches and tiredness. Sometimes simply reducing your wheat intake can help; but some people may have to avoid wheat altogether. Coeliac disease is a more serious condition than wheat intolerance. It is caused by an intolerance to gluten, a protein found in wheat, rye, barley and oats. A gluten-free diet means cutting out wheat, oats, barley, rye and all products made using them. Products labelled as being wheat free are not necessarily gluten free because they may contain other gluten-containing grains. Equally, products labelled gluten free are not necessarily wheat free because they may contain wheat starch (gluten is a protein and people with a gluten intolerance don't have a problem with the starchy part of the grain).

Foods to avoid on a gluten-free diet include:

- Wheat, oats, barley, rye
- Wheat flour (white, wholemeal, self-raising)
- All foods made with wheat flour (bread, pasta, cakes, biscuits, crackers, pastry, batter, semolina, couscous)
- All products made with barley meal or flour
- All products made with rye meal or flour (rye bread or rye crispbread)
- All products containing oatmeal or oat flour
- Breakfast cereals containing wheat, bran, oats, barley
- Any dish that includes breadcrumbs
- Sausages, except 100% meat sausages and those labelled gluten free
- Sauces and gravies thickened with flour
- Many manufactured goods contain flour as a thickening agent or filler so it is essential to check the label on individual products.

Substitute:

- Rice, corn, polenta (cornmeal), buckwheat, quinoa
- Rice, potato, soya, corn (maize) or chickpea flour
- Arrowroot, cornflour, sago or tapioca
- Cornflakes, Rice Crispies
- Rice or buckwheat noodles, gluten free pasta
- Gluten-free bread or bread mix, puffed rice cakes, rice crackers, taco shells

Watching your weight

Food gives us energy – in the form of calories – which is burnt up naturally with everyday living, but if we consume more calories than the body can use, even with increased exercise, excess calories are stored in the body as fat and the result is weight gain. If you need to shed excess pounds and achieve a healthy weight, avoid high-calorie, low-nutrient, unhealthy foods and swap them for something healthier. Try:

• Swapping fatty, sugary snacks for fruit and vegetables
• Reducing portion sizes
• Drinking plenty of water
• Remember, small changes add up.

Breakfast Swap white toast with jam and butter, an orange juice and a cup of tea with milk and two sugars for a slice of lemon in hot water and enjoy some homemade porridge with semi-skimmed milk and a little honey. The porridge will provide a much slower release of energy that will keep you going until lunch.

Coffee break Swap a whole milk latte for a skimmed milk latte and you'll still get your caffeine boost, but with nearly half the calories.

Snacks Swap a bag of crisps for a handful of fruit or nuts. Swap a chocolate biscuit for a piece of fruit. Bananas are good if you're craving something sweet.

Lunch Swap a cheese, tomato and pesto panini for a jacket potato with cottage cheese and a salad. This will fill you up without giving you that mid-afternoon energy slump.

A drink after work Swap a bottle of beer for a glass of white wine, which has far fewer calories, or stick to water for zero calories and a much healthier night out.

Dinner Swap roast beef, roast potatoes and Yorkshire pudding for a warming beef casserole with mash and vegetables. You'll save calories and it'll be just as satisfying.

EXTRA BOOSTS

There are many ingredients that you can add to your diet if you have specific nutritional requirements.

Acidophilus

A probiotic: 'friendly' bacteria that promote good health. Acidophilus is most beneficial when taken if you are suffering from diarrhoea or after a course of antibiotics, or if you have digestive problems such as irritable bowel syndrome (IBS). Available from most chemists and health shops in capsule form, which usually need to be kept in the refrigerator. Probiotics are now included in some ready-made drinks and yogurt products.

Bee pollen

A natural antibiotic and a source of antioxidants, bee pollen is a good general tonic. It contains plenty of protein and essential amino acids. Available as loose powder, granules or in tablet or capsule form.

Warning: it can cause an allergic reaction in pollen-sensitive individuals.

Brewers' yeast

A by-product of beer brewing, brewers' yeast is exceptionally rich in B vitamins, with high levels of iron, zinc, magnesium and potassium. Highly concentrated and an excellent pick-me-up, but the flavour is strong and needs to be mixed with other ingredients. Available as pills or powder.

Warning: it is high in purines so should be avoided by gout sufferers.

Echinacea

Recommended by herbalists for many years, echinacea is a native plant of North America, taken to support a healthy immune system. A great all-rounder with anti-viral and anti-bacterial properties. Comes in capsules and in extracts taken in drops.

Warning: not recommended for use during pregnancy or when breastfeeding.

Eggs

High in protein, but eggs also contain cholesterol so you might need to limit your intake; ask your GP. Egg white powder is low in fat and can be added to smoothies for a protein boost. Always use the freshest eggs.

Warning: raw egg should not be eaten by the elderly, children, babies, pregnant women or those with an impaired immune system as there can be a risk of contracting salmonella.

Ginseng

Derived from the roots of a plant grown in Russia, Korea and China. The active constituents are ginsenosides, reputed to stimulate the hormones and increase energy. Available in dry root form for grinding or ready powdered.

Warning: should not be taken by those suffering from hypertension.

Nuts

Packed with nutrients, nuts are a concentrated form of protein and are rich in antioxidants, vitamins B1, B6 and E, and many minerals. Brazil nuts are one of the best sources of selenium in the diet. Nuts do have a high fat content, but this is mostly unsaturated fat. Walnuts are particularly high in omega-3, an essential fatty acid that is needed for healthy heart and brain function. Brazil, cashew, coconut, peanut and macadamia nuts contain more saturated fat, so should be used sparingly. Almonds are particularly easy to digest. Finely chop or grind the nuts just before using for maximum freshness.

Oats

Sold in the form of whole grain, rolled, flaked or ground (oatmeal), oats are high in protein, vitamin B complex, vitamin E, potassium, calcium, phosphorus, iron and zinc; they are easy to digest and can soothe the digestive tract. They are also a rich source of soluble fibre, which helps to lower high blood cholesterol levels, which in turn will help reduce the risk of heart disease. Toasted oatmeal has a nutty flavour and is ideal for smoothies.

Warning: oats should be avoided by those on a gluten-free diet.

Seeds

Highly nutritious, seeds contain a good supply of essential fatty acids (EFAs). Flaxseed (linseed) is particularly beneficial as it is one of the richest sources of omega-3 EFAs, with 57% more than oily fish. Seeds are best bought in small amounts, as their fat content makes them go rancid quickly, so store in airtight containers in the fridge. Grind them just before use for maximum benefit, or use the oils – these have to be stored in the refrigerator.

Sprouting seeds

These are simply seeds from a variety of plants – such as sunflower, chickpea and mung bean – which have been given a little water and warmth and have started to grow. Sprouts are full of vitamins, minerals, proteins and carbohydrates.

Wheat bran and germ

Wheat bran is the outside of the wheat grain removed during milling; it is very high in fibre and adds bulk to the diet. It is bland in taste but adds a crunchy texture. Wheat germ, from the centre of the grain, is very nutritious and easy to digest, with a mild flavour. Highly perishable, store in the refrigerator once the pack is opened.

Warning: keep your intake of bran to moderate levels; large amounts can prevent vitamins and minerals from being absorbed.

Food Storage and Hygiene

Storing food properly and preparing it in a hygienic way is important to ensure that food remains as nutritious and flavourful as possible, and to reduce the risk of food poisoning.

Hygiene

When you are preparing food, always follow these important guidelines:

Wash your hands thoroughly before handling food and again between handling different types of food, such as raw and cooked meat and poultry. If you have any cuts or grazes on your hands, be sure to keep them covered with a waterproof plaster.

Wash down worksurfaces regularly with a mild detergent solution or multi-surface cleaner.

Use a dishwasher if available. Otherwise, wear rubber gloves for washing-up, so that the water temperature can be hotter than unprotected hands can bear. Change drying-up cloths and cleaning cloths regularly. Note that leaving dishes to drain is more hygienic than drying them with a teatowel.

Keep raw and cooked foods separate, especially meat, fish and poultry. Wash kitchen utensils in between preparing raw and cooked foods. Never put cooked or ready-to-eat foods directly on to a surface which has just had raw fish, meat or poultry on it.

Keep pets out of the kitchen if possible; or make sure they stay away from worksurfaces. Never allow animals on to worksurfaces.

Shopping

Always choose fresh ingredients in prime condition from stores and markets that have a regular turnover of stock to ensure you buy the freshest produce possible.

Make sure items are within their 'best before' or 'use by' date. (Foods with a longer shelf life have a 'best before' date; more perishable items have a 'use by' date.)

Pack frozen and chilled items in an insulated cool bag at the check-out and put them into the freezer or refrigerator as soon as you get home.

During warm weather in particular, buy perishable foods just before you return home. When packing items at the check-out, sort them according to where you will store them when you get home – the refrigerator, freezer, storecupboard, vegetable rack, fruit bowl, etc. This will make unpacking easier – and quicker.

The storecupboard

Although storecupboard ingredients will generally last a long time, correct storage is important:

Always check packaging for storage advice – even with familiar foods, because storage requirements may change if additives, sugar or salt have been reduced.

Check storecupboard foods for their 'best before' or 'use by' date and do not use them if the date has passed.

Keep all food cupboards scrupulously clean and make sure containers and packets are properly sealed.

Once opened, treat canned foods as though fresh. Always transfer the contents to a clean container, cover and keep in the refrigerator. Similarly, jars, sauce bottles and cartons should be kept chilled after opening. (Always check the label for safe storage times after opening.)

Transfer dry goods such as sugar, rice and pasta to moisture-proof containers. When supplies are used up, wash the container well and thoroughly dry before refilling with new supplies.

Store oils in a dark cupboard away from any heat source as heat and light can make them turn rancid and affect their colour. For the same reason, buy olive oil in dark green bottles.

Store vinegars in a cool place; they can turn bad in a warm environment.

Store dried herbs, spices and flavourings in a cool, dark cupboard or in dark jars. Buy in small quantities as their flavour will not last indefinitely.

Store flours and sugars in airtight containers.

Refrigerator storage

Fresh food needs to be stored in the cool temperature of the refrigerator to keep it in good condition and discourage the growth of harmful bacteria. Store day-to-day perishable items, such as opened jams and jellies, mayonnaise and bottled sauces, in the refrigerator along with eggs and dairy products, fruit juices, bacon, fresh and cooked meat (on separate shelves), and salads and vegetables (except potatoes, which don't suit being stored in the cold). A refrigerator should be kept at an operating temperature of 4–5°C. It is worth investing in a refrigerator thermometer to ensure the correct temperature is maintained. To ensure your refrigerator is functioning effectively for safe food storage, follow these guidelines:

To avoid bacterial cross-contamination, store cooked and raw foods on separate shelves, putting cooked foods on the top shelf. Ensure that all items are well wrapped.

Never put hot food into the refrigerator, as this will cause the internal temperature of the refrigerator to rise.

Avoid overfilling the refrigerator, as this restricts the circulation of air and prevents the appliance from working properly.

It can take some time for the refrigerator to return to the correct operating temperature once the door has been opened, so don't leave it open any longer than is necessary.

Clean the refrigerator regularly, using a specially formulated germicidal refrigerator cleaner. Alternatively, use a weak solution of bicarbonate of soda: 1 tbsp to 1 litre (1¾ pints) water.

If your refrigerator doesn't have an automatic defrost facility, then defrost regularly.

MAXIMUM REFRIGERATOR STORAGE TIMES

For pre-packed foods, always adhere to the 'use by' date on the packet. For other foods the following storage times should apply, providing the food is in prime condition when it goes into the refrigerator and that your refrigerator is in good working order

Vegetables and Fruit	
Green vegetables	3–4 days
Salad leaves	2–3 days
Hard and stone fruit	3–7 days
Soft fruit	1–2 days

Dairy Food	
Cheese, hard	1 week
Cheese, soft	2–3 days
Eggs	1 week
Milk	4–5 days

Fish	
Fish	1 day
Shellfish	1 day

Raw Meat	
Bacon	7 days
Game	2 days
Joints	3 days
Minced meat	1 day
Offal	1 day
Poultry	2 days
Raw sliced meat	2 days
Sausages	3 days

Cooked Meat	
Joints	3 days
Casseroles/stews	2 days
Pies	2 days
Sliced meat	2 days
Ham	2 days
Ham, vacuum-packed	1–2 weeks (or according to the instructions on the packet)

Start the Day

Toasted Oats with Berries

Preparation Time 10 minutes, plus cooling   Cooking Time 5–10 minutes   Serves 4   **EASY**

25g (1oz) hazelnuts, roughly chopped
125g (4oz) rolled oats
1 tbsp olive oil
125g (4oz) strawberries, sliced
250g (9oz) blueberries
200g (7oz) Greek yogurt
2 tbsp runny honey

1 Preheat the grill to medium. Put the hazelnuts into a bowl with the oats. Drizzle with the oil and mix well, then spread out on a baking sheet. Toast the oat mixture for 5–10 minutes until it starts to crisp up. Remove from the heat and set aside to cool.

2 Put the strawberries into a large bowl with the blueberries and yogurt. Stir in the oats and hazelnuts, drizzle with the honey and divide among four dishes. Serve immediately.

HEALTHY TIP

Oats are rich in soluble fibre, which helps regulate blood sugar levels and lower blood cholesterol levels. They also supply vitamins, iron and magnesium. Blueberries provide anthocyanins, which help protect against certain cancers and heart disease, while the strawberries provide a vitamin C boost.

TRY SOMETHING DIFFERENT

Use a mixture of raspberries, blackberries, or chopped nectarines or peaches instead of the strawberries and blueberries.

PER SERVING

327 calories
15g fat (of which 3g saturates)
44g carbohydrate
0.1g salt
vegetarian

Granola

Preparation Time 5 minutes   Cooking Time 1 hour 5 minutes   Serves 15   **EASY**

300g (11oz) rolled oats
50g (2oz) each chopped Brazil nuts,
    flaked almonds, wheatgerm or rye
    flakes, and sunflower seeds
25g (1oz) sesame seeds
100ml (3½fl oz) sunflower oil
3 tbsp runny honey
100g (3½oz) each raisins and dried
    cranberries
milk or yogurt to serve

1 Preheat the oven to 140°C (120°C
fan oven) mark 1. Put the oats,
nuts, wheatgerm or rye flakes, and
all the seeds into a bowl. Gently
heat the oil and honey in a pan.
Pour over the oats and stir to
combine. Spread on a shallow
baking tray and bake in the oven for
1 hour or until golden, stirring once.
Leave to cool.

2 Transfer to a bowl and stir in the
dried fruit. Store in an airtight
container – the granola will keep
for up to a week. Serve with milk
or yogurt.

PER SERVING

254 calories
14g fat (of which 2g saturates)
29g carbohydrate
0g salt
vegetarian

Energy-boosting Muesli

Preparation Time 5 minutes   Makes 15 servings   **EASY**

500g (1lb 2oz) porridge oats
100g (3½oz) toasted almonds, chopped
2 tbsp pumpkin seeds
2 tbsp sunflower seeds
100g (3½oz) ready-to-eat dried
   apricots, chopped
milk or yogurt to serve

Mix the oats with the almonds, seeds and apricots. Store in a sealable container: it will keep for up to one month. Serve with milk or yogurt.

HEALTHY TIP

This recipe includes dried apricots, which are rich in betacarotene. The body converts this into vitamin A, which is important for healthy vision and skin. Apricots are also a good source of iron, which helps make red blood cells to transport oxygen around the body. The pumpkin seeds supply good amounts of omega-3 oils called alpha linolenic acid, which help protect against heart disease and stroke.

PER SERVING

208 calories
9g fat (of which trace saturates),
28g carbohydrate
0g salt
vegetarian

Porridge with Dried Fruit

Preparation Time 5 minutes   Cooking Time 5 minutes   Serves 4   **EASY**

200g (7oz) porridge oats
400ml (14fl oz) milk, plus extra
  to serve
75g (3oz) mixture of chopped dried
  figs, apricots and raisins

1 Put the oats into a large pan and add the milk and 400ml (14fl oz) water. Stir in the figs, apricots and raisins and heat gently, stirring until the porridge thickens and the oats are cooked.

2 Divide among four bowls and serve with a splash of milk.

Porridge is an excellent way to start your day – it provides slow-release energy to sustain you through the morning, and keeps you feeling satisfied so you won't be struck by hunger pangs mid-morning. Figs are packed with calcium and the dried apricots supply high levels of beta-carotene and iron.

PER SERVING

279 calories
6g fat (of which 1g saturates)
49g carbohydrate
0.2g salt
vegetarian

Apple and Almond Yogurt

Preparation Time 5 minutes, plus overnight chilling   Serves 4   **EASY**

500g (1lb 2oz) natural yogurt
50g (2oz) each flaked almonds and
    sultanas
2 apples

1 Put the yogurt into a bowl and add
the almonds and sultanas.

2 Grate the apples, add to the bowl
and mix together. Chill in the fridge
overnight. Use as a topping for
breakfast cereal or serve as a snack.

HEALTHY TIP
Natural yogurt contains lactobacillus
bacteria, which aids digestion and
promotes a healthy immune system.
It is also a good source of protein,
B vitamins and bone-strengthening
calcium. The almonds add extra
calcium while the apples provide
useful amounts of fibre and the
antioxidant quercetin.

PER SERVING
193 calories
8g fat (of which 1g saturates),
22g carbohydrate
0.3g salt
vegetarian • gluten free

Apple Compôte

Preparation Time 10 minutes, plus chilling · Cooking Time 5 minutes · Serves 2 · **EASY**

250g (9oz) cooking apples, peeled and
    chopped
juice of ½ lemon
1 tbsp golden caster sugar
ground cinnamon

TO SERVE
25g (1oz) raisins
25g (1oz) chopped almonds
1 tbsp natural yogurt

1 Put the cooking apples into a pan with the lemon juice, caster sugar and 2 tbsp cold water. Cook gently for 5 minutes or until soft. Transfer to a bowl.

2 Sprinkle a little ground cinnamon over the top, cool and chill. It will keep for up to three days.

3 Serve with the raisins, chopped almonds and yogurt.

COOK'S TIP

To microwave, put the apples, lemon juice, sugar and water into a microwaveproof bowl, cover loosely with clingfilm and cook on full power in an 850W microwave oven for 4 minutes or until the apples are just soft.

PER SERVING

188 calories
7g fat (of which 1g saturates)
29g carbohydrate
0g salt
vegetarian • gluten free

Poached Eggs with Mushrooms

Preparation Time 15 minutes   Cooking Time 20 minutes   Serves 4   **EASY**

8 medium-sized flat or portabella
   mushrooms
25g (1oz) butter
8 medium eggs
225g (8oz) baby spinach leaves
4 tsp fresh Pesto (see Cook's Tip,
   page 71)

1 Preheat the oven to 200°C (180°C fan oven) mark 6. Arrange the mushrooms in a single layer in a small roasting tin and dot with the butter. Roast for 15 minutes or until golden brown and soft.

2 Meanwhile, bring a wide shallow pan of water to the boil. When the mushrooms are half-cooked and the water is bubbling furiously, break the eggs into the pan, spaced well apart, then take the pan off the heat. The eggs will take about 6 minutes to cook.

3 When the mushrooms are tender, put them on a warmed plate, cover and return to the turned-off oven to keep warm.

4 Put the roasting tin over a medium heat on the hob and add the spinach. Cook, stirring, for about 30 seconds or until the spinach has just started to wilt.

5 The eggs should be set by now, so divide the mushrooms among four warmed plates and top with a little spinach, a poached egg and a teaspoonful of pesto.

TRY SOMETHING DIFFERENT
For a more substantial meal, serve on 100% rye bread or German pumpernickel.

PER SERVING
263 calories
21g fat (of which 8g saturates)
1g carbohydrate
0.7g salt
vegetarian • gluten free

HEALTHY TIP
Eggs once had a bad press with many people believing (wrongly) that they raised blood cholesterol levels. However, scientists have found that most people can safely eat up to two eggs a day without any effect on their cholesterol levels. Eggs are a good source of protein – 2 eggs supply roughly one-third of an adult's daily requirement – as well as vitamins A and D.

Mozzarella Mushrooms

Preparation Time 2–3 minutes   Cooking Time 15–20 minutes   Serves 4   **EASY**

8 large portabella mushrooms
8 slices marinated red pepper
8 fresh basil leaves
150g (5oz) mozzarella cheese, cut into
   8 slices (see Cook's Tips, page 184)
4 English muffins, halved
salt and ground black pepper
green salad to serve

1 Preheat the oven to 200°C (180°C fan oven) mark 6. Lay the mushrooms side by side in a roasting tin and season with salt and pepper. Top each mushroom with a slice of red pepper and a basil leaf. Lay a slice of mozzarella on top of each mushroom and season again. Roast for 15–20 minutes or until the mushrooms are tender and the cheese has melted.

2 Meanwhile, toast the muffin halves until golden. Put a mozzarella mushroom on top of each muffin half. Serve immediately with a green salad.

HEALTHY TIP

Mushrooms are an excellent source of potassium – a mineral that helps lower elevated blood pressure and reduces the risk of stroke. One medium portabella mushroom has even more potassium than a banana or a glass of orange juice. Mushrooms contain antioxidant nutrients that help inhibit the development cancers of the breast and prostate.

PER SERVING

137 calories
9g fat (of which 5g saturates)
5g carbohydrate
0.4g salt
vegetarian

Creamy Baked Eggs

Preparation Time 5 minutes   Cooking Time 15–18 minutes   Serves 4   **EASY**

butter to grease
4 sun-dried tomatoes
4 medium eggs
1 tbsp double cream
salt and ground black pepper
Granary bread to serve (optional)

1 Preheat the oven to 180°C (160°C fan oven) mark 4. Grease four individual ramekins.

2 Put a tomato into each ramekin and season to taste with salt and pepper. Carefully break an egg on top of each tomato, then drizzle 1 tbsp cream over each egg.

3 Bake for 15–18 minutes – the eggs will continue to cook once they have been taken out of the oven.

4 Leave to stand for 2 minutes before serving. Serve with Granary bread, if you like.

PER SERVING

153 calories
14g fat (of which 7g saturates)
1g carbohydrate
0.2g salt
vegetarian • gluten free

Lemon and Blueberry Pancakes

Preparation Time 15 minutes   Cooking Time 10–15 minutes   Serves 4   **EASY**

125g (4oz) wholemeal plain flour
1 tsp baking powder
¼ tsp bicarbonate of soda
2 tbsp golden caster sugar
finely grated zest of 1 lemon
125g (4oz) natural yogurt
2 tbsp milk
2 medium eggs
40g (1½oz) butter
100g (3½oz) blueberries
1 tsp sunflower oil
natural yogurt and fruit compote
    to serve

1 Sift the flour, baking powder and bicarbonate of soda into a bowl, tipping in the contents left in the sieve. Add the sugar and lemon zest. Pour in the yogurt and milk. Break the eggs into the mixture and whisk together.

2 Melt 25g (1oz) butter in a pan, add to the bowl with the blueberries and stir everything together.

3 Heat a dot of butter with the oil in a frying pan over a medium heat until hot. Add four large spoonfuls of the mixture to the pan to make four pancakes. After about 2 minutes, flip them over and cook for 1–2 minutes. Repeat with the remaining mixture, adding a dot more butter each time.

4 Serve with natural yogurt and some fruit compote.

TRY SOMETHING DIFFERENT

Instead of blueberries and lemon, use 100g (3½ oz) chopped ready-to-eat dried apricots and 2 tsp grated fresh root ginger.

PER SERVING

290 calories
13g fat (of which 6g saturates)
39g carbohydrate
0.6g salt
vegetarian

Breakfast Bruschetta

Preparation Time 5 minutes   Cooking Time 5 minutes   Serves 4   **EASY**

1 ripe banana, peeled and sliced
250g (9oz) blueberries
200g (7oz) quark cheese
4 slices pumpernickel or wheat-free
   wholegrain bread
1 tbsp runny honey

1 Put the banana into a bowl with the blueberries. Spoon in the quark cheese and mix well.

2 Toast the slices of bread on both sides, then spread with the blueberry mixture. Drizzle with the honey and serve immediately.

PER SERVING

145 calories
1g fat (of which 0g saturates)
30g carbohydrate
0.4g salt
vegetarian

Soups and Salads

Autumn Barley Soup

Preparation Time 10 minutes   **Cooking Time** 1 hour 5 minutes   **Serves 4   EASY**

25g (1oz) pot barley, washed and
  drained
1 litre (1¾ pints) hot vegetable stock
2 large carrots, diced
1 turnip, diced
2 leeks, trimmed and sliced
2 celery sticks, diced
1 small onion, finely chopped
1 bouquet garni
2 tbsp freshly chopped parsley
salt and ground black pepper

1 Put the barley and hot stock into a
  pan and bring to the boil. Reduce
  the heat and simmer for 45 minutes
  or until the barley is tender.

2 Add the vegetables to the
  pan with the bouquet garni and
  season to taste with salt and
  pepper. Bring to the boil, then
  reduce the heat and simmer for
  about 20 minutes or until the
  vegetables are tender.

3 Discard the bouquet garni.
  Add the parsley to the soup, stir
  well and serve immediately.

HEALTHY TIP

Pot barley is a highly nutritious
addition to this soup. It is considered
a whole grain as it contains the outer
bran layer of the grain, which is rich in
the soluble fibres beta glucan and
pectin – the type that can help lower
high blood cholesterol. It contains
around 10g (¼g) protein per 100g
(3½oz), as well as good amounts of
folic acid, iron, phosphorus and zinc.

TRY SOMETHING DIFFERENT

Replace the barley with 75g (3oz)
soup pasta: add for the last
10 minutes of cooking.

PER SERVING

83 calories
1g fat (of which trace saturates)
16g carbohydrate
0.6g salt
vegetarian • dairy free

Spring Vegetable Broth

Preparation Time 20 minutes   **Cooking Time** 20 minutes   **Serves 4**   **EASY**

1 tbsp olive oil
4 shallots, chopped
1 fennel bulb, chopped
1 leek, trimmed and chopped
5 small carrots, chopped
1.1 litres (2 pints) hot vegetable stock
2 courgettes, chopped
1 bunch of asparagus, chopped
2 × 400g cans no-added-sugar-or-salt
    cannellini beans, drained and rinsed
50g (2oz) Gruyère or Parmesan cheese
    shavings to serve

1 Heat the oil in a large pan. Add the shallots, fennel, leek and carrots and fry for 5 minutes or until they start to soften

2 Add the hot stock, cover and bring to the boil. Add the courgettes, asparagus and beans, then reduce the heat and simmer for 5–6 minutes until the vegetables are tender.

3 Ladle into warmed bowls, sprinkle with a little cheese and serve.

HEALTHY TIP

This soup is a good source of potassium, which is important for regulating fluid balance and reducing blood pressure. Fennel contains beta-carotene, folate and potassium as well as the phytonutrients anethole, anisic acid, fenchone and limonine, which produce the unique flavour of the vegetable.

TRY SOMETHING DIFFERENT

This broth is also good with a tablespoon of Pesto (see page 71) added to each bowl, and served with chunks of crusty bread.

PER SERVING

228 calories
8g fat (of which 3g saturates)
26g carbohydrate
0.3g salt

Pepper and Lentil Soup

Preparation Time 15 minutes   **Cooking Time** 45 minutes   Serves 6   **EASY**

1 tbsp oil
1 medium onion, finely chopped
1 celery stick, chopped
1 leek, trimmed and chopped
1 carrot, chopped
2 red peppers, seeded and diced
225g (8oz) red lentils
400g can chopped tomatoes
1 litre (1¾ pints) hot light vegetable
    stock
25g pack flat-leafed parsley, chopped
salt and ground black pepper
toast to serve

1 Heat the oil in a pan. Add the onion, celery, leek and carrot and cook for 10–15 minutes until soft.

2 Add the red peppers and cook for 5 minutes. Stir in the red lentils, add the chopped tomatoes and hot stock and season to taste with salt and pepper.

3 Cover the pan and bring to the boil, then reduce the heat and cook, uncovered, for 25 minutes or until the lentils are soft and the vegetables are tender.

4 Stir in the parsley. Ladle the soup into warmed bowls and serve with toast.

HEALTHY TIP

Red lentils are a good source of protein, fibre, iron and B vitamins. They have a low GI (see page 12) thanks to their high content of soluble fibre, providing a sustained release of energy. The red peppers are rich in vitamin C and betacarotene, which are both powerful antioxidants that assist the immune system.

PER SERVING

165 calories
3g fat (of which 1g saturates)
27g carbohydrate
0.5g salt
vegetarian • dairy free

Full-of-goodness Broth

Preparation Time 10 minutes   Cooking Time 6–8 minutes   Serves 4   **EASY**

1–2 tbsp medium curry paste
  (see Cook's Tip)
200ml (7fl oz) reduced-fat coconut milk
600ml (1 pint) hot vegetable stock
200g (7oz) smoked tofu, cubed
2 pak choi, chopped
a handful of sugarsnap peas
4 spring onions, chopped
lime wedges to serve

1 Heat the curry paste in a pan for
  1–2 minutes. Add the coconut milk
  and hot stock and bring to the boil.

2 Add the smoked tofu, pak choi,
  sugarsnap peas and spring onions.
  Reduce the heat and simmer for
  1–2 minutes.

3 Ladle the soup into warmed bowls
  and serve with a wedge of lime to
  squeeze over the broth.

COOK'S TIP

Check the ingredients in the curry
paste: some may not be suitable for
vegetarians.

TRY SOMETHING DIFFERENT

Replace the smoked tofu with
shredded leftover roast chicken and
simmer for 2–3 minutes.

PER SERVING

107 calories
4g fat (of which trace saturates)
9g carbohydrate
1g salt
vegetarian • gluten free
dairy free

Leek and Potato Soup

Preparation Time 10 minutes   **Cooking Time** 45 minutes   **Serves** 4   **EASY**

25g (1oz) butter
1 onion, finely chopped
1 garlic clove, crushed
550g (1¼lb) leeks, trimmed and
   chopped
200g (7oz) floury potatoes, sliced
1.3 litres (2¼ pints) hot vegetable stock
crème fraîche and chopped chives to
   garnish

1 Melt the butter in a pan over a gentle heat. Add the onion and cook for 10–15 minutes until soft. Add the garlic and cook for a further 1 minute. Add the leeks and cook for 5–10 minutes until softened. Add the potatoes and toss together with the leeks.

2 Pour in the hot stock and bring to the boil, then reduce the heat and simmer for 20 minutes or until the potatoes are tender.

3 Leave the soup to cool a little, then whiz in batches in a blender or food processor until smooth.

4 To serve, reheat the soup gently. Ladle into warmed bowls, drizzle the crème fraîche over it and garnish with chives.

HEALTHY TIP

Leeks are an excellent source of vitamin C as well as iron and fibre. They provide many of the health-giving benefits associated with garlic and onions, such as promoting the functioning of the blood and the heart.

PER SERVING

117 calories
6g fat (of which 4g saturates)
13g carbohydrate
0.1g salt
vegetarian

Carrot and Sweet Potato Soup

Preparation Time 15 minutes   Cooking Time 45 minutes   Serves 8   **EASY**

1 tbsp olive oil
1 large onion, chopped
1 tbsp coriander seeds
900g (2lb) carrots, roughly chopped
2 medium sweet potatoes, roughly
    chopped
2 litres (3½ pints) hot vegetable or
    chicken stock
2 tbsp white wine vinegar
2 tbsp freshly chopped coriander, plus
    extra coriander leaves to garnish
4 tbsp half-fat crème fraîche
salt and ground black pepper

1 Heat the oil in a large pan. Add the onion and coriander seeds and cook over a medium heat for 5 minutes. Add the carrots and sweet potatoes and cook for a further 5 minutes.

2 Add the hot stock and bring to the boil, then reduce the heat and simmer for 25 minutes or until the vegetables are tender.

3 Leave the soup to cool a little, then whiz in batches in a blender or food processor until slightly chunky. Add the wine vinegar and season with salt and pepper.

4 Pour the soup into a clean pan, stir in the chopped coriander and reheat gently.

5 Drizzle the crème fraîche over it and sprinkle with the coriander leaves. Serve in warmed bowls.

FREEZING TIP

To freeze Freeze the soup at step 3 for up to one month.
To use Thaw overnight in the fridge. Reheat gently and simmer for 5 minutes.

PER SERVING

120 calories
3g fat (of which 1g saturates)
22g carbohydrate
0.7g salt
vegetarian • gluten free

Cauliflower Soup

Preparation Time 25 minutes   **Cooking Time** 40 minutes   **Serves 6**   **EASY**

2 × 400ml cans coconut milk
750ml (1¼ pints) vegetable stock
4 garlic cloves, finely chopped
5cm (2in) piece fresh root ginger,
    peeled and finely chopped
4 lemongrass stalks, roughly chopped
4 kaffir lime leaves, shredded (optional)
    or zest of 1 lime
4 red chillies
2 tbsp groundnut oil

2 tsp sesame oil
1 large onion, thinly sliced
2 tsp ground turmeric
2 tsp sugar
900g (2lb) cauliflower florets
2 tbsp lime juice
2 tbsp light soy sauce
4 spring onions, shredded
4 tbsp freshly chopped coriander
salt and ground black pepper

1 Put the coconut milk and stock into a pan. Add the garlic and ginger with the lemongrass, lime leaves, if using, or lime zest and chillies. Bring to the boil, then reduce the heat, cover and simmer for 15 minutes. Strain the mixture and keep the liquid to one side.

2 Heat the oils together in a clean pan. Add the onion, turmeric and sugar and fry gently for 5 minutes. Add the cauliflower and stir-fry for 5 minutes or until lightly golden.

3 Add the reserved liquid, the lime juice and soy sauce. Bring to the boil, then reduce the heat, cover and simmer for 10–15 minutes until the cauliflower is tender.

4 Season to taste with salt and pepper, then add the spring onions and coriander to the soup. Ladle into warmed bowls and serve.

PER SERVING

113 calories
5g fat (of which 1g saturates)
15g carbohydrate
1.4g salt
vegetarian • dairy free

Mushroom, Spinach and Miso Soup

Preparation Time 5 minutes   Cooking Time 25 minutes   Serves 6   **EASY**

1 tbsp vegetable oil

1 onion, finely sliced

125g (4oz) shiitake mushrooms, finely sliced

225g (8oz) baby spinach leaves

1.1 litres (2 pints) fresh fish stock

4 tbsp mugi miso (see Cook's Tip)

1 Heat the oil in a large pan over a low heat. Add the onion and cook gently for 15 minutes until soft.

2 Add the mushrooms and cook for 5 minutes, then stir in the spinach and stock. Heat for 3 minutes, then stir in the miso – don't boil, as miso is a live culture. Ladle the soup into warmed bowls and serve hot.

HEALTHY TIP

Although spinach contains high levels of iron and calcium, the presence of oxalic acid binds these minerals in a form that cannot be absorbed so readily by the body. But spinach is still very good for you – its high content of vitamins A and C and folic acid make this a versatile superfood.

COOK'S TIP

Miso (fermented barley and soy beans) is a living food in the same way that yogurt is, and contains bacteria and enzymes that are destroyed by boiling. Miso is best added as a flavouring at the end of cooking. It's available from Asian shops and larger supermarkets.

PER SERVING

55 calories

2g fat (of which trace saturates)

6g carbohydrate

1.3g salt

dairy free

Hot and Sour Soup

Preparation Time 20 minutes   Cooking Time 30–35 minutes   Serves 4   **EASY**

1 tbsp vegetable oil

2 turkey breasts, about 300g (11oz), or the same quantity of tofu, cut into strips

5cm (2in) piece fresh root ginger, peeled and grated

4 spring onions, finely sliced

1–2 tbsp Thai red curry paste

75g (3oz) long-grain wild rice

1.1 litres (2 pints) hot weak chicken or vegetable stock or boiling water

200g (7oz) mangetouts, sliced

juice of 1 lime

4 tbsp freshly chopped coriander to garnish

1 Heat the oil in a deep pan. Add the turkey or tofu and cook over a medium heat for 5 minutes or until browned. Add the ginger and spring onions and cook for a further 2–3 minutes. Stir in the curry paste and cook for 1–2 minutes to warm the spices.

2 Add the rice and stir to coat in the curry paste. Pour the hot stock or boiling water into the pan, stir once and bring to the boil. Reduce the heat, cover and simmer for about 20 minutes.

3 Add the mangetouts and cook for a further 5 minutes or until the rice is cooked. Just before serving, squeeze in the lime juice and stir to mix.

4 To serve, ladle into warmed bowls and sprinkle with the coriander.

HEALTHY TIP

This soup is a good source of protein, which comes from the turkey. It contains ginger, which is good for calming an upset stomach and providing relief from bloating and gas. Ginger is often recommended for alleviating and preventing nausea particularly in the form of seasickness, morning sickness and motion sickness.

PER SERVING

255 calories

10g fat (of which 1g saturates)

19g carbohydrate

0.7g salt

dairy free

Chicken Broth

Preparation Time 30 minutes   Cooking Time 15 minutes   Serves 4   **EASY**

1 tbsp olive oil

about 300g (11oz) boneless, skinless chicken thighs, cubed

3 garlic cloves, crushed

2 medium red chillies, seeded and finely diced (see Cook's Tips)

1 litre (1¾ pints) chicken stock

250g (9oz) each green beans, broccoli, sugarsnap peas and courgettes, chopped

50g (2oz) pasta shapes or spaghetti, broken into short lengths

1 Heat the oil in a large pan. Add the chicken, garlic and chillies and cook for 5–10 minutes or until the chicken is opaque all over.

2 Add the stock and bring to the boil. Add the vegetables, reduce the heat and simmer for 5 minutes or until the chicken is cooked through.

3 Meanwhile, cook the pasta in a separate pan of lightly salted boiling water for about 5–10 minutes, depending on the type of pasta or until just cooked.

4 Drain the pasta and add to the broth. Ladle into warmed bowls and serve immediately.

COOK'S TIPS

• Chillies vary enormously in strength, from quite mild to blisteringly hot, depending on the type of chilli and its ripeness. Taste a small piece first to check it's not too hot for you.

• Be extremely careful when handling chillies not to touch or rub your eyes with your fingers, as they will sting. Wash knives immediately after handling chillies for the same reason. As a precaution, use rubber gloves when preparing them if you like.

HEALTHY TIP

This highly nutritious soup provides an excellent balance of protein (from the chicken), carbohydrate (from the pasta) and healthy unsaturated fats (from the olive oil). The vegetables add valuable amounts of fibre, B vitamins, folate and iron, while the garlic provides numerous health benefits including protection against heart disease.

PER SERVING

229 calories
7g fat (of which 1g saturates)
16g carbohydrate
1.2g salt
dairy free

Cock-a-Leekie Soup

Preparation Time 30–40 minutes   Cooking Time 1 hour 20 minutes   Serves 8   **EASY**

1 oven-ready chicken, about
    1.4kg (3lb)
2 onions, roughly chopped
2 carrots, roughly chopped
2 celery sticks, roughly chopped
1 bay leaf
25g (1oz) butter
900g (2lb) leeks, trimmed and sliced
125g (4oz) ready-to-eat dried prunes,
    sliced
salt and ground black pepper
freshly chopped parsley to serve

FOR THE DUMPLINGS
125g (4oz) self-raising flour
a pinch of salt
50g (2oz) shredded suet
2 tbsp freshly chopped parsley
2 tbsp freshly chopped thyme

1 Put the chicken into a pan in which
it fits quite snugly, then add the
chopped vegetables, bay leaf and
chicken giblets (if available). Pour in
1.7 litres (3 pints) water and bring
to the boil, then reduce the heat,
cover and simmer gently for
1 hour.

2 Meanwhile, melt the butter in
a large pan. Add the leeks and
fry gently for 10 minutes or
until softened.

3 Remove the chicken from the
pan and leave until cool enough
to handle. Strain the stock and put
to one side. Strip the chicken from
the bones and shred roughly. Add
to the stock with the prunes and
softened leeks.

4 To make the dumplings, sift the
flour and salt into a bowl. Stir in the
suet, herbs and about 5 tbsp water
to make a fairly firm dough. Lightly
shape the dough into 2.5cm (1in)
balls. Bring the soup just to the boil
and season well. Reduce the heat,
add the dumplings and cover the
pan with a lid. Simmer for 15–20
minutes until the dumplings are light
and fluffy. Serve the soup scattered
with chopped parsley.

COOK'S TIP

Make the stock a day ahead, if
possible, then cool overnight.
The following day, remove any
fat from the surface.

PER SERVING

280 calories
4g fat (of which 1g saturates)
40g carbohydrate
0.2g salt

Fast Fish Soup

Preparation Time 10 minutes   **Cooking Time** 15 minutes   **Serves 4**   **EASY**

1 leek, trimmed and finely sliced
4 fat garlic cloves, crushed
3 celery sticks, finely sliced
1 small fennel bulb, finely sliced
1 red chilli, seeded and finely chopped
   (see Cook's Tip, page 49)
3 tbsp olive oil
50ml (2fl oz) dry white wine
about 750g (1lb 10oz) mixed fish and
   shellfish, such as haddock, monkfish
   and salmon, raw shelled prawns, and
   mussels, scrubbed, rinsed and beards
   removed (see Cook's Tip,
   page 135)

4 medium tomatoes, chopped
1½ tbsp freshly chopped thyme
salt and ground black pepper

1 Put the leek into a large pan and add the garlic, celery, fennel, chilli and oil. Cook over a medium heat for 5 minutes or until the vegetables are soft and beginning to colour.

2 Stir in 1.1 litres (2 pints) boiling water and the wine. Bring to the boil, then reduce the heat, cover and simmer for 5 minutes.

3 Meanwhile, cut the white fish into large chunks. Add to the soup with the tomatoes and thyme. Continue to simmer gently until the fish has just turned opaque. Add the prawns and simmer for 1 minute, then add the mussels. As soon as all the mussels have opened, season the soup and ladle into warmed bowls. Discard any mussels that remain closed, then serve immediately.

COOK'S TIP

Frozen seafood mix is a useful standby. Use it instead of the fish and shellfish in this recipe but take care not to overcook or it will become tough.

TRY SOMETHING DIFFERENT

• To give the soup more of a kick, stir in 2 tbsp Pernod instead of the wine.
• Garlic croûtes are traditionally served with fish soup; they can be made while the soup is simmering. Toast small slices of baguette, spread with garlic mayonnaise and sprinkle with grated cheese. Float in the hot soup just before serving.

PER SERVING

269 calories
10g fat (of which 2g saturates)
6g carbohydrate
0.6g salt
gluten free • dairy free

Roasted Root Vegetable Salad

Preparation Time 20 minutes, plus cooling   **Cooking Time** 40 minutes   **Serves 4**   **EASY**

1 butternut squash, halved, seeded and
   cubed
1½ large carrots, cut into chunks
3 fresh thyme sprigs
1½ tbsp olive oil
2 red onions, cut into wedges
1 tbsp balsamic vinegar
400g can chickpeas, drained and rinsed
25g (1oz) pinenuts, toasted
100g (3½oz) wild rocket
salt and ground black pepper

1 Preheat the oven to 190°C (170°C fan oven) mark 5. Put the squash and carrots into a large deep roasting tin. Scatter the thyme sprigs over them, drizzle with 1 tbsp oil and season with salt and pepper. Roast for 20 minutes.

2 Take the tin out of the oven, give it a good shake to make sure the vegetables aren't sticking, then add the onions. Drizzle the remaining oil over and toss to coat. Roast for a further 20 minutes or until all the vegetables are tender.

3 Remove the roasted vegetables from the oven and discard any twiggy sprigs of thyme. Drizzle the vinegar over, stir in and leave to cool.

4 To serve, put the chickpeas into a large serving bowl. Add the cooled vegetables, the pinenuts and rocket (reserving a few leaves to garnish). Toss everything together and garnish with the reserved rocket.

HEALTHY TIP

This salad gives you decent amounts of protein, carbohydrate and many vitamins and minerals. Chickpeas are an excellent source of soluble fibre, protein and iron. They contain fructo-oligosaccharides, a type of fibre that promotes healthy gut bacteria, which are important for healthy digestion and healthy immunity.

GET AHEAD

To prepare ahead Complete the recipe to the end of step 3, then cool, cover and chill for up to two days.
To use Complete the recipe.

PER SERVING
290 calories
14g fat (of which 2g saturates)
33g carbohydrate
0.7g salt
vegetarian

Melon, Mango and Cucumber Salad with Wasabi Dressing

Preparation Time 15 minutes, plus chilling **Serves 6** **EASY**

½ cucumber, halved lengthways and
   seeded
1 Charentais melon, halved and seeded
1 mango, peeled and stoned
freshly chopped flat-leafed parsley and
   lime wedges to serve

FOR THE WASABI DRESSING

3 tsp soy sauce
1 tbsp dry sherry
1 tbsp rice wine vinegar or white wine
   vinegar
¼ tsp wasabi paste (see Cook's Tip) or
   finely chopped green chilli (see
   Cook's Tip, page 49)

1 Cut the cucumber into slim diagonal slices. Cut the rind off the melon and cut the flesh into similar-size pieces to the cucumber. Cut the mango flesh into similar-size lengths. Mix the cucumber, melon and mango in a large bowl.

2 To make the wasabi dressing, put the soy sauce, sherry, vinegar and wasabi paste or chilli into a small bowl and whisk together, then toss with the salad. Sprinkle with chopped parsley and serve with lime wedges.

COOK'S TIP

Wasabi paste is a Japanese condiment, green in colour and extremely hot – a little goes a long way. It is available from larger supermarkets, but if you can't get it use creamed horseradish instead.

GET AHEAD

To prepare ahead Complete the recipe, store in an airtight container and keep chilled for up to one day.
To use Serve with lime wedges.

PER SERVING

62 calories
trace fat (of which 0g saturates)
14g carbohydrate
1.5g salt
**vegetarian • gluten free
dairy free**

Warm Tofu, Fennel and Bean Salad

Preparation Time 10 minutes   **Cooking Time** 15 minutes   **Serves 4**   **EASY**

1 tbsp olive oil, plus 1 tsp
1 red onion, finely sliced
1 fennel bulb, finely sliced
1 tbsp cider vinegar
400g can butter beans, drained
    and rinsed
2 tbsp freshly chopped flat-leafed
    parsley
200g (7oz) smoked tofu
salt and ground black pepper

1 Heat 1 tbsp oil in a large frying pan. Add the onion and fennel and cook over a medium heat for about 5–10 minutes until soft.

2 Add the cider vinegar and heat through for 2 minutes. Stir in the butter beans and parsley, season to taste with salt and pepper, then tip into a bowl.

3 Slice the smoked tofu horizontally into four and then into eight triangles. Add to the pan with the remaining 1 tsp oil. Cook for 2 minutes on each side or until golden brown.

4 Divide the bean mixture among four plates, then add two slices of tofu to each plate.

HEALTHY TIP

Tofu is rich in high-quality protein. It is also a good source of calcium, B vitamins and iron. Tofu is also very low in fat and sodium, making it a perfect food for people on sodium-restricted diets. Fennel is a good digestive aid, helping reduce gas and bloating. The butter beans provide good amounts of protein and iron as well as fibre.

PER SERVING

150 calories
6g fat (of which 1g saturates)
15g carbohydrate
0.8g salt
**vegetarian • gluten free
dairy free**

Cannellini Bean and Sunblush Tomato Salad

Preparation Time 5 minutes, plus marinating   **Serves 6**   **EASY**

½ red onion, very finely sliced
2 tbsp red wine vinegar
a small handful each of freshly chopped
   mint and flat-leafed parsley
2 × 400g cans cannellini beans, drained
   and rinsed
4 tbsp extra virgin olive oil
4 celery sticks, sliced
75g (3oz) sunblush tomatoes, snipped in
   half
salt and ground black pepper

1 Put the onion into a small bowl, add the vinegar and toss. Leave to marinate for 30 minutes – this stage is important as it takes the astringency out of the onion.

2 Tip the onion and vinegar into a large serving bowl, add the remaining ingredients, season to taste with salt and pepper and toss everything together.

PER SERVING

163 calories
8g fat (of which 1g saturates),
17g carbohydrate
1.3g salt
vegetarian • gluten free
dairy free

Vietnamese Rice Salad

Preparation Time 10 minutes   Cooking Time 20 minutes   Serves 6   **EASY**

225g (8oz) mixed basmati and wild rice
1 large carrot, coarsely grated
1 large courgette, coarsely grated
1 red onion, finely sliced
4 tbsp roasted salted peanuts, lightly
  chopped
20g (³⁄₄oz) each fresh coriander, mint
  and basil, roughly chopped
100g (3½oz) wild rocket

FOR THE VIETNAMESE
  DRESSING

2 tbsp light muscovado sugar
juice of 2 limes
4 tbsp fish sauce
6 tbsp rice wine vinegar or white wine
  vinegar
2 tbsp sunflower oil

1 Put the rice into a pan with 500ml (18fl oz) water. Cover and bring to the boil, then reduce the heat and cook for 20 minutes until the rice is just cooked. Tip on to a plastic tray, spread out and leave to cool.

2 Meanwhile, make the dressing. Put the sugar into a small pan and heat gently until it just begins to dissolve. Add the lime juice, fish sauce and vinegar. Stir over a low heat to dissolve the sugar. Take off the heat and add the oil. Stir into the rice with the grated carrot, courgette and sliced onion.

3 Spoon the salad into a large bowl and top with peanuts, herbs and rocket. Cover and keep chilled until ready to serve.

GET AHEAD

To prepare ahead Complete the recipe to the end of step 2 and store in an airtight container in the fridge for up to two days.
To use Complete the recipe.

PER SERVING

294 calories
14g fat (of which 2g saturates)
38g carbohydrate
0.6g salt
gluten free • dairy free

Orange and Chicken Salad

Preparation Time 15 minutes   Cooking Time 10 minutes   Serves 4   **EASY**

50g (2oz) cashew nuts
zest and juice of 2 oranges
2 tbsp marmalade
1 tbsp honey
1 tbsp oyster sauce
400g (14oz) roast chicken, shredded
a handful of chopped raw vegetables,
    such as cucumber, carrot, red and
    yellow pepper and Chinese leaves

1 Put the cashew nuts into a dry frying pan over a medium-high heat and cook for 2–3 minutes, tossing regularly, until golden brown. Tip into a large serving bowl.

2 To make the dressing, put the orange zest and juice into the frying pan with the marmalade, honey and oyster sauce. Bring to the boil, stirring, then simmer for about 2–3 minutes until slightly thickened.

3 Add the roast chicken to the serving bowl with the chopped raw vegetables. Pour the dressing over the salad, toss everything together and serve immediately.

COOK'S TIP

Toasting the cashew nuts in a dry frying pan before adding them to the salad brings out their flavour, giving them an intense, nutty taste and a wonderful golden colour.

PER SERVING

252 calories
8g fat (of which 2g saturates)
20g carbohydrate
0.5g salt
gluten free • dairy free

Easy Roast Chicken Salad

Preparation Time 10 minutes   Serves 1   **EASY**

100g (3½oz) shredded roast chicken, skin discarded
1 carrot, chopped
1 celery stick, chopped
¼ cucumber, chopped
a handful of ripe cherry tomatoes, chopped
1 tbsp hummus
¼ lemon to serve

1 Put the chicken into a shallow bowl. Add the carrot, celery, cucumber and cherry tomatoes.

2 Top with the hummus and serve with lemon for squeezing over the salad.

HEALTHY TIP

Chicken is lower in fat and higher in protein than red meat, and it is a good source of many nutrients, such as vitamins B6 and B12. It also contains selenium (an antioxidant that helps the body fight against cancer) and the amino acids that produce serotonin (the hormone that helps us feel happy).

TRY SOMETHING DIFFERENT

• For an even more nutritious salad, add a few pumpkin seeds or sunflower seeds, or a handful of sprouted seeds such as alfalfa, or chopped watercress.
• For extra bite, add a little finely chopped red chilli; for extra sweetness, add some strips of red pepper.
• For extra flavour, add some freshly chopped coriander or torn fresh basil leaves.

PER SERVING

323 calories
18g fat (of which 5g saturates)
17g carbohydrate,
0.9g salt
gluten free • dairy free

Zesty Orange, Chicken and Tarragon Salad

Preparation Time 15 minutes, plus chilling **Serves 4** **EASY**

50g (2oz) pecan nuts or walnuts
350g (12oz) smoked chicken or cooked
  chicken breast, skinned and cut into
  long strips
2 oranges
2 small chicory heads

FOR THE DRESSING
grated zest and juice of 2 oranges
2 tbsp white wine vinegar
1 tsp caster sugar
5 tbsp olive oil
3 tbsp freshly chopped tarragon
1 large egg yolk
salt and ground black pepper

1 Put the nuts into a dry pan and toast over a medium-high heat, tossing regularly, for 2–3 minutes until golden brown. Chop roughly.

2 Whisk all the dressing ingredients together in a small bowl. Put the chicken strips into a bowl, spoon over the dressing, cover and chill for at least 1 hour.

3 Use a sharp knife to remove the peel and pith from the oranges, then cut into slices.

4 Put a layer of chicory into a large flat salad bowl, add the orange slices, then spoon the chicken and dressing over. Sprinkle the toasted nuts over the top and serve.

COOK'S TIPS

Instant flavour ideas for chicken

• Snip bacon into a frying pan, cook until crisp and golden, then stir into warm, boiled new potatoes with shredded roast chicken and mustard mayonnaise. Serve with green salad.
• Roast a chicken with lots of tarragon, peppers, whole garlic cloves and olive oil. Serve with couscous, into which you've stirred the roasting juices.
• Pan-fry chicken breasts that have been marinating in olive oil with rosemary, thyme and crushed garlic. Serve with a fresh tomato sauce made by whizzing together ripe tomatoes, olive oil, basil and salt and pepper to taste.
• Pan-fry chicken breasts in butter and set aside. Add flaked almonds and pitted fresh cherries to the pan, toss over a high heat for 1–2 minutes and serve with the cooked chicken.

PER SERVING

252 calories
8g fat (of which 2g saturates)
20g carbohydrate
0.5g salt
gluten free • dairy free

Warm Chicken Liver Salad

Preparation Time 20 minutes   **Cooking Time** 8–10 minutes   **Serves 4**   **EASY**

450g (1lb) chicken livers
1–2 tbsp balsamic vinegar
1 tsp Dijon mustard
3 tbsp olive oil
50g (2oz) streaky bacon rashers,
  rind removed and cut into small, neat
  pieces (lardons)
50g (2oz) sun-dried tomatoes or
  roasted red peppers, cut into thin
  strips
½ curly endive, about 175g (6oz)
100g (3½oz) rocket
1 bunch of spring onions, sliced
salt and ground black pepper

1 Drain the chicken livers on kitchen paper, then trim and cut into pieces.

2 To make the dressing, put the vinegar, mustard, 2 tbsp oil, and salt and pepper to taste into a small bowl. Whisk together and put to one side.

3 Fry the lardons in a non-stick frying pan until beginning to brown, stirring from time to time. Add the tomatoes or red peppers and heat through for 1 minute. Add the remaining oil and the chicken livers and stir-fry over a high heat for 2–3 minutes until the livers are just pink in the centre.

4 Meanwhile, toss the endive, rocket and spring onions with the dressing in a large bowl. Divide among four plates, arrange the warm livers and bacon on top and serve at once.

HEALTHY TIP

Chicken livers provide the richest source of folic acid, with nearly five times the RDA in 100g (3½oz). They are rich in iron, which is needed for healthy red blood cells and energy, and provide enough vitamin B12 in one portion to satisfy the body's requirements for a month.

PER SERVING

236 calories
15g fat (of which 3g saturates)
3g carbohydrate
0.8g salt
gluten free • dairy free

Warm Bacon Salad

Preparation Time 10 minutes   **Cooking Time** 10–15 minutes   **Serves 2**   **EASY**

4 handfuls of soft salad leaves
1 small red onion, thinly sliced
75g (3oz) cubed pancetta
1 thick slice white bread, diced
2 medium eggs
25g (1oz) Parmesan shavings
salt and ground black pepper
fresh flat-leafed parsley sprigs to garnish

FOR THE DRESSING
1 tbsp Dijon mustard
2 tbsp red wine vinegar
2 tbsp fruity olive oil

1 Put the salad leaves and onion into a large bowl. Fry the pancetta in a non-stick frying pan until it begins to release some fat. Add the diced bread and continue to fry until the pancetta is golden and crisp.

2 Put all the dressing ingredients into a small bowl, season with salt and pepper and whisk together.

3 Half-fill a small pan with cold water and bring to the boil. Turn the heat right down – there should be just a few bubbles on the base of the pan. Break the eggs into a cup, then tip them gently into the pan and cook for 3–4 minutes, using a metal spoon to baste the tops with a little of the hot water. Lift the eggs out of the water with a slotted spoon and drain on kitchen paper.

4 Tip the pancetta, bread and any pan juices over the salad leaves. Add the Parmesan, then pour the dressing over the salad. Toss well, then divide between two plates. Top each with an egg, season to taste, then garnish with flat-leafed parsley sprigs and serve.

PER SERVING
375 calories
29g fat (of which 9g saturates)
11g carbohydrate
1.7g salt

Couscous and Haddock Salad

Preparation Time 15 minutes   Cooking Time 15 minutes   Serves 4   **EASY**

175g (6oz) couscous

125g (4oz) cooked smoked haddock, flaked

50g (2oz) cooked peas

a pinch of curry powder

2 spring onions, sliced

1 tbsp freshly chopped flat-leafed parsley

1 small hard-boiled egg, chopped

2 tbsp olive oil

2 tsp lemon juice

salt and ground black pepper

1 Cook the couscous according to the packet instructions. Drain if necessary.

2 Mix the couscous with the smoked haddock, peas, curry powder, spring onions, parsley and egg.

3 Toss with the oil, lemon juice and plenty of salt and pepper to taste, then serve.

HEALTHY TIP

Couscous is made by rolling and shaping moistened semolina wheat and then coating the granules with finely ground wheat flour. It is very healthy, with a low GI (see page 12), thus providing sustained energy, and a good profile of vitamins, including thiamin, riboflavin, niacin, vitamin B6 and folate. It is low in fat and sodium and contains useful amounts of selenium.

PER SERVING

408 calories

15g fat (of which 2g saturates)

48g carbohydrate

1.3g salt

dairy free

Tuna Salad

Preparation Time 10 minutes   Serves 4   **EASY**

2 × 400g can mixed beans, drained and
  rinsed
250g (9oz) flaked tuna
1 cucumber, chopped
1 large red onion, finely sliced
4 ripe tomatoes, chopped
4 celery sticks, chopped
80g bag baby spinach leaves
2 tbsp olive oil
1 tsp red wine vinegar
salt and ground black pepper

1 Put the beans into a bowl and add
  the tuna, cucumber, red onion,
  tomatoes, celery and spinach.

2 Mix together the oil and vinegar,
  season with salt and pepper, then
  toss through the bean mix and
  serve immediately.

COOK'S TIP
If you prefer tuna in oil, replace the
olive oil with the same amount from
the tuna can.

PER SERVING
157 calories
4g fat (of which trace saturates)
9g carbohydrate
0.5g salt
gluten free • dairy free

Trout with Apple and Watercress Salad

Preparation Time 15 minutes   **Cooking Time** 15–20 minutes   **Serves 4**   **EASY**

4 × 150g (5oz) trout fillets
1 tbsp olive oil, plus extra to oil
250g (9oz) cooked baby new potatoes,
   cut into chunks
2 apples, cored and cut into chunks
4 cooked beetroot in natural juice, cut
   into chunks
150g (5oz) watercress
salt and ground black pepper

FOR THE DRESSING

1 tbsp extra virgin olive oil
juice of ½ lemon
2 tsp Dijon mustard
1 tbsp freshly chopped dill

1 Preheat the oven to 200°C (180°C
fan oven) mark 6. Put each piece of
fish on a piece of oiled foil, brush
the top of the fish with olive oil and
season with salt and pepper.
Scrunch the foil around the fish and
roast for 15–20 minutes until the
fish is cooked.

2 Put the potatoes, apples, beetroot
and watercress into a large bowl
and mix lightly.

3 Mix all the dressing ingredients
together In a small bowl and season
with salt and pepper. Add to the
salad and toss through, then serve
with the fish.

PER SERVING

320 calories
12g fat (of which 1g saturates)
21g carbohydrate
0.4g salt
gluten free • dairy free

Smoked Mackerel Citrus Salad

Preparation Time 10 minutes **Cooking Time** 5 minutes **Serves 6** **EASY**

200g (7oz) green beans
200g (7oz) smoked mackerel fillets
125g (4oz) mixed watercress, spinach
  and rocket
4 spring onions, sliced
1 avocado, halved, stoned, peeled and
  sliced

FOR THE DRESSING

1 tbsp olive oil
1 tbsp freshly chopped coriander
grated zest and juice of 1 orange

1 Preheat the grill. Blanch the green beans in boiling water for 3 minutes until they are just tender. Drain, rinse under cold running water, drain well, then tip into a bowl.

2 Cook the mackerel under the hot grill for 2 minutes until warmed through. Flake into bite-size pieces, discard the skin and add the fish to the bowl with the salad leaves, spring onions and avocado.

3 Whisk all the dressing ingredients together in a small bowl. Pour over the salad, toss well and serve immediately.

COOK'S TIP

Leftover mackerel fillets can be turned into a quick pâté. Whiz in a food processor with the zest of a lemon and enough crème fraîche to make a spreadable consistency.

PER SERVING

299 calories
26g fat (of which 5g saturates)
4g carbohydrate
1g salt
gluten free • dairy free

Lunch and Light Bites

Cheesy Polenta with Tomato Sauce

Preparation Time 15 minutes, plus cooling   Cooking Time 45 minutes   Serves 6   **EASY**

oil to oil
225g (8oz) polenta
4 tbsp freshly chopped herbs, such as
    oregano, chives and flat-leafed parsley
100g (3½oz) freshly grated Parmesan,
    plus fresh Parmesan shavings to serve
salt and ground black pepper

**FOR THE TOMATO AND
    BASIL SAUCE**
1 tbsp vegetable oil
3 garlic cloves, crushed
500g carton creamed tomatoes or
    passata
1 bay leaf
1 fresh thyme sprig
caster sugar
3 tbsp freshly chopped basil, plus extra
    to garnish

1 Lightly oil a 25.5 × 18cm (10 × 7in) dish. Bring 1.1 litres (2 pints) water and ¼ tsp salt to the boil in a large pan. Sprinkle in the polenta, whisking constantly. Reduce the heat and simmer, stirring frequently, for 10–15 minutes until the mixture leaves the sides of the pan.

2 Stir in the herbs and Parmesan and season to taste with salt and pepper. Turn into the prepared dish and leave to cool.

3 Next, make the tomato and basil sauce. Heat the oil in a pan and fry the garlic for 30 seconds (do not brown). Add the creamed tomatoes or passata, the bay leaf, thyme and a large pinch of sugar. Season with salt and pepper and bring to the boil, then reduce the heat and simmer, uncovered, for 5–10 minutes. Remove the bay leaf and thyme sprig and add the chopped basil.

4 To serve, prehat a griddle or grill. Cut the polenta into pieces and lightly brush with oil. Fry on the hot griddle for 3–4 minutes on each side or under the hot grill for about 7–8 minutes on each side. Serve with the tomato and basil sauce, fresh Parmesan shavings and chopped basil.

PER SERVING
249 calories
9g fat (of which 4g saturates)
31g carbohydrate
0.9g salt
gluten free • dairy free

GET AHEAD
To prepare ahead Complete the recipe to the end of step 3. Cover and chill separately for up to two days.
To use Complete the recipe.

Mixed Mushroom Frittata

Preparation Time 15 minutes   Cooking Time 15–20 minutes   Serves 4   **EASY**

1 tbsp olive oil
300g (11oz) mixed mushrooms, sliced
2 tbsp freshly chopped thyme
zest and juice of ½ lemon
50g (2oz) watercress, chopped
6 medium eggs, beaten
salt and ground black pepper
stoneground wholegrain bread
    (optional) and a crisp green salad to
    serve

1 Heat the oil in a large deep frying pan over a medium heat. Add the mushrooms and thyme and stir-fry for 4–5 minutes until starting to soften and brown. Stir in the lemon zest and juice, then bubble for 1 minute. Reduce the heat.

2 Preheat the grill. Add the watercress to the beaten eggs, season with salt and pepper and pour into the pan. Cook on the hob for 7–8 minutes until the sides and base are firm but the centre is still a little soft.

3 Transfer to the grill and cook for 4–5 minutes until just set. Cut into wedges and serve with chunks of bread, if you like, and a salad.

HEALTHY TIP

This dish is rich in protein and a good source of vitamin D. The mushrooms supply useful amounts of fibre, vitamin B6 and potassium while the watercress adds iron and folate.

PER SERVING

148 calories
12g fat (of which 3g saturates)
0g carbohydrate
0.3g salt
vegetarian • gluten free
dairy free

Roast Mushrooms with Pesto

Preparation Time 5 minutes   Cooking Time 15 minutes   Serves 4   **EASY**

8 portabella mushrooms
8 tbsp fresh Pesto (see Cook's Tip)
toasted ciabatta, salad and basil leaves
    to serve

1 Preheat the oven to 200°C
(180°C fan oven) mark 6. Put the
mushrooms into an ovenproof dish,
then spoon 1 tbsp fresh Pesto on
top of each one.

2 Pour 150ml (¼ pint) boiling
water into the dish, then cook for
15 minutes or until the mushrooms
are soft and the topping is hot.
Serve with toasted ciabatta and
salad, and scatter a few small basil
leaves over the mushrooms.

Pesto
Roughly chop 75g (3oz) basil, 50g
(2oz) Parmesan, 25g (1oz) pinenuts
and ½ crushed garlic clove and put
into a food processor. With the
motor running, add 50–75ml (2–3fl
oz) extra virgin olive oil and whiz to a
rough paste. Alternatively, grind in a
pestle and mortar. Season with salt
and pepper.

PER SERVING

258 calories
23g fat (of which 6g saturates)
1g carbohydrate
0.5g salt

Chickpea Patties

Preparation Time 20 minutes, plus chilling   Cooking Time 15 minutes   Serves 4   **EASY**

2 × 400g cans chickpeas, drained and
 rinsed
4 garlic cloves, crushed
1 tsp ground cumin
1 small red onion, chopped
20g pack fresh coriander
2 tbsp plain flour, plus extra to dust
olive oil for frying
Mixed Salad (see Cook's Tip, page 99)
 and lemon wedges to serve

1 Pat the chickpeas dry with kitchen
 paper, then put them into a food
 processor with the garlic, cumin,
 onion and coriander. Whiz until
 smooth, then stir in the flour.

2 With floured hands, shape the
 chickpea mixture into 12 small,
 round patties and chill in the fridge
 for 20 minutes.

3 Heat a little oil in a non-stick frying
 pan over a medium heat and fry the
 patties in batches for about
 2 minutes on each side or until
 heated through and golden. Serve
 the patties warm with mixed salad
 and lemon wedges.

HEALTHY TIP

Chickpeas are highly nutritious,
packed with protein, fibre, B vitamins
and iron. They also supply complex
carbohydrates and have a low GI,
which means they provide long-
lasting energy (see page 12). Frying
the patties in olive oil is a healthy
alternative to frying in a blended
vegetable oil, as it contains high
levels of heart-healthy
monounsaturated fats.

FREEZING TIP

To freeze Make the patties, then
cool, put in a freezerproof container
and freeze. They will keep for up to
one month.
To use Thaw overnight at a cool
room temperature, then reheat in
the oven at 180°C (160°C fan oven)
mark 4 for 20 minutes.

PER SERVING

344 calories
17g fat (of which 2g saturates)
37g carbohydrate
1g salt
vegetarian • dairy free

Bubble and Squeak Cakes

Preparation Time 15 minutes   Cooking Time 45 minutes, plus cooling   Makes 12   **EASY**

550g (1¼lb) old potatoes
125g (4oz) butter
175g (6oz) leeks, trimmed and finely
 shredded
175g (6oz) green cabbage, finely
 shredded
plain flour to dust
1 tbsp oil
salt and ground black pepper

1 Cook the potatoes in a large pan of lightly salted boiling water until tender, then drain and mash.

2 Heat 50g (2oz) butter in a large non-stick frying pan. Add the leeks and cabbage and fry for 5 minutes, stirring, or until soft and beginning to colour. Combine the leeks and cabbage with the potatoes then season well with salt and pepper. Leave to cool. When cool enough to handle, mould into 12 cakes and dust with flour.

3 Heat the oil and remaining butter in a non-stick frying pan and cook the cakes for 4 minutes on each side or until they are golden, crisp and hot right through. Serve.

PER CAKE
130 calories
10g fat (of which 6g saturates)
10g carbohydrate
0.2g salt
vegetarian

Rosti Potatoes with Fried Eggs

Preparation Time 20 minutes   Cooking Time 20–25 minutes plus cooling   Serves 4   **EASY**

900g (2lb) red potatoes, scrubbed and
    left whole
40g (1½oz) butter
4 large eggs
salt and ground black pepper
fresh flat-leafed parsley sprigs to garnish

1 Put the potatoes into a pan of cold water. Cover, bring to the boil and parboil for 5–8 minutes. Drain and leave to cool for 15 minutes.

2 Preheat the oven to 150°C (130°C fan oven) mark 2. Put a baking tray inside to warm. Peel the potatoes and coarsely grate them lengthways into long strands. Divide into eight portions and shape into mounds.

3 Melt half the butter in a large non-stick frying pan. When it is beginning to brown, add four of the potato mounds, spacing them well apart, and flatten them a little. Fry slowly for 6–7 minutes until golden brown, then turn them and brown the other side for 6–7 minutes. Transfer to a warmed baking tray and keep warm in the oven while you fry the rest.

4 Just before serving, carefully break the eggs into the hot pan and fry for about 2 minutes until the white is set and the yolk is still soft. Season with salt and pepper and serve at once, with the rosti and garnished with parsley sprigs.

PER SERVING

324 calories
16g fat (of which 7g saturates)
36g carbohydrate
0.4g salt
vegetarian • gluten free

Egg and Pepper Pizza

Preparation Time 15 minutes   Cooking Time 12 minutes   Serves 4   **EASY**

150g (5oz) red and yellow marinated peppers in oil, drained and oil reserved

8 tbsp passata

4 small (4 × 100g/3½oz) pizza bases

4 medium eggs

125g (4oz) watercress, washed and stalks removed

1 Preheat the oven to 220°C (200°C fan oven) mark 7. Put two large baking sheets, big enough to hold two pizzas each, into the oven to heat up.

2 Chop the peppers into thin strips. Spoon 2 tbsp passata over each pizza base and scatter strips of pepper around the edges. Make a dip in the passata in the middle of each pizza and break an egg into it. Carefully slide the pizzas on to the preheated baking sheets. Place in the oven and cook for 12 minutes or until the egg is cooked.

3 Top the pizzas with the watercress, drizzle with a little of the reserved oil from the peppers and serve.

COOK'S TIP

Watercress is the salad superfood par excellence. It is a good source of iron, and vitamins C and E.

PER SERVING

448 calories

16g fat (of which 3g saturates)

63g carbohydrate

1.2g salt

vegetarian • gluten free

Tomato Crostini with Feta and Basil

Preparation Time 20 minutes   Cooking Time 3 minutes   Serves 4   **EASY**

1 small garlic clove, crushed

3 tbsp freshly chopped basil, plus extra
basil leaves to garnish

25g (1oz) pinenuts

2 tbsp extra virgin olive oil

grated zest and juice of 1 lime

50g (2oz) vegetarian feta cheese

4 large tomatoes, preferably vine-
ripened, thickly sliced

150g tub fresh tomato salsa

50g (2oz) pitted black olives, roughly
chopped

4 thick slices country-style bread

salt and ground black pepper

1 Put the garlic, chopped basil, pinenuts, oil, lime zest and juice into a food processor and whiz to a smooth paste. Add the feta cheese and whiz until smooth. Thin with 1 tbsp water if necessary. Season with salt and pepper.

2 Put the tomatoes, salsa and olives into a bowl and gently toss together.

3 Toast the bread. Divide the tomato mixture among the slices of toast and spoon the basil and feta mixture on top. Garnish with basil leaves and serve immediately.

PER SERVING

242 calories

17g fat (of which 3g saturates)

18g carbohydrate

1.5g salt

vegetarian

Easy Wrap

Preparation Time 10 minutes Serves 4 **EASY**

salt and ground black pepper to taste
2 cooked chicken breasts, about 125g
    (4oz) each, cut into bite-size pieces
1 carrot, grated
1 avocado, halved, stoned, peeled and
    chopped
a small handful of rocket
juice of ½ lemon
3 tbsp mayonnaise
4 flour tortillas

1 Mix the salt with the pepper in a
large bowl. Add the chicken, carrot,
avocado and rocket and mix well.

2 In a separate bowl, mix the lemon
juice with the mayonnaise, then
spread over the tortillas. Divide the
chicken mixture among the tortillas,
then roll up and serve in napkins,
if you like.

HEALTHY TIP

Tortillas make a sustaining light meal
as they have a lower GI (see page 12)
than many other types of bread.
These wraps are filled with chicken,
which provides protein and
B vitamins; as well as avocados, rich
in heart-protective vitamin E and
healthy unsaturated fats.

PER SERVING

269 calories
16g fat (of which 3g saturates)
17g carbohydrate,
1.5g salt

Red Pepper Pesto Croûtes

Preparation Time 20 minutes   Cooking Time 15–20 minutes   Makes 24   **EASY**

1 thin French stick, sliced into
   24 rounds
olive oil to brush
fresh Pesto (see Cook's Tip, page 71)
4 pepper pieces (from a jar of
   marinated peppers), each sliced into
   6 strips
pinenuts to garnish

1 Preheat the oven to 200°C (180°C
fan oven) mark 6. Brush both sides
of the bread with oil and put on a
baking sheet. Cook in the oven for
15–20 minutes.

2 Spread 1 tsp pesto on each croûte,
top with a pepper strip and pinenuts
and serve.

PER SERVING

90 calories
5g fat (of which 1g saturates)
10g carbohydrate
0.3g salt

Bruschetta with Tapenade

Preparation Time 10 minutes   **Cooking Time** 5 minutes   **Makes** 12   **EASY**

1 ciabatta loaf
olive oil to brush
6 tbsp tapenade (see Cook's Tips)
selection of vegetable antipasti, such as
    marinated red peppers and
    artichokes, drained
a few basil sprigs to garnish

1 Cut the ciabatta on the diagonal to make 12 slices. Brush both sides of the slices with a little oil. Heat a griddle pan until hot, add the ciabatta slices and toast for a couple of minutes on each side.

2 Spread a thin layer of tapenade on each slice of bread, then top with a little of the antipasti. Garnish with basil and serve. Alternatively, arrange the antipasti in separate bowls and let your guests assemble their own bruschettas.

HEALTHY TIP

Tapenade is a fantastic source of healthy monounsaturated fats, which help lower blood cholesterol levels and reduce heart disease risk. It is also packed with vitamin E, a powerful antioxidant that also protects against heart disease.

COOK'S TIPS

• Tapenade is a black olive paste from Provence in the south of France. You can buy ready-made tapenade, or make your own by whizzing 75g (3oz) pitted black olives in a food processor with 4 anchovies, 2 tbsp olive oil and 1 tbsp freshly chopped flat-leafed parsley.
• Instead of spreading it on bread, serve tapenade as a dip for crisp raw carrots, red pepper strips or chicory leaves.

PER SLICE

119 calories
4g fat (of which trace saturates)
19g carbohydrate
0.7g salt
dairy free

Chicken and Salsa Verde Crostini

Preparation Time 20 minutes, plus chilling   Cooking Time 2 minutes   Makes 15   **EASY**

50g (2oz) walnuts
1 loaf walnut bread, cut into
   15 × 1cm (½in) slices
2 tbsp olive oil
1 tbsp sea salt flakes
175g (6oz) cooked chicken breast,
   thinly sliced
125g (4oz) sun-dried tomatoes in oil,
   drained and thinly sliced
freshly chopped flat-leafed parsley to
   garnish

FOR THE SALSA VERDE

3 tbsp each freshly chopped coriander,
   mint and basil
1 garlic clove, roughly chopped
2 tbsp Dijon mustard
3 anchovy fillets
1 tbsp capers
50ml (2fl oz) olive oil
juice of ½ lemon

1 Put the walnuts into a dry pan and toast over a medium-high heat, tossing regularly, for 2–3 minutes until golden brown. Finely chop and set aside.

2 Put all the salsa verde ingredients into a food processor or blender and whiz until it is smooth. (Alternatively, use a pestle and mortar.) Cover and chill.

3 Preheat the grill to high. Put the bread on a baking sheet, brush with oil and sprinkle with sea salt flakes. Grill for 1 minute on each side or until lightly toasted.

4 To serve, put two or three chicken slices on each crostini base, top with a spoonful of salsa verde and slices of sun-dried tomato, then garnish with a sprinkling of walnuts and flat-leafed parsley.

PER SERVING

208 calories
9g fat (of which 1g saturates)
24g carbohydrate
1.7g salt
dairy free

Squid with Haricot Beans and Rocket

Preparation Time 20 minutes, plus marinating   Cooking Time about 2 minutes   Serves 6   **EASY**

450g (1lb) prepared squid, cut into
   thick rings
3 tbsp extra virgin olive oil
1 rosemary sprig, cut into four pieces
1 chilli, seeded and finely chopped (see
   Cook's Tip, page 49)
zest and juice of 1 lemon
2 × 400g cans no-added-sugar-or-salt
   haricot beans, drained and rinsed
2 tbsp olive oil
6 slices sourdough bread (about 40g
   each slice)
55g pack rocket
salt and ground black pepper
lemon wedges to serve

1 Put the squid into a non-metallic bowl. Add 1 tbsp extra virgin olive oil, the rosemary, chilli and half the lemon zest. Season to taste with salt and pepper, then leave to marinate for 30 minutes.

2 Put the beans into a large bowl with the remaining lemon zest and extra virgin olive oil and the lemon juice. Season with salt and pepper, then use a potato masher to pound into a rough purée.

3 Heat the olive oil in a wok or a non-stick frying pan. Add the squid and cook for 1–2 minutes until opaque. Toast the bread.

4 Spread the bean purée over the toast. Top with the squid and rocket and serve with lemon wedges.

PER SERVING

308 calories
12g fat (of which 2g saturates)
33g carbohydrate
0.8g salt

Sardines on Toast

Preparation Time 5 minutes   Cooking Time 8–10 minutes   Serves 4   **EASY**

4 thick slices wholemeal bread

2 large tomatoes, sliced

2 × 120g cans sardines in olive oil, drained

juice of ½ lemon

a small handful of parsley, chopped

1 Preheat the grill. Toast the slices of bread on both sides.

2 Divide the tomato slices and the sardines among the toast slices, squeeze the lemon juice over them, then put back under the grill for 2–3 minutes to heat through. Scatter the parsley over the sardines and serve immediately.

COOK'S TIP

Oily fish such as sardines are one of the best sources of essential heart-protecting omega-3 oils. Eat them at least once a week. Fresh Cornish sardines, when they are available, are a treat and are cheap. Look out for them at your fishmonger's or on the fresh fish counter at the supermarket.

TRY SOMETHING DIFFERENT

Instead of sardines, use a 200g can salmon in oil.

PER SERVING

240 calories

9g fat (of which 2g saturates)

25g carbohydrate

1.6g sal

dairy free

Quick Crab Cakes

Preparation Time 15 minutes   Cooking Time 6 minutes   Serves 4   **EASY**

200g (7oz) fresh crabmeat

2 spring onions, finely chopped

2 red chillies, seeded and finely chopped
(see Cook's Tip, page 49)

finely grated zest of 1 lime

4 tbsp freshly chopped coriander

about 40g (1½oz) wholemeal
breadcrumbs

1 tbsp groundnut oil

1 tbsp plain flour

salt and ground black pepper

1 red chilli, seeded and thinly sliced, to
garnish (see Cook's Tip, page 49)

1 lime, cut into wedges, and salad leaves
to serve

1 Put the crabmeat into a bowl, then add the spring onions, chillies, lime zest, coriander and salt and pepper to taste and stir to mix. Add enough breadcrumbs to hold the mixture together, then form the mixture into four small patties.

2 Heat ½ tbsp oil in a pan. Dredge the patties with flour and fry on one side for 3 minutes. Add the rest of the oil, then turn the patties over and fry for a further 2–3 minutes. Garnish the crab cakes with the sliced red chilli and serve with lime wedges to squeeze over them, and salad leaves.

HEALTHY TIP

Crabmeat is low in fat and relatively low in calories. It contains high levels of protein, vitamin B6 and the antioxidant selenium. The overall salt content of this recipe is low thanks to the addition of strongly flavoured ingredients such as chilli, lime and spring onions.

COOK'S TIP

Use leftover bread to make breadcrumbs and then freeze them – they're a great timesaver. You can use them from frozen.

PER SERVING

124 calories

4g fat (of which 1g saturates)

12g carbohydrate

0.9g salt

dairy free

Trout and Dill Fishcakes

Preparation Time 15 minutes · Cooking Time 25 minutes · Serves 4 · **EASY**

4 medium potatoes, roughly chopped

2 trout fillets

3 spring onions, finely chopped

2 fresh dill sprigs, finely chopped

zest of 1 lemon

1 tbsp olive oil

a little plain gluten-free flour

salt

watercress to serve

1 Cook the potatoes in a pan of lightly salted boiling water for about 6–8 minutes until tender. Drain, put back into the pan and mash.

2 Preheat the grill to high. Grill the trout fillets for 8–10 minutes until cooked through and firm to the touch. Skin the fish, flake into pieces, removing any bones, then put into the pan with the mashed potato.

3 Add the spring onions, dill and lemon zest to the pan with the oil, season with salt and mix well.

4 Shape the mixture into eight small patties. Dust with flour and put on a non-stick baking sheet. Cook the fishcakes under the hot grill for 3 minutes on each side. Serve the fishcakes hot, with watercress.

HEALTHY TIP

Trout is lower in fat than other types of oily fish. It contains omega-3 fatty acids, which help protect against heart disease, stroke, rheumatoid arthritis and depression. In this recipe the fishcakes are grilled rather than fried, which helps reduce the overall fat content of the dish.

TRY SOMETHING DIFFERENT

Replace the trout with 225g (8oz) cooked salmon, haddock or smoked haddock: skin, flake and add at step 2.

PER SERVING

196 calories

5g fat (of which 1g saturates)

27g carbohydrate

0.1g salt

gluten free · dairy free

Cheese Coleslaw with Roast Chicken

Preparation Time 15 minutes   Serves 4   **EASY**

1 baby white cabbage, thinly shredded
4 spring onions, finely chopped
1 large carrot, finely shredded
75g (3oz) mature Cheddar, grated
6 tbsp mayonnaise
ground black pepper
cress to garnish
sliced roast chicken to serve

1 Put the white cabbage, spring onions, carrot, cheese and mayonnaise into a large bowl and season with pepper.

2 Divide the coleslaw among four small bowls or plates and snip some cress over them. Serve with slices of roast chicken.

HEALTHY TIP

Cabbage is rich in fibre, vitamin C and cancer-protective nutrients called glucosinolates. It may aid the liver's detoxifying function. Carrots are rich in betacarotene, an antioxidant that helps fight cancer and heart disease. The cheese adds protein and calcium.

TRY SOMETHING DIFFERENT

• Use either Gruyère or Emmenthal instead of Cheddar.
• Add freshly chopped chives or flat-leafed parsley.
• Sprinkle with 1 tbsp mixed seeds just before serving.

PER SERVING

270 calories
23g fat (of which 7g saturates)
8g carbohydrate,
0.6g salt
gluten free

Lime and Chilli Chicken Goujons

Preparation Time 15 minutes   Cooking Time 20 minutes   Serves 4   **EASY**

300g (11oz) boneless, skinless chicken
   thighs
50g (2oz) fresh breadcrumbs
50g (2oz) plain flour
2 tsp dried chilli flakes
grated zest of 1 lime
1 medium egg, beaten
2 tbsp sunflower oil
salt and ground black pepper
lime wedges to serve

FOR THE DIP
6 tbsp (240g) natural yogurt
6 tbsp (60g) mayonnaise
¼ cucumber, halved lengthways, seeded
   and finely diced
25g (1oz) freshly chopped coriander
juice of 1 lime

1 Put all the dip ingredients into a bowl. Season to taste with salt and pepper and mix well, then chill.

2 Cut the chicken into strips. Put the breadcrumbs into a bowl with the flour, chilli flakes and lime zest and mix well. Pour the egg on to a plate. Dip the chicken in egg, then coat in the breadcrumbs.

3 Heat the oil in a frying pan over a medium heat. Fry the chicken in batches for 7–10 minutes until golden and cooked through. Keep each batch warm while cooking the remainder. Transfer to a serving plate, sprinkle with a little salt, then serve with the dip and lime wedges.

COOK'S TIP

For a lower-fat version, bake the goujons in the oven. Preheat the oven to 200°C (180°C fan oven) mark 6. Put the goujons on a lightly oiled baking sheet, brush each with a little oil and bake for 12–15 minutes until golden and cooked through.

PER SERVING

337 calories
21g fat (of which 4g saturates)
24g carbohydrate
0.7g salt

Chicken Tarragon Burgers

Preparation Time 30 minutes, plus chilling   Cooking Time 12 minutes   Serves 2   **EASY**

225g (8oz) minced chicken
2 shallots, finely chopped
1 tbsp freshly chopped tarragon
25g (1oz) fresh breadcrumbs
1 large egg yolk
vegetable oil to oil
salt and ground black pepper
toasted burger buns, mayonnaise or
    Greek yogurt, salad leaves and
    tomato salad to serve

1   Put the chicken into a bowl with the shallots, tarragon, breadcrumbs and egg yolk. Mix well, then beat in about 75ml (2½fl oz) cold water and season with salt and pepper.

2   Lightly oil a foil-lined baking sheet. Divide the chicken mixture into two or four portions (depending on how large you want the burgers) and put on the foil. Using the back of a wet spoon, flatten each portion to a thickness of 2.5cm (1in). Cover and chill for 30 minutes.

3   Preheat the barbecue or grill. If cooking on the barbecue, lift the burgers straight on to the grill rack; if cooking under the grill, slide the baking sheet under the grill. Cook the burgers for 5–6 minutes on each side until cooked through, then serve in a toasted burger bun with a dollop of mayonnaise or Greek yogurt, a few salad leaves and tomato salad.

TRY SOMETHING DIFFERENT

Pork and Apricot Burgers
Replace the chicken with minced pork, use freshly chopped sage instead of the tarragon, and add 100g (3½oz) chopped ready-to-eat dried apricots to the mixture before shaping into burgers.

PER SERVING

205 calories
4g fat (of which 1g saturates)
12g carbohydrate
0.4g salt

Speedy Burgers

Preparation Time 10 minutes   Cooking Time 8–12 minutes   Serves 4   **EASY**

450g (1lb) lean minced beef
1 onion, very finely chopped
1 tbsp dried Herbes de Provence
2 tsp sun-dried tomato paste
1 medium egg, beaten
ground black pepper
Chilli Coleslaw to serve (see
    Cook's Tip)

1 Put the minced beef, onion, herbs, tomato paste and beaten egg into a large bowl and mix well. Season with pepper, then shape the mixture into four round burgers about 2cm (¾in) thick.

2 Preheat the grill or griddle pan. Cook the burgers for 4–6 minutes on each side and serve immediately with chilli coleslaw.

COOK'S TIP

Chilli Coleslaw
Put 3 peeled and finely shredded carrots into a large bowl. Add ½ finely shredded white cabbage, 1 seeded and finely sliced red pepper and ½ chopped cucumber. Mix ½ tsp harissa paste with 100g (3½oz) natural yogurt and 1 tbsp white wine vinegar. Add to the vegetables and toss well.

PER SERVING

80 calories
20g fat (of which 8g saturates)
2g carbohydrate
0.3g salt
gluten free • dairy free

Piperade

Preparation Time 20 minutes   Cooking Time 20 minutes   Serves 4   **EASY**

2 tbsp olive oil

1 medium onion, finely chopped

1 garlic clove, finely chopped

1 red pepper, seeded and chopped

375g (13oz) tomatoes, peeled, seeded
    and chopped

a pinch of cayenne pepper

8 large eggs

salt and ground black pepper

freshly chopped flat-leafed parsley to
    garnish

fresh bread to serve (optional)

1 Heat the oil in a heavy-based frying pan. Add the onion and garlic and cook gently for 5 minutes. Add the red pepper and cook for 10 minutes or until softened.

2 Add the tomatoes, increase the heat and cook until they are reduced to a thick pulp. Season well with cayenne pepper, salt and pepper.

3 Lightly whisk the eggs and add to the frying pan. Using a wooden spoon, stir gently until they've just begun to set but are still creamy. Garnish with parsley and serve with bread, if you like.

PER SERVING

232 calories

17g fat (of which 4g saturates)

7g carbohydrate

0.4g salt

vegetarian • gluten free

dairy free

Weekday Suppers

Italian Meatballs

Preparation Time 15 minutes   **Cooking Time** 50 minutes   **Serves 4**   **EASY**

50g (2oz) fresh breadcrumbs
450g (1lb) minced lean pork
1 tsp fennel seeds, crushed
1/4 tsp chilli flakes, or to taste
3 garlic cloves, crushed
4 tbsp freshly chopped flat-leafed
    parsley
3 tbsp red wine
oil-water spray (see Cook's Tip)
roughly chopped fresh oregano to
    garnish
spaghetti to serve

FOR THE TOMATO SAUCE

oil-water spray
2 large shallots, finely chopped
3 pitted black olives, shredded
2 garlic cloves, crushed
2 pinches of chilli flakes
250ml (9fl oz) vegetable or chicken
    stock
500g carton passata
2 tbsp each freshly chopped flat-leafed
    parsley, basil and oregano
salt and ground black pepper

1 To make the tomato sauce, spray a pan with the oil-water spray and add the shallots. Cook gently for 5 minutes. Add the olives, garlic, chilli flakes and stock and bring to the boil, then reduce the heat, cover and simmer for 3–4 minutes.

2 Uncover and simmer for 10 minutes or until the shallots and garlic are soft and the liquid syrupy. Stir in the passata and season with salt and pepper. Bring to the boil, then reduce the heat and simmer for 10–15 minutes. Stir in the herbs.

3 Meanwhile, put the breadcrumbs, pork, fennel seeds, chilli flakes, garlic, parsley and wine into a large bowl, season and mix together, using your hands, until thoroughly combined. (If you wish to check the seasoning, fry a little mixture, taste and adjust if necessary.)

4 Preheat the grill. Line a grill pan with foil, shiny side up, and spray with the oil-water spray. With wet hands, roll the mixture into balls. Cook the meatballs under the hot grill for 3–4 minutes on each side. Serve with the tomato sauce and spaghetti, garnished with oregano.

PER SERVING

275 calories
12g fat (of which 4g saturates)
16g carbohydrate
1.8g salt
dairy free

COOK'S TIP

Oil-water spray is far lower in calories than oil alone and, as it sprays on thinly and evenly, you'll use less. Fill one-eighth of a travel-sized spray bottle with oil such as sunflower, light olive or vegetable (rapeseed) oil, then top up with water.
To use, shake well before spraying. Store in the fridge.

Steak and Chips

Preparation Time 10 minutes   **Cooking Time** 35–45 minutes   **Serves 4**   **EASY**

2 large potatoes, cut into chips
2 tbsp olive oil
4 sirloin steaks, 125g (4oz) each,
  fat trimmed
25g (1oz) Roquefort cheese, cut
  into four small pieces
salt and ground black pepper
watercress to garnish

1 Preheat the oven to 220°C (200°C fan oven) mark 7. Put the potato chips into a pan of lightly salted water. Bring to the boil, then reduce the heat and simmer for about 4–5 minutes. Drain well.

2 Put the chips into a roasting tin, toss with 1 tbsp oil and bake, turning once, for about 30–40 minutes until cooked through and golden.

3 When the chips are nearly done, heat a non-stick frying pan until really hot. Brush the remaining oil over the steaks and season with salt and pepper. Add to the pan and fry for 3 minutes on each side for medium-rare, or 2 minutes more if you prefer the meat well done. Put on to warmed plates, top each steak with a small piece of Roquefort while still hot and serve with the chips. Garnish with watercress.

HEALTHY TIP

The overall fat and saturated fat content of dish is dramatically lower than steak and chips cooked the traditional way. Here the chips are sealed with just a little oil and baked in the oven instead of deep-frying them, which saves around 10g (¼oz) fat per portion. Pan-frying the steak in minimal oil further cuts the fat and calorie content.

PER SERVING
318 calories
13g fat (of which 5g saturates)
18g carbohydrate
0.4g salt
gluten free

Spicy Pork and Bean Stew

Preparation Time 15 minutes **Cooking Time** 50–55 minutes **Serves** 4 **EASY**

3 tbsp olive oil

400g (14oz) pork escalopes, cut into
   cubes

1 red onion, sliced

2 leeks, trimmed and cut into chunks

2 celery sticks, cut into chunks

1 tbsp harissa paste

1 tbsp tomato purée

400g (14oz) cherry tomatoes

300ml (½ pint) hot vegetable or
   chicken stock

400g can cannellini beans, drained and
   rinsed

1 marinated red pepper, sliced

salt and ground black pepper

freshly chopped flat-leafed parsley to
   garnish

Greek yogurt, lemon wedges and bread
   to serve

1 Preheat the oven to 180°C (160°C fan oven) mark 4. Heat 2 tbsp oil in a flameproof casserole and fry the pork in batches until golden. Remove from the pan and put to one side.

2 Heat the remaining oil in the pan and fry the onion for 5–10 minutes until softened. Add the leeks and celery and cook for about 5 minutes. Return the pork to the pan, and add the harissa and tomato purée. Cook for 1–2 minutes, stirring all the time. Add the tomatoes and hot stock and season well with salt and pepper. Bring to the boil, then transfer to the oven and cook for 25 minutes.

3 Add the drained beans and red pepper to the mixture and put back into the oven for 5 minutes to warm through. Garnish with parsley and serve with a dollop of Greek yogurt, lemon wedges for squeezing over the stew, and chunks of crusty baguette or wholegrain bread.

PER SERVING

348 calories

14g fat (of which 3g saturates)

27g carbohydrate

1.5g salt

gluten free

Garlic Pork

Preparation Time 5 minutes   **Cooking Time** 20–25 minutes   **Serves 4**   **EASY**

1 tbsp olive oil
2 garlic cloves, crushed
5cm (2in) piece fresh root ginger, peeled and grated
4 pork chops
salt
stir-fried shredded cabbage to serve

1 Preheat the grill to high. Put the oil into a small bowl, add the garlic and ginger and a pinch of salt and stir well to mix.

2 Cook the pork chops under the hot grill for 7–10 minutes on each side, then remove from the grill. Brush the oil mixture all over the chops, then put back under the grill and cook for a further 2 minutes on each side. Serve with stir-fried shredded cabbage.

HEALTHY TIP

Garlic contains allicin, an antioxidant nutrient that helps combat heart disease, high blood pressure, high blood cholesterol levels and certain cancers, particularly cancer of the colon. It also has anti-viral and antibacterial properties.

PER SERVING

181 calories
8g fat (of which 2g saturates)
1g carbohydrate
0.2g salt
gluten free • dairy free

Pork Fillet with Apricots

Preparation Time 10 minutes, plus marinating   **Cooking Time** about 20 minutes, plus resting   **Serves 4**   **EASY**

700g (1½lb) pork fillet (tenderloin), trimmed
4 tbsp light soy sauce
150ml (5fl oz) red wine
4 tbsp dry sherry
1 tbsp clear honey
1 fresh thyme sprig or a pinch of dried thyme
75g (3oz) dried apricots
100ml (3½fl oz) dry white wine
2 tbsp olive oil
175g (6oz) onions, sliced
2 tsp cornflour
ground black pepper
green vegetables to serve

1 Put the pork into a non-metallic dish. Combine the soy sauce, red wine, sherry, honey and thyme, season with pepper and spoon over the pork. Cover with clingfilm and leave to marinate in the fridge for at least 2 hours or overnight.

2 Meanwhile, put the apricots and white wine into a pan. Bring to the boil, then reduce the heat, cover and simmer for 20 minutes or until the apricots are soft. Strain, reserving the liquid, and chop the apricots roughly.

3 Preheat the oven to 200°C (180°C fan oven) mark 6. Lift the pork from the marinade; reserve the marinade. Heat 1 tbsp oil in a casserole. Add the meat and brown over a high heat. Roast in the oven for about 20 minutes or until cooked.

4 Meanwhile, heat 1 tbsp oil in a pan. Add the onions and cook, stirring, for 10–12 minutes until softened. Add the apricots. Keep warm.

5 When the meat is cooked, remove from the casserole and keep warm. Add the marinade and the reserved liquid from the apricots to the juices in the casserole. Blend the cornflour with 1 tbsp cold water and stir into the sauce. Bring to the boil and cook over a medium heat, stirring constantly, for 2 minutes until the sauce thickens.

6 Cut the pork into slices about 1cm (½ in) thick. To serve, spoon a little apricot and onion mixture on to four warmed plates. Put the sliced pork on top and pour a little sauce over it. Serve with green vegetables.

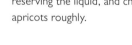

PER SERVING

387 calories
13g fat (of which 3g saturates)
16g carbohydrate
0.3g salt
dairy free

Sticky Chicken Thighs

Preparation Time 5 minutes   **Cooking Time** 20 minutes   **Serves 4**   **EASY**

I garlic clove, crushed
I tbsp clear honey
I tbsp Thai sweet chilli sauce
4 chicken thighs
rice (optional) and green salad
    to serve

1 Preheat the oven to 200°C (180°C fan oven) mark 6. Put the garlic into a bowl with the honey and chilli sauce and stir to mix. Add the chicken thighs and toss to coat.

2 Put the chicken into a roasting tin and roast in the oven for 15–20 minutes until golden and cooked through and the juices run clear when the thighs are pierced with a skewer. Serve with rice, if you like, and a crisp green salad.

TRY SOMETHING DIFFERENT
• Try this with sausages instead of the chicken, if you like.
• **Italian Marinade**
Mix I crushed garlic clove with 4 tbsp olive oil, the juice of I lemon and I tsp dried oregano. If you like, then leave to marinate for 1–2 hours before cooking.
• **Oriental Marinade**
Mix 2 tbsp soy sauce with I tsp demerara sugar, 2 tbsp dry sherry or apple juice, I tsp chopped fresh root ginger and I crushed garlic clove.
• **Honey and Mustard Marinade**
Mix together 2 tbsp grain mustard, 3 tbsp clear honey and the grated zest and juice of I lemon.

PER SERVING
218 calories
12g fat (of which 3g saturates)
5g carbohydrate
0.4g salt
gluten free • dairy free

Spiced Tikka Kebabs

Preparation Time 10 minutes   **Cooking Time** 20 minutes   **Serves 4**   **EASY**

2 tbsp tikka paste

150g (5oz) natural yogurt

juice of ½ lime

4 spring onions, chopped

350g (12oz) skinless chicken, cut into
   bite-size pieces

lime wedges and Mixed Salad (see
   Cook's Tip) to serve

1 Preheat the grill. Put the tikka paste,
   yogurt, lime juice and spring onions
   into a large bowl. Add the chicken
   and toss well. Thread the chicken
   on to metal skewers.

2 Grill the chicken for 8–10 minutes
   on each side, turning and basting
   with the paste, until cooked
   through. Serve with lime wedges to
   squeeze over the kebabs, and
   mixed salad.

HEALTHY TIP

This dish is cooked in a yogurt
marinade, which means that no
additional oil is required for cooking
and is therefore a great low fat
cooking method. Chicken is a rich
source of protein and B vitamins; the
yogurt adds valuable calcium.

COOK'S TIP

Mixed Salad

Put 75g (3oz) green salad leaves into
a large bowl. Add ¼ chopped
avocado, a handful of halved cherry
tomatoes, ½ chopped cucumber and
the juice of 1 lime. Season to taste
with salt and pepper and mix
together well.

PER SERVING

150 calories

5g fat (of which 1g saturates)

4g carbohydrate

0.3g salt

gluten free

One-pan Chicken with Tomatoes

Preparation Time 5 minutes Cooking Time 20–25 minutes Serves 4 **EASY**

4 chicken thighs
1 red onion, sliced
400g can chopped tomatoes with herbs
400g can mixed beans, drained and
    rinsed
2 tsp balsamic vinegar
freshly chopped flat-leafed parsley to
    garnish

1 Heat a non-stick pan and fry
  the chicken thighs, skin side down,
  until golden. Turn over and fry for
  5 minutes.

2 Add the onion and fry for a further
  5 minutes. Add the tomatoes,
  mixed beans and vinegar, cover the
  pan and simmer for 10–12 minutes
  until piping hot. Garnish with
  parsley and serve immediately.

HEALTHY TIP

Tomatoes are packed with vitamin C
and lycopene, a powerful antioxidant
linked with a lower risk of cancer of
the prostate. It is absorbed more
readily from cooked tomatoes,
including the canned variety, which
makes this dish a healthy option.
The mixed beans add useful amounts
of fibre, protein and iron.

TRY SOMETHING DIFFERENT

Use flageolet beans or other canned
beans instead of mixed beans, and
garnish with fresh basil or oregano.

PER SERVING

238 calories
4g fat (of which 1g saturates)
20g carbohydrate
1g salt
gluten free • dairy free

Chicken Stir-fry with Noodles

Preparation Time 20 minutes   Cooking Time 20 minutes   Serves 4   **EASY**

2 tbsp vegetable oil

2 garlic cloves, crushed

4 boneless, skinless chicken breasts, each sliced into 10 pieces

3 medium carrots, about 450g (1lb), cut into thin strips, about 5cm (2in) long

250g pack thick egg noodles

1 bunch of spring onions, sliced

200g (7oz) mangetouts

155g jar sweet chilli and lemongrass sauce

1 Cook the noodles in boiling water according to the pack instructions.

2 Meanwhile, heat the oil in a wok or frying pan. Add the garlic and stir-fry for 1–2 minutes. Add the chicken pieces and stir-fry for 5 minutes, then add the carrot strips and stir-fry for a further 5 minutes.

3 Add the spring onions, mangetouts and sauce to the wok and stir-fry for 5 minutes.

4 Drain the cooked noodles well and add to the wok. Toss everything together and serve.

TRY SOMETHING DIFFERENT
Use turkey or pork escalopes instead of the chicken: you will need 450g (1lb), cut into thin strips.

PER SERVING
355 calories
10g fat (of which 2g saturates)
29g carbohydrate
0.5g salt
dairy free

Chicken Falafels

Preparation Time 20 minutes, plus soaking   **Cooking Time** 20 minutes   **Serves 4** **EASY**

450g (1lb) minced chicken
3 shallots, finely chopped
125g (4oz) canned chickpeas (about ½ can), drained and rinsed
2.5cm (1in) piece fresh root ginger, peeled and grated
½ tsp salt
20g (¾oz) freshly chopped coriander
1 medium egg
3 tbsp olive oil
400g can chopped tomatoes
1 tsp caster sugar

FOR THE COUSCOUS SALAD
200g (7oz) couscous
350ml (12fl oz) hot chicken stock
grated zest and juice of ½ lemon
25g (1oz) pinenuts
seeds from ½ pomegranate
3 tbsp extra virgin olive oil
2–3 tbsp freshly chopped parsley

1 First, make the couscous salad. Put the couscous into a bowl and add the hot stock and lemon zest. Leave to soak for 20 minutes. Meanwhile, toast the pinenuts in a dry pan, tossing regularly, until golden. Use a fork to fluff up the couscous, then stir in the pinenuts, pomegranate seeds, lemon juice, extra virgin olive oil and parsley.

2 Put the chicken mince into a food processor. Add 1 chopped shallot, the chickpeas, grated ginger and salt and whiz to combine.

3 Add the coriander and egg and whiz again briefly. With damp hands, shape into 12 balls, each measuring 6.5cm (2½in).

4 Heat 2 tbsp olive oil in a frying pan. Fry the patties for 2–3 minutes on each side until golden brown.

5 Meanwhile, fry the remaining shallots in a pan with the remaining olive oil. Stir in the tomatoes and sugar and simmer for 10 minutes or until slightly thickened. Serve the patties with the couscous salad, and with the sauce on the side.

PER SERVING
287 calories
14g fat (of which 3g saturates)
10g carbohydrate
1.1g salt
dairy free

Chicken with Spicy Couscous

Preparation Time 15 minutes, plus soaking **Serves 4** **EASY**

125g (4oz) couscous
1 ripe mango, peeled, stoned and cut
 into 2.5cm (1in) chunks
1 tbsp lemon or lime juice
125g tub fresh tomato salsa
3 tbsp mango chutney
3 tbsp orange juice
2 tbsp freshly chopped coriander, plus
 extra to garnish
200g (7oz) chargrilled chicken fillets
4 tbsp fromage frais (optional)
salt and ground black pepper
freshly chopped coriander and lime
 wedges to garnish

1 Put the couscous into a large bowl and pour 300ml (½ pint) boiling water over. Season well with salt and pepper, then leave to soak for 15 minutes.

2 Put the mango chunks on a large plate and sprinkle with the lemon or lime juice.

3 Mix the tomato salsa with the mango chutney, orange juice and coriander in a small bowl.

4 Drain the couscous if necessary, fluff the grains with a fork, then stir in the salsa mixture and check the seasoning. Turn out on to a large serving dish and arrange the chicken and mango on top.

5 Just before serving, spoon the fromage frais over the chicken, if you like, then garnish with chopped coriander and lime wedges.

HEALTHY TIP

Couscous is made from semolina flour and has a low GI (see page 12), helping to make you feel fuller longer. It provides B vitamins and valuable amounts of selenium. Mango is rich in betacarotene, an antioxidant which helps combat harmful free radicals and promotes healthy skin.

PER SERVING
223 calories
6g fat (of which 2g saturates),
30g carbohydrate
0.2g salt

Mild Spiced Chicken and Quinoa

Preparation Time 15 minutes   **Cooking Time** 20 minutes   **Serves 4**   **EASY**

2 tbsp mango chutney
juice of ½ lemon
1 tbsp olive oil
2 tsp mild curry powder
1 tsp paprika
350g (12oz) skinless chicken breast, cut
    into thick strips
200g (7oz) quinoa (see Cook's Tip)
1 cucumber, roughly chopped
½ bunch of spring onions, sliced
75g (3oz) ready-to-eat dried apricots,
    sliced
2 tbsp freshly chopped mint, basil or
    tarragon
salt and ground black pepper
fresh mint sprigs to garnish

1 Put the chutney, lemon juice, ½ tbsp oil, the curry powder, paprika and salt and pepper into a bowl and mix together. Add the chicken strips and toss to coat.

2 Cook the quinoa in boiling water for 10–12 minutes until tender or according to the pack instructions. Drain thoroughly. Put into a bowl, then stir in the cucumber, spring onions, apricots, herbs and remaining oil.

3 Put the chicken and marinade into a pan and fry over a high heat for 2–3 minutes, then add 150ml (¼ pint) water. Bring to the boil, then reduce the heat and simmer for 5 minutes or until the chicken is cooked through. Serve with the quinoa garnished with mint.

COOK'S TIP

Quinoa is a tiny, bead-shaped grain with a slightly nutty flavour. It's easy to prepare and nearly quadruples in size and looks translucent when cooked. It can be substituted for rice or couscous.

PER SERVING

268 calories
3g fat (of which trace saturates)
37g carbohydrate
0.4g salt
gluten free • dairy free

Quick Chicken Stir-fry

Preparation Time 10 minutes **Cooking Time** 12 minutes **Serves 4** **EASY**

1 tsp groundnut oil

300g (11oz) boneless, skinless chicken breasts, sliced

4 spring onions, chopped

200g (7oz) medium rice noodles

100g (3½oz) mangetouts

200g (7oz) purple sprouting broccoli, chopped

2–3 tbsp sweet chilli sauce

coriander leaves to garnish

lime wedges (optional) to serve

1 Heat the oil in a wok or large frying pan. Add the chicken and spring onions and stir-fry over a high heat for 5–6 minutes until the chicken is golden brown.

2 Meanwhile, soak the rice noodles in boiling water for 4 minutes or according to the pack instructions.

3 Add the mangetouts, broccoli and chilli sauce to the chicken. Continue to stir-fry for 4 minutes.

4 Drain the noodles, then add to the pan and toss everything together. Scatter the coriander over the top and serve with lime wedges to squeeze over the stir-fry, if you like.

HEALTHY TIP

Stir-frying is a healthy cooking method as it uses only minimal amounts of oil, thus helping keep the calorie and overall fat content of the dish low. It also seals in the vitamins so losses are kept to a minimum. Purple sprouting broccoli contains the phytochemical sulphoraphane (thought to help prevent cancer) and may provide resistance against heart disease and type 2 diabetes. It is packed with vitamin C and is a good source of carotenoids, iron, folate, calcium, fibre and vitamin A.

TRY SOMETHING DIFFERENT

Other vegetables are just as good in this dish: try pak choi, button mushrooms, carrots cut into matchsticks, or baby sweetcorn.

PER SERVING

316 calories

3g fat (of which 1g saturates)

46g carbohydrate

0.5g salt

gluten free • dairy free

Grilled Spicy Chicken

Preparation Time 10 minutes, plus marinating   **Cooking Time** about 20 minutes   **Serves 4**   **EASY**

4 boneless, skinless chicken breasts
1 tbsp coriander seeds, crushed
1 tsp ground cumin
2 tsp mild curry paste
1 garlic clove, crushed
450g (1lb) natural yogurt
3 tbsp freshly chopped coriander
salt and ground black pepper
fresh coriander sprigs to garnish
Mixed Salad (see Cook's Tip, page 99)
    and rice to serve

1 Prick the chicken breasts all over with a fork, cover with clingfilm and lightly beat with a rolling pin to flatten them slightly.

2 Mix the coriander seeds with the cumin, curry paste, garlic and yogurt in a large shallow dish. Season with salt and pepper and stir in the chopped coriander.

3 Add the chicken and turn to coat with the spiced yogurt. Cover and leave to marinate in the fridge for at least 30 minutes or overnight.

4 Preheat the barbecue or griddle. Lift the chicken out of the marinade and cook over a medium-high heat, turning occasionally, for about 20 minutes or until cooked through. Serve immediately, with rice and a mixed salad, garnished with coriander sprigs.

HEALTHY TIP

This dish is low in fat as it is marinated in a low fat yogurt mixture instead of an oil-based version. Yogurt is rich in calcium, important for maintaining bone strength and, according to recent studies has been linked with reduced blood pressure and heart disease risk.

PER SERVING

157 calories,
2g fat (of which 1g saturates)
3g carbohydrate
0.2g salt
gluten free

Moroccan Spiced Chicken Kebabs

Preparation Time 10 minutes, plus marinating   **Cooking Time** 10–12 minutes   **Serves 4**   **EASY**

2 tbsp olive oil

15g (½oz) fresh flat-leafed parsley

1 garlic clove

½ tsp paprika

1 tsp ground cumin

zest and juice of 1 lemon

4 skinless chicken breasts, cut into bite-size chunks

salt

shredded lettuce, sliced cucumber and tomatoes, and lime wedges to serve

1 Put the oil into a blender and add the parsley, garlic, paprika, cumin, lemon zest and juice and a pinch of salt. Whiz to make a paste.

2 Put the chicken into a medium-sized shallow dish and rub in the spice paste. Leave to marinate for at least 20 minutes. Preheat the grill to high. Soak some wooden skewers in water.

3 Thread the marinated chicken on to the skewers and grill for 10–12 minutes, turning every now and then, until the meat is cooked through. Serve with shredded lettuce, sliced cucumber and tomatoes, and lime wedges.

TRY SOMETHING DIFFERENT

Instead of chicken, use 700g (1½lb) lean lamb fillet or leg of lamb, cut into chunks.

PER SERVING

190 calories,

7g fat (of which 1g saturates)

1g carbohydrate

0.2g salt

gluten free • dairy free

Spiced Chicken with Garlic Butter Beans

Preparation Time 10 minutes   **Cooking Time** 15 minutes   **Serves 4**   **EASY**

4 boneless, skinless chicken breasts,
    about 100g (3½oz) each
1 tbsp olive oil
1 tsp ground coriander
1 tsp ground cumin
100g (3½oz) couscous
3 tbsp extra virgin olive oil
1 garlic clove, sliced
2 × 400g cans no-added-sugar-or-salt
    butter beans, drained and rinsed
juice of 1 lemon

1 small red onion, thinly sliced
50g (2oz) marinated roasted peppers,
    drained
2 medium tomatoes, seeded and
    chopped
1 tbsp freshly chopped coriander
1 tbsp freshly chopped flat-leafed
    parsley
salt and ground black pepper
green salad and lemon wedges
    to serve

1 Put the chicken on a board,
cover with clingfilm and flatten
lightly with a rolling pin. Put the
olive oil into a large bowl with the
ground coriander and cumin.
Mix together, then add the chicken
and turn to coat.

2 Heat a large frying pan and cook
the chicken for 5–7 minutes on
each side until golden and the
juices run clear when pierced with
a sharp knife.

3 While the chicken is cooking, put
the couscous into a bowl and add
100ml (3½fl oz) boiling water.
Cover with clingfilm and set aside.

4 Put the extra virgin olive oil into a
small pan with the garlic and butter
beans and warm through for 3–4
minutes over a low heat. Stir in the
lemon juice and season with salt
and pepper.

5 Fluff up the couscous with a fork
and tip in the warm butter beans.
Add the onion, peppers, tomatoes
and herbs and stir together. Slice
each chicken breast into four pieces
and arrange alongside the bean
salad. Serve with a green salad and
lemon wedges to squeeze over it.

PER SERVING

443 calories
16g fat (of which 3g saturates)
42g carbohydrate
0.2g salt
dairy free

Oven-baked Mediterranean Chicken

Preparation Time 5 minutes   **Cooking Time** 20 minutes   **Serves 4**   **EASY**

1 red pepper, seeded and chopped
2 tbsp capers
2 tbsp freshly chopped rosemary
2 tbsp olive oil
4 skinless chicken breasts, about 125g
   (4oz) each
salt and ground black pepper
rice or new potatoes to serve

1 Preheat the oven to 200°C (180°C fan oven) mark 6. Put the red pepper into a bowl with the capers, rosemary and oil. Season with salt and pepper and mix well.

2 Put the chicken breasts into an ovenproof dish and spoon the pepper mixture over the top. Roast for 15–20 minutes or until the chicken is cooked through and the topping is hot. Serve with rice or new potatoes.

HEALTHY TIP

Red peppers are a rich source of vitamin C, betacarotene and beta-cryptoxanthin, all powerful antioxidants that help protect the body from heart disease and certain cancers. Oven-roasting in olive oil is a healthy way of preserving the vitamin content.

TRY SOMETHING DIFFERENT

Use chopped black olives instead of the capers.

PER SERVING

223 calories
7g fat (of which 1g saturates)
3g carbohydrate
0.2g salt
gluten free • dairy free

Oven-baked Chicken with Garlic Potatoes

Preparation Time 10 minutes   **Cooking Time** 1½ hours   **Serves 6**   **EASY**

2 medium baking potatoes,
   thinly sliced
a little freshly grated nutmeg
600ml (1 pint) white sauce (use a
   ready-made sauce or make your
   own, see Cook's Tip)
½ × 390g can fried onions
250g (9oz) frozen peas
450g (1lb) cooked chicken, shredded
20g pack garlic butter, sliced
a little butter to grease
salt and ground black pepper
Granary bread to serve (optional)

1 Preheat the oven to 180°C (160°C fan oven) mark 4. Layer half the potatoes over the base of a 2.4 litre (4¼ pint) shallow ovenproof dish and season with the nutmeg, salt and pepper. Pour the white sauce over and shake the dish, so that the sauce settles through the gaps in the potatoes.

2 Spread half the onions on top, then scatter on half the peas. Arrange the shredded chicken on top, then add the remaining peas and onions. Finish with the remaining potatoes, arranged in an even layer, and dot with garlic butter. Season with salt and pepper.

3 Cover tightly with buttered foil and cook in the oven for 1 hour. Increase the heat to 200°C (180°C fan oven) mark 6, remove the foil and cook for 20–30 minutes until the potatoes are golden and tender. Serve with Granary bread, if you like, to mop up the juices.

COOK'S TIP

White Sauce
To make 600ml (1 pint) white sauce, melt 25g (1oz) butter in a pan, then stir in 25g (1oz) plain flour. Cook, stirring constantly, for 1 minute. Remove from the heat and gradually pour in 600ml (1 pint) milk, beating after each addition. Return to the heat and cook, stirring, until the sauce has thickened and is velvety and smooth. Season with salt, pepper and freshly grated nutmeg.

PER SERVING

376 calories
16g fat (of which 5g saturates)
32g carbohydrate
1.2g salt

Oven-poached Cod with Spring Onions and Herbs

Preparation Time 10 minutes   **Cooking Time** 10 minutes   **Serves 4   EASY**

10 spring onions, sliced

2 garlic cloves, crushed

6 tbsp shredded fresh mint

6 tbsp freshly chopped flat-leafed parsley

juice of ½ lemon

150ml (¼ pint) fish, chicken or vegetable stock

4 cod fillets, about 200g (7oz) each

salt and ground black pepper

lemon wedges to garnish

mashed potatoes to serve

1 Preheat the oven to 230°C (210°C fan oven) mark 8. Combine the spring onions (putting some of the green part to one side), garlic, mint, parsley, lemon juice and stock in an ovenproof dish that can hold the cod in a single layer.

2 Put the cod on the herb and garlic mixture and turn to moisten. Season with salt and pepper, then roast for 8–10 minutes.

3 Sprinkle with the reserved spring onion, garnish with lemon wedges and serve with mashed potatoes.

HEALTHY TIP

The flat-leafed parsley used in this dish is rich in vitamin C (it contains three times as much vitamin C as oranges weight for weight), betacarotene, folate and iron. It contains flavonoids and other phytochemicals, recognised as having cancer-fighting properties. Mint is also a source of anti-cancer substances and well-recognised for soothing the digestive tract.

TRY SOMETHING DIFFERENT

There are lots of alternatives to cod: try sea bass, gurnard or pollack.

PER SERVING

170 calories

2g fat (of which trace saturates)

1g carbohydrate

0.5g salt

gluten free • dairy free

Cod Steaks with Fennel

Preparation Time 10 minutes, plus marinating   **Cooking Time** 30 minutes   Serves 4   **EASY**

1 tbsp hoisin sauce

4 tbsp light soy sauce

4 tbsp dry vermouth

4 tbsp orange juice

½ tsp Chinese five-spice powder

½ tsp ground cumin

1 garlic clove, crushed

4 × 150g (5oz) thick cod fillets or steaks (see Cook's Tip)

1 tbsp vegetable oil

2 fennel bulbs, about 700g (1½lb), thinly sliced and tops put to one side

2 tsp sesame seeds

1 For the marinade, combine the hoisin sauce, soy sauce, vermouth, orange juice, five-spice powder, cumin and garlic. Put the cod into a shallow dish and pour the marinade over it. Cover and leave to marinate in a cool place for at least 1 hour.

2 Preheat the grill or a lightly oiled griddle. Remove the fish and put the marinade to one side. Cook the fish under the hot grill or on the hot griddle for 4 minutes, then turn over and cook for 3–4 minutes until cooked.

3 Heat the oil in a sauté pan. Add the fennel and cook briskly for 5–7 minutes until brown and beginning to soften. Add the marinade, bring to the boil and bubble until reduced and sticky.

4 Put the fish on a bed of fennel, spoon any pan juices around it and sprinkle with the sesame seeds. Garnish with the reserved fennel tops.

HEALTHY TIP

Fennel is packed with antioxidants that help protect the body from free radical damage. It is believed to help combat certain cancers. It is also a good source of fibre, vitamin C, folate, magnesium, calcium, iron and phosphorus, and helpful in easing digestive problems such as gas and bloating.

COOK'S TIP

Ask your fishmonger to remove the scales from the cod's skin. When grilled, the skin will be crisp and delicious to eat.

PER SERVING

209 calories

6g fat (of which 1g saturates)

6g carbohydrate

1.4g salt

dairy free

Garlic and Thyme Fish Steaks

Preparation Time 10 minutes, plus marinating   **Cooking Time** 5–10 minutes   **Serves 4**   **EASY**

2 garlic cloves, crushed
2 tbsp chopped thyme leaves
4 tbsp olive oil
2 lemons
4 × 200g (7oz) firm fish steaks, such as
    tuna, swordfish or shark
salt and ground black pepper
Barbecued Red Peppers (see Cook's
    Tip) and salad leaves to serve

1 Put the garlic, thyme, oil and juice of one lemon into a large shallow container and mix well.

2 Add the fish steaks and season with salt and pepper, then cover and chill for 20 minutes. Cut the other lemon into four slices and put to one side.

3 Preheat the barbecue or a griddle pan.

4 Cook the fish on the barbecue or griddle for 4–5 minutes on one side and brush with a little of the marinade. Turn over, put a slice of reserved lemon on top of each steak and continue to cook for 3–4 minutes until cooked through. Serve with Barbecued Red Peppers and salad leaves.

COOK'S TIP

Barbecued Red Peppers
Halve 3 red peppers, seed, then cut into thick strips. Brush with 1 tbsp olive oil and season with salt and pepper. Cook on the barbecue or on a preheated griddle pan for 15–20 minutes until the peppers are tender.

PER SERVING
299 calories,
12g fat (of which 3g saturates)
trace carbohydrate
0.2g salt
gluten free • dairy free

Sardines with Mediterranean Vegetables

Preparation Time 15 minutes   Cooking Time 20 minutes   Serves 4   **EASY**

3 tbsp olive oil

2 red onions, about 300g (11oz), halved and cut into petals

2 garlic cloves, crushed

2 red peppers, about 375g (12oz), seeded and cut into chunks

225g (8oz) courgettes, cut into small chunks

900g (2lb) sardines (about 16), cleaned

olive oil and lemon juice to drizzle

salt and ground black pepper

small fresh basil sprigs to garnish

1 Heat the oil in a large griddle pan, or preheat the grill. Add the onion and fry for 2–3 minutes until almost soft. Add the garlic and peppers and stir-fry for 5 minutes, then add the courgettes and stir-fry for 4–5 minutes until almost soft. Remove from the griddle and keep warm.

2 Season the sardines and cook on the griddle or under the hot grill for 3–4 minutes on each side until cooked in the centre.

3 Drizzle the sardines with a little olive oil and lemon juice. Garnish with basil sprigs and serve with the vegetables.

HEALTHY TIP

Sardines are an excellent source of omega-3 fats, which help prevent clots forming in the arteries (thrombosis), stroke and high blood pressure. They are also beneficial for promoting healthy joints and alleviating rheumatoid arthritis. They also provide plenty of protein and iron.

GET AHEAD

To prepare ahead Complete the recipe to the end of step 1, cover and chill for up to 3 hours.

To use Stir-fry the vegetables for 2–3 minutes until hot. Complete the recipe.

PER SERVING

409 calories

23g fat (of which 5g saturates)

13g carbohydrate

0.5g salt

gluten free • dairy free

Crispy Crumbed Fish

Preparation Time 5 minutes **Cooking Time** 10–15 minutes **Serves 4** **EASY**

50g (2oz) fresh breadcrumbs
a small handful of freshly chopped
    flat-leafed parsley
2 tbsp capers, chopped
grated zest of 1 lemon
4 haddock or pollack fillets, about 150g
    (5oz) each
½ tbsp Dijon mustard
juice of ½ lemon
salt and ground black pepper
new potatoes and Mixed Salad (see
    Cook's Tip, page 99) to serve

1 Preheat the oven to 180°C
(160°C fan oven) mark 4. Put the
breadcrumbs into a bowl with the
parsley, capers and lemon zest.
Mix well, then set aside.

2 Put the fish fillets on a baking tray.
Mix the mustard and half the lemon
juice in a bowl with a little salt and
pepper, then spread over the top
of each piece of fish. Spoon the
breadcrumb mixture on top –
don't worry if some falls off.

3 Cook in the oven for 10–15
minutes until the fish is cooked and
the breadcrumbs are golden. Pour
the remaining lemon juice over the
top and serve with new potatoes
and a mixed salad.

PER SERVING
171 calories
1g fat (of which trace saturates)
10g carbohydrate
0.8g salt
dairy free

Chinese-style Sesame-crusted Trout

Preparation Time 10 minutes   **Cooking Time** 10–13 minutes   **Serves 4**   **EASY**

1 tbsp sesame oil

1 tbsp soy sauce

juice of 1 lime

4 × 150g (5oz) trout fillets

2 tbsp sesame seeds

lime wedges, herb salad and fennel to serve

1 Preheat the grill. Put the oil into a bowl, add the soy sauce and lime juice and whisk together.

2 Put the trout fillets on a baking sheet, pour the sesame mixture over them and cook under the hot grill for 8–10 minutes. Sprinkle with the sesame seeds and grill for a further 2–3 minutes until the seeds are golden. Serve with lime wedges, a herb salad and finely sliced fennel.

COOK'S TIP

Sesame seeds are deliciously nutty and highly nutritious. They are a valuable source of protein, good omega fats and vitamin E. Lightly toasted sesame seeds, crushed with a little salt and stirred into 1–2 tbsp olive oil, make an excellent dressing for cooked green beans, broccoli and carrots.

PER SERVING

259 calories

15g fat (of which 3g saturates)

1g carbohydrate

0.8g salt

gluten free • dairy free

Red Mullet with Cherry Tomatoes and Basil Oil

Preparation Time 10 minutes   **Cooking Time** about 40 minutes   **Serves 6**   **EASY**

450g (1lb) cherry tomatoes, mixture of
   red and yellow
2 tbsp green peppercorns in brine,
   drained
8 garlic cloves, bruised not peeled
zest and juice of 1 small lemon
75ml (2½fl oz) basil oil
12 × 50g (2oz) red mullet fillets,
   descaled
a small handful of fresh basil leaves
salt and ground black pepper

1 Preheat the oven to 180°C (160°C fan oven) mark 4. Halve the larger tomatoes, then put them all into a shallow roasting tin. Add the peppercorns, garlic and lemon zest, drizzle with half the oil and bake for 20 minutes.

2 Add the fish to the tin and drizzle with the remaining oil. Cook for a further 15–20 minutes until golden and cooked through.

3 Pour the lemon juice over the fish and sprinkle with basil leaves, salt and pepper. Serve with steamed new potatoes.

HEALTHY TIP

Red mullet is classified as a white fish but it has a richer and more satisfying flavour than most other white fish thanks to its slightly higher fat content – around 4g per fillet. It is baked with basil oil – a good source of monounsaturates – and tomatoes, which are a rich source of vitamin C and betacarotene.

PER SERVING

(without potatoes) 282 calories
17g fat (of which 2g saturates)
4g carbohydrates
0.4g salt
dairy free

Cod with Cherry Tomatoes

Preparation Time 15 minutes   **Cooking Time** 20–25 minutes   **Serves 4**   **EASY**

4 × 100g (3½oz) cod steaks
1 tbsp plain flour
2 tbsp olive oil
1 small onion, sliced
1 large red chilli, seeded and chopped
   (see Cook's Tips, page 49)
1 garlic clove, crushed
250g (9oz) cherry tomatoes, halved
4 spring onions, chopped
2 tbsp freshly chopped coriander
salt and ground black pepper

1 Season the cod with salt and pepper, then dust lightly with the flour. Heat 1 tbsp oil in a large frying pan. Add the onion and fry for 5–10 minutes until golden.

2 Pour the remaining oil into the pan. Add the cod and fry for 3 minutes on each side. Add the chilli, garlic, cherry tomatoes, spring onions and coriander and season with salt and pepper. Cover and continue to cook for 5–10 minutes until everything is heated through. Serve immediately.

TRY SOMETHING DIFFERENT
Use another white fish such as sea bass or pollack fillets instead of the cod, if you like.

PER SERVING
168 calories
7g fat (of which 1g saturates)
8g carbohydrate
0.2g salt
dairy free

Spicy Beans with Jazzed-up Potatoes

Preparation Time 12 minutes   **Cooking Time** about 1½ hours   **Serves 4**   **EASY**

4 baking potatoes
1 tbsp olive oil, plus extra to rub
1 tsp smoked paprika, plus a pinch
2 shallots, finely chopped
1 tbsp freshly chopped rosemary
400g can cannellini beans, drained and
   rinsed
400g can chopped tomatoes
1 tbsp light muscovado sugar
1 tsp vegetarian Worcestershire sauce
75ml (2½fl oz) red wine
75ml (2½fl oz) hot vegetable stock
a small handful of freshly chopped
   flat-leafed parsley
grated mature vegetarian Cheddar to
   sprinkle
sea salt and ground black pepper

1 Preheat the oven to 200°C (180°C fan oven) mark 6. Rub the potatoes with a little oil and put them on a baking tray. Scatter with sea salt and a pinch of smoked paprika. Bake for 1–1½ hours.

2 Meanwhile, heat 1 tbsp oil in a large pan, then fry the shallots over a low heat for 1–2 minutes until they start to soften.

3 Add the rosemary and 1 tsp paprika and fry for 1–2 minutes, then add the beans, tomatoes, sugar, Worcestershire sauce, wine and hot stock. Season, then bring to the boil and simmer, uncovered, for 10–15 minutes. Serve with the baked potatoes, scattered with parsley and grated Cheddar.

HEALTHY TIP

Baked potatoes are a useful source of vitamin C, which is preserved well in this cooking method. Much of the vitamin content is found just beneath the skin so you should eat the skin for maximum nutritional benefits. The cannellini beans add protein, fibre, iron and zinc while the canned tomatoes are rich in the anti-cancer phytochemical lycopene.

TRY SOMETHING DIFFERENT

For a quick meal that takes less than 25 minutes, the spicy beans are just as good served with toast .

PER SERVING

298 calories
4g fat (of which 1g saturates)
56g carbohydrate
0.8g salt
vegetarian • gluten free

Pasta, Rice, Noodles and Grains

Sunblush Tomato and Artichoke Pasta

Preparation Time 10 minutes   Cooking Time 10–12 minutes   Serves 4   **EASY**

300g (11oz) penne
6 pieces sunblush tomatoes in oil
1 red onion, sliced
about 10 pieces roasted artichoke
  hearts in oil, drained and roughly
  chopped
50g (2oz) pitted black olives, roughly
  chopped
50g (2oz) pecorino cheese, grated
100g (3½oz) rocket

1 Cook the pasta in a large pan of lightly salted boiling water according to the pack instructions until al dente. Drain well.

2 Meanwhile, drain the sunblush tomatoes, reserving the oil, and roughly chop. Heat 1 tbsp oil from the tomatoes in a large frying pan. Add the onion and fry for 5–6 minutes until softened and turning golden. Add the tomatoes, artichokes and olives to the pan and heat for 3–4 minutes until hot.

3 Add half the pecorino cheese and stir through. Remove from the heat and stir in the rocket and pasta. Divide the pasta among four bowls and sprinkle the remaining pecorino over the top to serve.

HEALTHY TIP

Artichokes are a good source of vitamin C, folate, magnesium and dietary fibre. They contain the powerful phytonutrients cynarin and silymarin, which have beneficial effects on the liver. The olives contain useful amounts of vitamin E while the rocket adds iron and folate.

PER SERVING

380 calories
11g fat (of which 4g saturates)
59g carbohydrate
1.3g salt

Pasta with Goat's Cheese and Sunblush Tomatoes

Preparation Time 5 minutes   Cooking Time 10 minutes   Serves 4   **EASY**

300g (11oz) conchiglie pasta

2 tbsp olive oil

1 red pepper, seeded and chopped

1 yellow pepper, seeded and chopped

½ tbsp sun-dried tomato paste

75g (3oz) sunblush tomatoes

75g (3oz) soft goat's cheese (see Cook's
    Tips, page 184)

2 tbsp freshly chopped parsley

salt and ground black pepper

1 Cook the pasta in a large pan of lightly salted boiling water according to the pack instructions until al dente.

2 Meanwhile, heat the oil in a pan and fry the red and yellow peppers for 5–7 minutes until softened and just beginning to brown. Add the tomato paste and cook for a further minute. Add a ladleful of pasta cooking water to the pan and simmer for 1–2 minutes to make a sauce.

3 Drain the pasta and put back in the pan. Pour the sauce on top, then add the tomatoes, goat's cheese and parsley. Toss together until the cheese begins to melt, then season with pepper and serve.

PER SERVING

409 calories

12g fat (of which 4g saturates)

64g carbohydrate

0.4g salt

vegetarian

Borlotti, Anchovy and Spinach Pasta

Preparation Time 10 minutes   Cooking Time 1 hour   Serves 4   **EASY**

300g (11oz) conchiglie pasta
30g can anchovies, drained and
    chopped, oil from the can put to
    one side
400g can borlotti beans, drained and
    rinsed
a handful of spinach leaves

FOR THE TOMATO SAUCE
2 tbsp oil from the drained anchovies
2 carrots, diced
1 large onion, diced
2 celery sticks, diced
1 bay leaf
250ml (9fl oz) dry white wine
300ml (½ pint) hot vegetable stock
2 × 400g cans chopped tomatoes
1 tsp caster sugar or to taste
salt and ground black pepper

1 To make the tomato sauce, preheat the oven to 180°C (160°C fan oven) mark 4. Heat the oil in a flameproof casserole on the hob. Add the carrots, onion, celery and bay leaf and season to taste. Cook gently for 15–20 minutes, stirring occasionally, until soft and golden.

2 Add the wine, hot stock and tomatoes. Bring to the boil, then cover and cook in the oven for 20 minutes. Uncover and cook for a further 20 minutes until the sauce is thick. Taste the sauce – if it's a little acidic, add the sugar.

3 Cook the pasta in a large pan of lightly salted boiling water according to the pack instructions until al dente.

4 Meanwhile, add the anchovies to the simmering tomato sauce with 1 tbsp of the oil from the can, the beans and spinach. Heat for 5 minutes. Drain the pasta and toss through the sauce. Serve.

PER SERVING
518 calories
9g fat (of which 1g saturates)
86g carbohydrate
1.8g salt
dairy free

Ham and Mushroom Pasta

Preparation Time 5 minutes   Cooking Time 15 minutes   Serves 4   **EASY**

350g (12oz) penne pasta

1 tbsp olive oil

2 shallots, sliced

200g (7oz) small button mushrooms

3 tbsp crème fraîche

125g (4oz) smoked ham, roughly
    chopped

2 tbsp freshly chopped flat-leafed
    parsley

salt and ground black pepper

1 Cook the pasta in a large pan of lightly salted boiling water according to the pack instructions until al dente.

2 Meanwhile, heat the oil in a pan. Add the shallots and fry gently for 3 minutes or until starting to soften. Add the mushrooms and fry for 5–6 minutes.

3 Drain the pasta, put back in the pan and add the shallots and mushrooms. Stir in the crème fraîche, ham and parsley. Toss everything together, season to taste with salt and pepper and heat through to serve.

HEALTHY TIP

Mushrooms contain significant amounts of selenium, which may help prevent certain cancers, in particular prostate cancer. They also supply B vitamins and potassium and are very low in fat.

PER SERVING

415 calories

10g fat (of which 4g saturates)

67g carbohydrate

1g salt

Pappardelle with Spinach

Preparation Time 5 minutes   Cooking Time 12 minutes   Serves 4   **EASY**

350g (12oz) pappardelle
350g (12oz) baby leaf spinach, roughly
    chopped
2 tbsp olive oil
75g (3oz) ricotta (see Cook's Tips,
    page 184)
freshly grated nutmeg
salt and ground black pepper

1 Cook the pappardelle in a large pan of boiling water according to the pack instructions until al dente.

2 Drain the pasta well, put back in the pan and add the spinach, oil and ricotta, tossing for 10–15 seconds until the spinach has wilted. Season with a little nutmeg, salt and pepper and serve immediately.

HEALTHY TIP

Spinach is rich in iron, calcium, beta-carotene (which the body converts to vitamin A), vitamin C and folate. Ricotta is a type of whey cheese, containing just 9g (¼oz) of fat per 100g (3½oz) – considerably less than cream cheese at 45g (1¾oz) per 100g (3½oz). It is a good source of protein, calcium, magnesium and also selenium.

PER SERVING

404 calories
11g fat (of which 3g saturates)
67g carbohydrate
0.3g salt
vegetarian

Penne with Smoked Salmon

Preparation Time 5 minutes   Cooking Time 10–15 minutes   Serves 4   **EASY**

350g (12oz) penne or other short
    tubular pasta
200ml (7fl oz) half-fat crème fraîche
150g (5oz) smoked salmon, roughly
    chopped
20g (¾oz) fresh dill, finely chopped
salt and ground black pepper
lemon wedges to serve (optional)

1 Cook the pasta in a large pan
of lightly salted boiling water
according to the pack instructions
until al dente. Drain well.

2 Meanwhile, put the crème fraîche
into a large bowl. Add the smoked
salmon and dill, season well with
salt and pepper and mix together.
Gently stir into the drained penne
and serve immediately with lemon
wedges, if you like, to squeeze over
the salmon and pasta.

PER SERVING

432 calories
11g fat (of which 6g saturates)
67g carbohydrate
1.7g salt

Pea, Mint and Ricotta Pasta

Preparation Time 5 minutes   Cooking Time 10 minutes   Serves 4   **EASY**

300g (11oz) farfalle pasta
200g (7oz) frozen peas
175g (6oz) ricotta cheese (see Cook's
    Tips, page 184)
3 tbsp freshly chopped mint
2 tbsp extra virgin olive oil
salt and ground black pepper

1 Cook the pasta according to
the pack instructions until al dente.
Add the frozen peas for the last
4 minutes of cooking.

2 Drain the pasta and peas, reserving
a ladleful of pasta cooking water,
then put back in the pan. Stir in the
ricotta and mint with the pasta
water. Season well with salt and
pepper, drizzle with the oil and
serve at once.

PER SERVING

431 calories
14g fat (of which 5g saturates)
63g carbohydrate
trace salt
vegetarian

Seafood Spaghetti with Pepper and Almond Sauce

Preparation Time 20 minutes   Cooking Time 25 minutes   Serves 4   **EASY**

1 small red pepper
1 red chilli (see Cook's Tip, page 49)
50g (2oz) blanched almonds
2–3 garlic cloves, chopped
2 tbsp red wine vinegar
350ml (12fl oz) tomato juice
a small handful of flat-leafed parsley
300g (11oz) spaghetti
450g (1lb) mixed cooked seafood, such as prawns, mussels and squid
salt and ground black pepper

1 Preheat the grill. Grill the red pepper and chilli, turning occasionally, until the skins char and blacken. Cover and leave to cool slightly, then peel off the skins. Halve, discard the seeds, then put the flesh into a food processor.

2 Toast the almonds under the grill until golden. Add the toasted almonds and garlic to the processor with the vinegar, tomato juice and half the parsley, then season with salt and pepper. Whiz until almost smooth, then transfer the sauce to a large pan.

3 Meanwhile, cook the spaghetti in a pan of lightly salted boiling water according to the pack instructions until al dente.

4 Heat the sauce gently until it simmers, then add the seafood. Simmer for 3–4 minutes until the sauce and seafood have heated through, stirring frequently.

5 Roughly chop the remaining parsley. Drain the pasta and put back in the pan, then add the sauce together with the parsley and toss well. Serve immediately.

HEALTHY TIP

Red peppers are rich in vitamin C, betacarotene and other phytochemicals that help combat cancer and heart disease. Almonds supply useful amounts of calcium and protein and although high in fat, it is the healthy unsaturated kind. Seafood such as prawns and mussels are good sources of protein and zinc, and low in fat.

PER SERVING
426 calories
9g fat (of which 1g saturates)
62g carbohydrate
0.9g salt
dairy free

Clams with Chilli

Preparation Time 15 minutes   Cooking Time about 10 minutes   Serves 4   **EASY**

300g (11oz) linguine pasta

2 tbsp olive oil

1 garlic clove, crushed

1 red chilli, seeded and finely chopped
   (see Cook's Tips, page 49)

4 tomatoes, seeded and chopped

900g (2lb) clams in their shells, washed
   and scrubbed

150ml (¼ pint) light dry white wine

2 tbsp freshly chopped parsley

1 Cook the linguine in a pan of lightly salted boiling water according to the pack instructions until al dente.

2 Meanwhile, heat the oil in a large pan. Add the garlic, chilli and tomatoes and fry for 4 minutes, stirring gently. Add the clams and wine. Cover and cook over a high heat for 3–4 minutes until the clam shells spring open – discard any that remain closed.

3 Drain the pasta and put back in the pan, then add the clams with the sauce and the parsley. Toss together gently and serve immediately.

PER SERVING

512 calories

9g fat (of which 1g saturates)

64g carbohydrate

0.3g salt

dairy free

Stuffed Pasta Shells

Preparation Time 15 minutes   Cooking Time about 1 hour   Serves 6   **EASY**

2 tbsp olive oil
1 large onion, finely chopped
a few fresh rosemary or oregano sprigs,
    chopped
125g (4oz) small flat mushrooms, sliced
6 plump coarse sausages, skinned
175ml (6fl oz) red wine
300ml (½ pint) passata
4 tbsp sun-dried tomato paste
sugar to taste, if necessary
250g (9oz) large pasta shells, such as
    conchiglioni rigati
150ml (¼ pint) half-fat single cream
    (optional)
freshly grated Parmesan to garnish
green salad to serve

1 Preheat the oven to 180°C (160°C fan oven) mark 4. Heat the oil in a deep frying pan. Stir in the onion and rosemary or oregano and cook over a gentle heat for 10 minutes or until the onion is soft and golden. Add the mushrooms and cook over a medium heat until the vegetables are soft and beginning to brown at the edges. Tip the onion mixture into a bowl.

2 Crumble the sausagemeat into the hot pan and stir over a high heat with a wooden spoon, breaking the meat up as you do so, until browned all over. Reduce the heat slightly and pour in the wine. Leave to bubble and reduce by about half. Return the onion mixture to the pan and add the passata and sun-dried tomato paste. Bubble gently for a further 10 minutes. Add a pinch of sugar if the sauce tastes a little sharp.

3 Meanwhile, cook the pasta shells in a large pan of lightly salted boiling water for 10 minutes or until al dente. Drain well and run under the cold tap to cool.

4 Fill the shells with the sauce and put into a shallow ovenproof dish. Drizzle with any extra sauce and the cream, if using, and bake for 30 minutes or until piping hot. Sprinkle with Parmesan and serve with a big bowl of green salad.

TRY SOMETHING DIFFERENT

• Turkey or chicken mince would make a lighter alternative to the sausages: you will need 450g (1lb).
• Use a small aubergine, diced, instead of the mushrooms.

PER SERVING

378 calories
17g fat (of which 5g saturates)
41g carbohydrate
1.1g salt

Classic Lasagne

Preparation Time about 1 hour 20 minutes   Cooking Time 45 minutes   Serves 6   **EASY**

butter to grease
350g (12oz) fresh lasagne, or 225g (8oz)
   'no need to pre-cook' lasagne
   (12–15 sheets, see Cook's Tip)
3 tbsp freshly grated Parmesan
mixed salad leaves to serve

FOR THE BOLOGNESE
   SAUCE

2 tbsp olive oil
1 onion, finely chopped
2 garlic cloves, crushed
450g (1lb) extra-lean minced beef
2 tbsp sun-dried tomato paste
300ml (½ pint) red wine
400g can chopped tomatoes
125g (4oz) chestnut mushrooms, sliced
2 tbsp Worcestershire sauce
salt and ground black pepper

FOR THE BÉCHAMEL SAUCE

300ml (½ pint) semi-skimmed milk
1 onion slice
6 peppercorns
1 mace blade
1 bay leaf
15g (½oz) butter
15g (½oz) plain flour
freshly grated nutmeg
salt and ground black pepper

1 To make the Bolognese sauce, heat the oil in a large pan, add the onion and fry over a medium heat for 10 minutes or until softened and golden. Add the garlic and cook for 1 minute. Add the beef and brown evenly, using a wooden spoon to break up the pieces. Stir in the tomato paste and wine, cover and bring to the boil. Add the tomatoes, mushrooms and Worcestershire sauce and season well with salt and pepper. Bring back to the boil, reduce the heat and simmer for 20 minutes.

2 To make the béchamel sauce, pour the milk into a pan and add the onion, peppercorns, mace and bay leaf. Bring almost to the boil, then remove from the heat, cover and leave to infuse for about 20 minutes. Strain. Melt the butter in a pan, stir in the flour and cook, stirring, for 1 minute or until cooked but not coloured. Remove from the heat and gradually pour in the milk, whisking constantly. Season lightly with nutmeg, salt and pepper. Put back on the heat and cook, stirring constantly, until the sauce is thickened and smooth. Simmer gently for 2 minutes.

3 Preheat the oven to 180°C (160°C fan oven) mark 4. Spoon one-third of the Bolognese sauce over the base of a greased 2.3 litre (4 pint) ovenproof dish. Cover with a layer of lasagne sheets, then a layer of béchamel. Repeat these layers twice more, finishing with a layer of béchamel to cover the lasagne.

4 Sprinkle the Parmesan over the top and stand the dish on a baking sheet. Cook in the oven for 45 minutes or until well browned and bubbling. Serve with mixed salad leaves.

PER SERVING

326 calories
13g fat (of which 6g saturates)
37g carbohydrate
0.5g salt

COOK'S TIP

If using 'no need to pre-cook' lasagne, add a little extra stock or water to the sauce.

Butternut Squash and Spinach Lasagne

Preparation Time 30 minutes   Cooking Time about 1 hour   Serves 6   **EASY**

1 butternut squash, peeled, halved, seeded and cut into 3cm (1¼in) cubes
2 tbsp olive oil
1 onion, sliced
25g (1oz) butter
25g (1oz) plain flour
600ml (1 pint) milk
250g (9oz) ricotta cheese
1 tsp freshly grated nutmeg
225g bag baby leaf spinach
6 'no need to pre-cook' lasagne sheets
50g (2oz) pecorino cheese or Parmesan, freshly grated
salt and ground black pepper

1 Preheat the oven to 200°C (180°C fan oven) mark 6. Put the squash into a roasting tin with the oil, onion and 1 tbsp water. Mix well and season with salt and pepper. Roast for 25 minutes, tossing halfway through.

2 To make the sauce, melt the butter in a pan, then stir in the flour and cook over a medium heat for 1–2 minutes. Gradually add the milk, stirring constantly. Reduce the heat to a simmer and cook, stirring, for 5 minutes or until the sauce has thickened. Crumble the ricotta into the sauce and add the nutmeg. Mix together thoroughly and season with salt and pepper.

3 Heat 1 tbsp water in a pan. Add the spinach, cover and cook until just wilted. Season generously.

4 Spoon the squash mixture into a 1.7 litre (3 pint) ovenproof dish. Layer the spinach on top, then cover with one-third of the sauce, then the lasagne. Spoon the remaining sauce on top, season and sprinkle with the grated cheese. Cook for 30–35 minutes until the cheese topping is golden and the pasta is cooked.

HEALTHY TIP

Butternut squash is super-rich in betacarotene, which has powerful antioxidant properties, helping to protect against heart disease and cancer. It also benefits the skin and can be converted into vitamin A in the body. Spinach adds folate, vitamin C, calcium and iron to the dish.

PER SERVING

273 calories
17g fat (of which 7g saturates)
18g carbohydrate
0.6g salt

Spaghetti with Mussels

Preparation Time 20 minutes Cooking Time 35 minutes Serves 4 **EASY**

1kg (2lb) fresh mussels in their shells,
    cleaned (see Cook's Tip)
1kg (2lb) ripe, flavourful tomatoes,
    quartered
1 onion, chopped
4 garlic cloves
6 basil leaves, plus extra to garnish
150ml (¼ pint) white wine
400g (14oz) dried spaghetti
2 tbsp olive oil
2 red chillies, halved, seeded and
    chopped (see Cook's Tip, page 49)
salt and ground black pepper

1 Put the mussels into a large pan with a cupful of water. Cover and cook for 3–4 minutes, shaking the pan occasionally, until the mussels open. Using a slotted spoon, transfer the mussels to a bowl; discard any unopened ones. Strain the cooking juices through a muslin lined sieve and put to one side.

2 Put the tomatoes and onion into a shallow pan. Crush 2 garlic cloves and add them to the pan with the basil. Bring to the boil, then reduce the heat and simmer for 20 minutes or until the tomatoes disintegrate. Press the tomato mixture through a nylon sieve into a clean pan. Pour in the cooking juices and the wine. Bring to the boil and leave to bubble until reduced by half.

3 Cook the spaghetti according to the pack instructions. Meanwhile, heat the oil in another pan. Chop the remaining garlic and add to the pan with the chillies. Cook until golden, then stir in the tomato sauce and mussels. Cover and simmer for 2–3 minutes. Season.

4 Drain the spaghetti, keeping 2 tbsp of the pasta cooking water. Toss the spaghetti and reserved water with the sauce. Serve, garnished with basil.

COOK'S TIP

To clean mussels, scrape off the fibres (beards) attached to the shells. If the mussels are very clean, give them a quick rinse under the cold tap. If they are very sandy, scrub them with a stiff brush, then rinse thoroughly. If the shells have sizeable barnacles on them, it's best (though not essential) to remove them. Rap them sharply with a metal spoon or the back of a washing-up brush, then scrape off. Discard any open mussels that don't shut when sharply tapped; this means they are dead and may cause food poisoning.

PER SERVING

530 calories
10g fat (of which 2g saturates)
83g carbohydrate
0.5g salt
dairy free

Pasta and Pastrami Salad

Preparation Time 10 minutes   Cooking Time 20 minutes   Serves 4   **EASY**

300g (11oz) cooked pasta, cooled
125g (4oz) pastrami, diced
4 tomatoes, chopped
1 cucumber, chopped
3 tbsp freshly chopped parsley
1 medium red onion, finely chopped

FOR THE DRESSING
wholegrain mustard to taste
6 tbsp Vinaigrette Dressing (see
   Cook's Tip)

1 Combine all the ingredients for the
   salad in a salad bowl.

2 Mix the mustard into the
   vinaigrette, pour on to the salad
   and toss.

COOK'S TIP

Vinaigrette Dressing
Put 100ml (3½fl oz) extra virgin olive
oil, 100ml (3½fl oz) grapeseed oil,
75ml (2fl oz) white wine vinegar,
pinch each sugar and English mustard
powder and 1 crushed garlic clove
(optional) in a large screw-topped jar.
Shake well, season to taste with salt
and ground black pepper and store in
a cool place. Makes about 300ml
(½ pint).

PER SERVING
72 calories
1g fat (of which 0.5g saturates)
12g carbohydrate
0.4g salt
dairy free

Greek Pasta Salad

Preparation Time 10 minutes   Cooking Time 10–15 minutes   Serves 2   **EASY**

3 tbsp olive oil

2 tbsp lemon juice

150g (5oz) cooked pasta shapes, cooled

75g (3oz) vegetarian feta cheese, crumbled

3 tomatoes, roughly chopped

2 tbsp small pitted black olives

½ cucumber, roughly chopped

1 small red onion, finely sliced

salt and ground black pepper

freshly chopped mint and lemon zest to garnish

crusty bread to serve

1 Mix the oil and lemon juice together in a salad bowl, then add the pasta, feta cheese, tomatoes, olives, cucumber and onion.

2 Season with salt and pepper and stir to mix, then garnish with chopped mint and lemon zest and serve with chunks of bread.

HEALTHY TIP

This salad provides many vitamins and minerals. Tomatoes are rich in vitamins A and C, as well as the cancer-protective phytochemical lycopene. Olives supply high levels of vitamin E and heart-healthy monounsaturated fats while the cucumber supplies potassium, important for regulating blood pressure and fluid balance.

PER SERVING

382 calories

27g fat (of which 8g saturates)

25g carbohydrate

2.5g salt

vegetarian

Salmon and Bulgur Wheat Pilau

Preparation Time 5 minutes   **Cooking Time** 20 minutes   **Serves** 4   **EASY**

1 tbsp olive oil
1 onion, chopped
175g (6oz) bulgur wheat
450ml (¾ pint) vegetable stock
400g can pink salmon, drained and
    flaked
125g (4oz) spinach, roughly chopped
225g (8oz) frozen peas
zest and juice of 1 lemon
salt and ground black pepper

1 Heat the oil in a large pan. Add the onion and cook until softened. Stir in the bulgur wheat to coat in the oil, then stir in the stock and bring to the boil. Cover, reduce the heat and simmer for 10–15 minutes until the stock has been fully absorbed.

2 Stir in the salmon, spinach, peas and lemon juice and cook until the spinach has wilted and the salmon and peas are heated through. Season to taste with salt and pepper and sprinkle with lemon zest before serving.

HEALTHY TIP

Salmon is a rich source of omega-3 fats, which help promote cardiovascular health and protect against heart disease. They also help maintain brain function and eyesight. Bulgur wheat is made from whole-grain wheat so is a good source of fibre, iron and B vitamins.

TRY SOMETHING DIFFERENT

Instead of salmon, use 200g (7oz) cooked peeled prawns and 200g (7oz) cherry tomatoes.

PER SERVING

323 calories
11g fat (of which 2g saturates)
30g carbohydrate
1.5g salt
dairy free

Prawn and Vegetable Pilau

Preparation Time 10 minutes   Cooking Time 15–20 minutes   Serves 4   **EASY**

250g (9oz) long-grain rice
1 broccoli head, broken into florets
150g (5oz) baby sweetcorn, halved
200g (7oz) sugarsnap peas
1 red pepper, seeded and sliced into
    thin strips
400g (14oz) cooked and peeled king
    prawns

FOR THE DRESSING
1 tbsp sesame oil
5cm (2in) piece fresh root ginger,
    peeled and grated
juice of 1 lime
1–2 tbsp light soy sauce

1 Put the rice into a large wide pan – it needs to be really big, as you'll be cooking the rice and steaming the vegetables on top, then tossing it all together. Add 600ml (1 pint) boiling water. Cover and bring to the boil, then reduce the heat to low and cook the rice according to the pack instructions.

2 About 10 minutes before the end of the rice cooking time, add the broccoli, corn, sugarsnaps and red pepper. Stir well, then cover the pan and cook until the vegetables and rice are just tender.

3 Meanwhile, put the prawns into a bowl. Add the sesame oil, ginger, lime and soy sauce. Mix the prawns and dressing into the cooked vegetables and rice and toss well. Serve immediately.

> **COOK'S TIP**
>
> The word 'pilau', or 'pilaf', comes from the Persian 'pilaw'. The dish consists of rice flavoured with spices, to which vegetables, poultry, meat, fish or shellfish are added.

PER SERVING
360 calories
5g fat (of which 1g saturates)
61g carbohydrate
1.8g salt
dairy free

Coconut Fish Pilau

Preparation Time 15 minutes   **Cooking Time** 30 minutes   **Serves** 4   **EASY**

2 tsp olive oil

1 shallot, chopped

1 tbsp Thai green curry paste

225g (8oz) brown basmati rice

600ml (1 pint) hot fish or vegetable
   stock

150ml (¼ pint) reduced-fat coconut
   milk

350g (12oz) skinless white fish fillet, cut
   into bite-size pieces

350g (12oz) sugarsnap peas

125g (4oz) cooked and peeled prawns

25g (1oz) flaked almonds, toasted

a squeeze of lemon juice

salt and ground black pepper

2 tbsp freshly chopped coriander
   to garnish

1 Heat the oil In a frying pan. Add the shallot and 1 tbsp water and fry for 4–5 minutes until golden. Stir in the curry paste and cook for a further 1–2 minutes.

2 Add the rice, hot stock and coconut milk and bring to the boil. Cover the pan, reduce the heat and simmer for 15–20 minutes until all the liquid has been absorbed.

3 Add the fish and cook for 3–5 minutes. Add the sugarsnap peas, prawns, almonds and lemon juice and stir over the heat for about 3–4 minutes or until heated through. Check the seasoning and serve immediately, garnished with chopped coriander.

TRY SOMETHING DIFFERENT

There are plenty of alternatives to cod: try coley (saithe), sea bass or pollack.

PER SERVING

398 calories

7g fat (of which 1g saturates)

53g carbohydrate

0.4g salt

gluten free • dairy free

Aubergine and Chickpea Pilau

Preparation Time 10 minutes   Cooking Time 20 minutes, plus standing   Serves 4   **EASY**

4–6 tbsp olive oil
275g (10oz) aubergine, roughly chopped
225g (8oz) onions, finely chopped
25g (1oz) butter
½ tsp cumin seeds
175g (6oz) long-grain rice
600ml (1 pint) vegetable stock
400g can chickpeas, drained and rinsed
225g (8oz) baby spinach leaves
salt and ground black pepper

1 Heat half the oil in a large pan or flameproof casserole over a medium heat. Fry the aubergine for 4–5 minutes, in batches, until deep golden brown. Remove from the pan with a slotted spoon and put to one side. Add the remaining oil to the pan, then add the onions and cook for 5 minutes until golden.

2 Add the butter, then stir in the cumin seeds and rice. Fry for 1–2 minutes. Pour in the stock, season with salt and pepper and bring to the boil. Reduce the heat, then simmer, uncovered, for 10–12 minutes until most of the liquid has evaporated and the rice is tender.

3 Remove the pan from the heat. Stir in the chickpeas, spinach and reserved aubergine. Cover with a tight-fitting lid and leave to stand for 5 minutes until the spinach has wilted and the chickpeas are heated through. Adjust the seasoning to taste. Fork through the rice grains to separate and make the rice fluffy before serving.

HEALTHY TIP

Chickpeas are excellent sources of fibre, protein and iron. They contain a type of fibre called fructo-oligosaccharides, which help promote the friendly gut bacteria, and boost immunity. Spinach supplies plenty of vitamins A and C.

COOK'S TIP

To prepare ahead Fry the aubergine and onion as in step 1. Cover and keep in a cool place for 1½ hours.
To use Complete the recipe.

PER SERVING

462 calories
20g fat (of which 5g saturates)
58g carbohydrate
0.9g salt
vegetarian

Prawn and Lemon Risotto

Preparation Time 15 minutes   Cooking Time 40 minutes   Serves 4   **EASY**

225g (8oz) sugarsnap peas, sliced
   diagonally
175g (6oz) baby courgettes, sliced
   diagonally
2 tbsp olive oil
1 onion, finely chopped
¼ tsp saffron (optional)
225g (8oz) arborio rice
1 garlic clove, crushed
225g (8oz) brown-cap mushrooms,
   quartered
zest and juice of 1 lemon
750ml (1¼ pints) hot fish, chicken or
   vegetable stock
300g (11oz) cooked and peeled prawns
3 tbsp freshly chopped chives

salt and ground black pepper
spring onion curls (see Cook's Tips) and
   grated lemon zest to garnish

1 Put the sugarsnap peas and
courgettes into a pan of lightly
salted boiling water and bring to the
boil. Cook for 1–2 minutes. Drain
and plunge into ice-cold water.

2 Heat the oil in a medium non-stick
pan. Add the onion and saffron, if
using, and cook over a medium heat
for 10 minutes or until soft. Add the
rice, garlic and mushrooms and
cook, stirring, for 1–2 minutes.
Season with salt and pepper.

3 Add the grated lemon zest and
about one-third of the hot stock.
Simmer gently, stirring frequently,
until most of the liquid has been
absorbed. Add another one-third of
the stock, then repeat the process.

4 Add the remaining stock. Cook,
stirring, for 10 minutes or until the
rice is tender and most of the stock
has been absorbed. Add the prawns,
drained vegetables, 1–2 tbsp lemon
juice and the chives, then heat for
3–4 minutes. Garnish with spring
onion curls and lemon zest.

PER SERVING
405 calories
8g fat (of which 1g saturates)
59g carbohydrate
0.9g salt
gluten free • dairy gree

Prawn, Courgette and Leek Risotto

Preparation Time 10 minutes   Cooking Time 30 minutes, plus standing   Serves 6   **EASY**

1 tbsp olive oil
25g (1oz) butter
1 leek, finely chopped
2 courgettes, thinly sliced
2 garlic cloves, crushed
350g (12oz) arborio rice
1.6 litres (2¾ pints) vegetable stock
200g (7oz) cooked and peeled prawns
small bunch of parsley or mint, or a
    mixture of both, chopped
salt and ground black pepper

1 Heat the oil and half the butter in a large shallow pan. Add the leek, courgettes and garlic and soften over a low heat. Add the rice and cook, stirring well, for 1 minute.

2 Meanwhile, heat the stock in a separate pan to a steady low simmer. Add a ladleful of the hot stock to the rice and simmer, stirring, until absorbed. Continue adding the hot stock, a ladleful at a time.

3 When nearly all the stock has been added and the rice is al dente, add the prawns. Season to taste with salt and pepper and stir in the remaining stock and the rest of the butter. Stir through and remove from the heat. Cover and leave to stand for a couple of minutes, then stir the chopped herbs through it. Serve immediately.

HEALTHY TIP

Arborio rice is the classic risotto rice. It is a medium- to long-grain white rice that can absorb a lot of cooking liquid yet still retain a good 'bite' when fully cooked. Like other types of white rice it is low in fat and high in complex carbohydrates, and contains small amounts of B vitamins. The prawns add protein to the dish while the courgettes provide valuable vitamins A and C.

PER SERVING

320 calories
7g fat (of which 3g saturates)
49g carbohydrate
1.3g salt
gluten free

Squash and Bacon Risotto

Preparation Time 10 minutes   Cooking Time 40 minutes   Serves 4   **EASY**

125g (4oz) smoked bacon, chopped
1 small butternut squash, peeled and cut
   into small chunks
1 onion, finely chopped
300g (11oz) arborio rice
1 litre (1¾ pints) hot vegetable stock

1 Put the bacon and the butternut squash into a large deep frying pan and fry over a medium heat for 8–10 minutes.

2 When the bacon is golden and the squash has softened, add the onion to the pan and continue to fry for 5 minutes until softened.

3 Stir in the rice, cook for 1–2 minutes, then add the hot stock. Bring to the boil and simmer for 15–20 minutes, stirring occasionally to ensure the rice doesn't stick, until almost all the stock has been absorbed and the rice and squash are tender. Serve immediately.

HEALTHY TIP

Butternut squash is a very good source of betacarotene and vitamin C as well as magnesium, manganese, calcium and potassium. Smoked bacon supplies protein to the dish but is high in salt so keep portion sizes small.

TRY SOMETHING DIFFERENT

• Instead of the squash, use 750g (1lb 11oz) peeled and seeded pumpkin.
• Instead of the onion, use a fennel bulb.

PER SERVING

390 calories
9g fat (of which 3g saturates)
65g carbohydrate
2g salt
gluten free • dairy free

Simple Fried Rice

Preparation Time 5 minutes   **Cooking Time** 15–20 minutes   **Serves 4**   **EASY**

150g (5oz) long-grain rice
2 tbsp sesame oil
3 medium eggs, lightly beaten
250g (9oz) frozen petits pois
250g (9oz) cooked and peeled prawns

1 Cook the rice in boiling water for about 10 minutes or according to the pack instructions. Drain well.

2 Heat 1 tsp oil in a large non-stick frying pan. Pour in half the beaten eggs and tilt the pan around over the heat for about 1 minute until the egg is set. Tip the omelette on to a warmed plate. Repeat with another 1 tsp oil and the remaining beaten egg to make another omelette. Tip on to another warmed plate.

3 Add the remaining oil to the pan and stir in the rice and peas. Stir-fry for 2–3 minutes until the peas are cooked. Stir in the prawns.

4 Roll up the omelettes, roughly chop one-third of one, then slice the remainder into strips. Add the chopped omelette to the rice, peas and prawns and cook for 1–2 minutes until heated through. Divide the fried rice among four bowls, top with the sliced omelette and serve immediately.

PER SERVING

339 calories
11g fat (of which 2g saturates)
37g carbohydrate
0.4g salt
gluten free • dairy free

Rice and Red Pepper Stir-fry

Preparation Time 5 minutes   Cooking Time 15 minutes   Serves 1   **EASY**

75g (3oz) long-grain rice
200ml (7fl oz) hot vegetable stock
2 tsp vegetable oil
½ onion, sliced
2 rashers streaky bacon
1 small red pepper, halved, seeded and
    cut into chunks
a handful of frozen peas
a dash of Worcestershire sauce

1 Put the rice into a pan and pour in the hot stock. Cover and bring to the boil, then reduce the heat and simmer for 10 minutes or until the rice is tender and the liquid has been absorbed.

2 Heat the oil in a frying pan over a medium heat. Add the onion and fry for 5 minutes, then add the bacon and red pepper. Fry for 5 minutes or until the bacon is crisp. Stir in the cooked rice and the peas. Cook, stirring occasionally, for 2–3 minutes until the rice is hot and the peas are tender. Add a dash of Worcestershire sauce and serve.

HEALTHY TIP

Red peppers are rich in vitamin C – one pepper supplies 100% of your daily needs – as well as betacarotene, a powerful cancer-fighting nutrient. Peas add valuable amounts of fibre to the dish as well as vitamin C and protein. Streaky bacon is high in fat so use smaller amounts if you want to reduce the overall fat content of the dish.

PER SERVING

584 calories
20g fat (of which 5g saturates)
82g carbohydrate
1.7g salt
dairy free

Prawn and Peanut Noodles

Preparation Time 10 minutes, plus soaking   Serves 4   **EASY**

300g (11oz) straight-to-wok noodles
360g pack stir-fry vegetables
4 tbsp coconut cream
4 tbsp smooth peanut butter
1 tbsp Thai red or green curry paste
juice of ½ lime
225g (8oz) cooked and peeled king
   prawns
a small handful of freshly chopped
   coriander
25g (1oz) peanuts, chopped

1 Put the noodles and stir-fry vegetables into a large bowl or wok and cover with boiling water. Cover with clingfilm and leave for 5 minutes.

2 Meanwhile, mix the coconut cream with the peanut butter, curry paste and lime juice in a bowl.

3 Drain the noodles and vegetables in a colander. Put back into the bowl and toss with the prawns, coriander and half the dressing. Sprinkle with the peanuts and serve with the remaining dressing.

PER SERVING

579 calories
24g fat (of which 7g saturates)
67g carbohydrate
0.7g salt
dairy free

Weekends and Special Meals

Lamb, Orange and Apricot Kebabs

Preparation Time 45 minutes, plus marinating **Cooking Time** 25–30 minutes **Serves 8** **EASY**

700g (1½lb) boned leg of lamb
75g (3oz) ready-to-eat dried apricots
150g (5oz) ready-to-eat dried figs
1 garlic clove, crushed
50g (2oz) spring onions, finely chopped
juice of 2 lemons
6 tbsp Greek yogurt
5 tbsp smooth peanut butter
2 tsp each ground coriander and cumin
   seeds
1 tsp ground fenugreek
½ tsp chilli powder
3 tbsp olive oil
225g (8oz) onions
2 large oranges
salt and ground black pepper
salad leaves to serve

1 Trim the lamb and cut into large cubes, allowing about three pieces per skewer. Put the apricots and figs into a bowl and add enough water to cover completely, then cover and chill.

2 In a large bowl, mix the garlic and spring onions with 8 tbsp lemon juice and all the remaining ingredients except the whole onions and oranges. Add the lamb to the marinade, season and stir to coat well. Cover and chill for at least 6 hours or overnight.

3 Preheat the barbecue and, if using wooden skewers, soak eight in water for 20 minutes. Quarter the onions, then separate the quarters into petals. Thickly slice the oranges. Thread the meat, onions, oranges, apricots and figs on to skewers.

4 Barbecue for 25–30 minutes until the lamb is pink to the centre. Serve hot, with salad leaves.

PER SERVING

260 calories
14g fat (of which 5g saturates)
15g carbohydrate
0.2g salt
gluten free

Leek, Artichoke and Mushroom Croûte

Preparation Time 30 minutes, plus chilling   Cooking Time 30–35 minutes, plus cooling   Serves 8   **EASY**

3 tbsp olive oil

2 garlic cloves, crushed

125g (4oz) shiitake mushrooms, sliced

1 tbsp balsamic vinegar

50g (2oz) peeled cooked (or vacuum-packed) chestnuts, roughly chopped

1½ tsp fresh thyme leaves

400g can artichoke hearts, drained and quartered

350g (12oz) leeks, sliced

375g pack ready-rolled puff pastry

butter to grease

1 medium egg, lightly beaten

salt and ground black pepper

cranberry sauce and a little extra virgin olive oil to serve

1 Heat 2 tbsp olive oil in a large pan and fry the garlic for 1 minute. Add the mushrooms and cook over a low heat for 3 minutes to soften. Add the vinegar, chestnuts, ½ tsp thyme leaves and the artichokes, then cook for 1 minute. In a separate pan, soften the leeks in the remaining 1 tbsp oil for 4 minutes. Tip into a bowl and leave to cool for 5 minutes.

2 Unroll the pastry and sprinkle with the remaining thyme; roll it lightly into the pastry. Flip the pastry over so that the herbs are on the underside, then lightly roll out to a 38 × 25.5cm (15 × 10in) rectangle. Using a sharp knife, cut the pastry in half to create two long thin rectangles. Spoon half the mushroom mixture down the centre of each. Top with the leeks and season. Brush the pastry edges with water, then fold each side of the pastry up over the filling and seal. Cut both rolls in half and put on to a greased baking sheet. Cover and chill overnight.

3 Preheat the oven to 200°C (180°C fan oven) mark 6. Brush the pastry with beaten egg to glaze. Cook for 20 minutes until the pastry is golden. Slice each croûte into six and serve three slices per person, with cranberry sauce and a light drizzle of olive oil.

FREEZING TIP

To freeze Complete the recipe to the end of step 2, then wrap and freeze for up to one month.

To use Cook from frozen in a preheated oven at 200°C (180°C fan oven) mark 6 for 25 minutes until the pastry is golden brown. Complete the recipe.

PER SERVING

236 calories

17g fat (of which 1g saturates)

20g carbohydrate

0.4g sal

vegetarian

Fennel Pork with Cabbage and Apple

Preparation Time 10 minutes   **Cooking Time** 6–10 minutes   **Serves 4**   **EASY**

2 tbsp olive oil
½l tbsp fennel seeds, crushed
1 tbsp freshly chopped sage
4 lean pork medallions, 125g (4oz) each
½ small red cabbage, shredded
450g (1lb) purple sprouting broccoli,
    tough ends removed
1 apple, cored and sliced into rings
salt and ground black pepper

1 Put 1 tbsp oil into a large shallow bowl. Add the fennel seeds and sage, season with salt and pepper and mix well. Add the pork and rub the mixture into the meat.

2 Heat the remaining oil in a wok or large frying pan and stir-fry the cabbage and broccoli for 6–8 minutes until starting to char.

3 Meanwhile, heat a non-stick griddle until hot and fry the pork for 2–3 minutes on each side until cooked through. Remove and put to onee side. Add the apple rings to the griddle and cook for 1–2 minutes on each side until starting to char and caramelise. Serve with the pork and vegetables.

PER SERVING

276 calories
12g fat (of which 3g saturates)
9g carbohydrate
0.3g salt
gluten free • dairy free

Lemon-roasted Pork with Garlic and Basil

Preparation Time 20 minutes, plus marinating   Cooking Time 40 minutes   Serves 6   **EASY**

2 pork tenderloins, about 350g (12oz)
    each, trimmed
finely grated zest and juice of
    2 lemons, sieved
6 tbsp freshly chopped basil or parsley
12 garlic cloves, blanched and halved if
    large
2–3 bay leaves
2 tbsp olive oil
fresh herbs and lemon slices to garnish
sautéed shallots to serve

1 Split the pork lengthways without cutting right through and open each piece out flat. Sprinkle with the lemon zest and basil or parsley. Lay the garlic cloves evenly along the middle of each fillet and season with salt and pepper.

2 Close the pork and tie loosely at 2.5cm (1in) intervals with string. Put in a shallow non-metallic dish with the bay leaves and sieved lemon juice. Cover, chill and leave to marinate overnight.

3 Preheat the oven to 200°C (180°C fan oven) mark 6. Remove the pork and put the marinade to one side. Heat the oil in a sauté pan. Add the meat and fry until browned. Transfer to a shallow roasting tin with the marinade. Season the pork and cook in the oven for about 35 minutes, basting frequently.

4 Serve the pork sliced, garnished with herbs and lemon slices, and with sautéed shallots.

HEALTHY TIP

Garlic is rich in antioxidants and other chemicals that support many aspects of health, from heart and circulatory health to immunity and anti-ageing. Garlic has been found to lower LDL ('bad') cholesterol, blood pressure, and atherosclerosis.

PER SERVING

185 calories
9g fat (of which 2g saturates)
1.5g carbohydrate
0.2g salt
gluten free • dairy free

Pork with Basil, Tomato and Stilton

Preparation Time 10 minutes   Cooking Time 10–14 minutes   Serves 4   **EASY**

4 pork loin steaks
1 ripe beef tomato, sliced
a few basil leaves
50g (2oz) Stilton, sliced
new potatoes and runner beans
    to serve

1 Preheat the grill. Grill the pork for
  1–5 minutes on each side.

2 Divide the sliced tomato among the
  steaks, add a few basil leaves and
  the sliced Stilton and grill for a
  further 1–2 minutes or until the
  cheese has melted and the pork is
  cooked through. Serve with new
  potatoes and runner beans.

TRY SOMETHING DIFFERENT

Instead of pork, use 4 boneless,
skinless chicken breasts: season
lightly, place between two pieces of
clingfilm and beat with a rolling pin
until about 1cm ($\frac{1}{2}$in) thick. Brush
lightly with olive oil before grilling.

PER SERVING

212 calories
9g fat (of which 5g saturates)
2g carbohydrate
0.5g salt
gluten free

Calf's Liver with Fried Sage and Balsamic Vinegar

Preparation Time 5 minutes   Cooking Time 5 minutes   Serves 4   **EASY**

15g (½oz) butter plus a little olive oil
   to fry
12 sage leaves
4 thin slices of calf's liver
1–2 tbsp balsamic vinegar
rice, with freshly chopped parsley
   stirred through, or grilled polenta
   to serve

1 Preheat the oven to a low setting. Melt the butter with a little oil in a heavy-based frying pan and when hot add the sage leaves. Cook briefly for 1 minute or so until crisp. Remove, put in a single layer in a shallow dish and keep hot in the oven.

2 Add a little extra oil to the pan, put in two slices of calf's liver and cook quickly for 30 seconds on each side over a high heat. Remove and place on a plate while you quickly cook the remaining two slices.

3 Return all four slices to the pan, splash the balsamic vinegar over the top and cook for another minute or so. Serve immediately with rice or grilled polenta.

HEALTHY TIP

Liver is an excellent source of the minerals iron and selenium as well as vitamin A, vitamin B2, vitamin B12 and folate. In addition, it is also a good source of protein, zinc, niacin and vitamin B6.

PER SERVING

88 calories
6g fat (of which 3g saturates)
trace carbohydrate
0.1g salt
gluten free

Mustard Roast Beef

Preparation Time 10 minutes, plus marinating   **Cooking Time** 50–60 minutes, plus resting   **Serves 4**   **EASY**

1.1kg (2½lb) boned, rolled sirloin
   of beef
1 tbsp olive oil
5 bay leaves
200ml (7fl oz) red wine
2 onions, sliced
2 tbsp English mustard
300ml (½ pint) hot vegetable stock
salt and ground black pepper
new potatoes and broccoli to serve

1 Put the beef into a bowl and add the oil, bay leaves, wine and onions. Cover and marinate in the fridge for 4 hours or overnight.

2 Preheat the oven to 200°C (180°C fan oven) mark 6. Put the beef into a roasting tin with all the marinade ingredients. Spread the mustard over the meat, then season well with salt and pepper. Pour in the stock, then roast in the oven for 50–60 minutes. Cover and leave to rest for 10 minutes, then carve and serve with new potatoes and broccoli.

PER SERVING

469 calories
19g fat (of which 6g saturates)
3g carbohydrate
0.5g salt
gluten free • dairy free

Sesame Beef

Preparation Time 20 minutes **Cooking Time** 10 minutes **Serves 4** **EASY**

2 tbsp soy sauce

2 tbsp Worcestershire sauce

2 tsp tomato purée

juice of 1/2 lemon

1 tbsp sesame seeds

1 garlic clove, crushed

400g (14oz) rump steak, sliced

1 tbsp vegetable oil

3 small pak choi, chopped

1 bunch of spring onions, sliced

egg noodles or tagliatelle to serve

1 Put the soy and Worcestershire sauces, tomato purée, lemon juice, sesame seeds and garlic into a bowl and mix well. Add the steak and toss to coat.

2 Heat the oil in a large wok or non-stick frying pan until hot. Add the steak and sear well. Remove from the wok and put to one side.

3 Add any sauce from the bowl to the wok and heat for 1 minute. Add the pak choi, spring onions and steak and stir-fry for 5 minutes. Add freshly cooked and drained noodles or pasta, then toss and serve immediately.

HEALTHY TIP

In addition to being a very good source of protein, beef is a good source of vitamin B12, and vitamin B6. It is one of the richest dietary sources of iron, needed to carry oxygen around the body.

TRY SOMETHING DIFFERENT

Use 400g (14oz) pork escalope cut into strips instead of beef. Cook for 5 minutes before removing from the pan at step 2.

PER SERVING

207 calories

10g fat (of which 3g saturates)

4g carbohydrate

2g salt

dairy free

Chicken and Artichoke Pie

Preparation Time 20 minutes · Cooking Time 45 minutes · Serves 4 **EASY**

3 boneless, skinless chicken breasts,
    about 350g (12oz)
150ml (¼ pint) dry white wine
225g (8oz) reduced-fat cream cheese
    with garlic and herbs
400g can artichoke hearts, drained and
    quartered
4 sheets filo pastry, thawed
    if frozen
olive oil
1 tsp sesame seeds
salt and ground black pepper

1 Preheat the oven to 200°C (180°C fan oven) mark 6. Put the chicken and wine into a pan and bring to the boil, then cover, reduce the heat and simmer for 10 minutes. Remove the chicken with a slotted spoon and put to one side. Add the cheese to the wine and mix until smooth. Bring to the boil, then reduce the heat and simmer until thickened.

2 Cut the chicken into bite-size pieces, then add to the sauce with the artichokes. Season and mix well.

3 Put the mixture into an ovenproof dish. Brush the pastry lightly with oil, scrunch slightly and put on top of the chicken. Sprinkle with sesame seeds, then cook in the oven for 30–35 minutes until crisp. Serve hot.

HEALTHY TIP

This recipe uses filo pastry, which is almost fat free, and therefore a healthy alternative to traditional shortcrust pastry, which contains around 30g (1oz) of fat and 500 calories per 100g (3½oz). Artichokes have cholesterol-lowering properties and help protect the liver from damage by toxins.

TRY SOMETHING DIFFERENT

Replace the artichoke hearts with 225g (8oz) brown-cap mushrooms, cooked in a little water with some salt and pepper and lemon juice.

PER SERVING

241 calories
9g fat (of which 5g saturates)
7g carbohydrate
0.2g salt

Stuffed Chicken Breasts

Preparation Time 5 minutes   Cooking Time 20 minutes   Serves 4   **EASY**

vegetable oil to oil
150g (5oz) ball mozzarella
4 skinless chicken breasts, about 125g
    (4oz) each
4 sage leaves
8 slices Parma ham
ground black pepper
new potatoes and spinach to serve

1 Preheat the oven to 200°C (180°C fan oven) mark 6. Lightly oil a baking sheet. Slice the mozzarella into eight, then put two slices on each chicken piece. Top each with a sage leaf.

2 Wrap each piece of chicken in two slices of Parma ham, covering the mozzarella. Season with pepper.

3 Put on the prepared baking sheet and cook in the oven for 20 minutes or until the chicken is cooked through. Serve with new potatoes and spinach.

COOK'S TIP

Sage has a strong, pungent taste, so you need only a little to flavour the chicken. Don't be tempted to add more than just one leaf to each chicken breast or it will overpower the finished dish.

PER SERVING

297 calories
13g fat (of which 7g saturates)
trace carbohydrate
1.4g salt
gluten free

Chicken with Wine and Capers

Preparation Time 5 minutes Cooking Time 25 minutes Serves 4 **EASY**

1 tbsp olive oil
15g (½oz) butter
4 small skinless chicken breasts
lemon wedges to garnish
boiled rice to serve

FOR THE WINE AND CAPER SAUCE

125ml (4fl oz) white wine
3 tbsp capers, rinsed and drained
juice of 1 lemon
15g (½oz) butter
1 tbsp freshly chopped flat-leafed
    parsley

1 Heat the oil and butter in a frying pan over a medium heat. Add the chicken breasts and fry for 10–12 minutes on each side until cooked through. Transfer to a warmed plate, cover and keep warm.

2 To make the sauce, add the wine and capers to the same pan. Bring to the boil, then reduce the heat and simmer for 2–3 minutes until the wine is reduced by half. Add the lemon juice and butter and stir in the parsley.

3 Divide the chicken among four warmed plates, pour the sauce over the chicken, garnish each serving with a lemon wedge and serve immediately with boiled rice.

PER SERVING

234 calories
10g fat (of which 5g saturates)
trace carbohydrate
0.3g salt
gluten free

Chicken Cacciatore

Preparation Time 5 minutes   Cooking Time 40 minutes   Serves 4   **EASY**

2 tbsp olive oil

0 boneless, skinless chicken thighs

2 garlic cloves, crushed

1 tsp dried thyme

1 tsp dried tarragon

150ml (¼ pint) white wine

400g can chopped tomatoes

12 pitted black olives

12 capers, rinsed and drained

ground black pepper

brown rice and broad beans or peas
   to serve

1 Heat the oil in a flameproof casserole over a high heat. Add the chicken and brown all over. Reduce the heat and add the garlic, thyme, tarragon and wine to the casserole. Stir for 1 minute, then add the tomatoes and season with pepper.

2 Bring to the boil, then reduce the heat, cover the casserole and simmer for 20 minutes or until the chicken is tender.

3 Lift the chicken out of the casserole and put to one side. Bubble the sauce for 5 minutes or until thickened, add the olives and capers, stir well and cook for a further 2–3 minutes.

4 Put the chicken into the sauce. Serve with brown rice and broad beans or peas.

PER SERVING

327 calories

17g fat (of which 4g saturates)

3g carbohydrate

1.3g salt

gluten free • dairy free

Chicken with Mango and Fennel Salsa

Preparation Time 12 minutes   **Cooking Time** 20 minutes   **Serves 4**   **EASY**

4 skinless chicken breasts
juice of ½ lime
oil-water spray (see Cook's Tip,
   page 92)
salt and ground black pepper
rocket to serve

FOR THE SALSA
1 mango, peeled, stoned and diced
1 small fennel bulb, trimmed and diced
1 fresh chilli, seeded and finely diced
   (see Cook's Tip, page 49)
1 tbsp balsamic vinegar
juice of ½ lime
2 tbsp freshly chopped flat-leafed
   parsley
2 tbsp freshly chopped mint

1 Preheat the grill to medium. Put the chicken on a grill pan and season well. Pour the lime juice over it and spray with the oil-water. Grill for 8–10 minutes on each side until cooked and the juices run clear when pierced with a skewer. Remove from the grill and put the chicken to one side.

2 Combine all the salsa ingredients in a bowl and season generously with salt and pepper. Spoon on top of the chicken and serve with rocket.

TRY SOMETHING DIFFERENT
Replace the chicken with 4 duck breasts with skin; score the skin in a criss-cross pattern and grill for 5–8 minutes on each side.

PER SERVING
161 calories
2g fat (of which trace saturates)
6g carbohydrate
0.2g salt
gluten free • dairy free

Garlic and Thyme Chicken

Preparation Time 10 minutes   **Cooking Time** 10–15 minutes   **Serves 4**   **EASY**

2 garlic cloves, crushed
2 tbsp freshly chopped thyme leaves
2 tbsp olive oil
4 chicken thighs
salt and ground black pepper

1 Preheat the barbecue or grill. Mix the garlic with the thyme and oil in a large bowl. Season with salt and pepper.

2 Using a sharp knife, make two or three slits in each chicken thigh. Put the chicken into the bowl and toss to coat thoroughly. Barbecue or grill for 5–7 minutes on each side until golden and cooked through.

HEALTHY TIP

Chicken is a rich source of protein and B vitamins. Chicken thighs contain more iron than chicken breast. Garlic has many health benefits: it has been shown to lower the risk of heart disease, high blood pressure, high blood cholesterol levels and certain cancers.

PER SERVING

135 calories
6g fat (of which 1g saturates)
trace carbohydrate
0.2g salt
gluten free • dairy free

Chicken in Lemon Vinaigrette

Preparation Time 10 minutes   **Cooking Time** 40 minutes   **Serves 6**   **EASY**

2 lemons

175g (6oz) shallots or onions, sliced

2 tbsp balsamic vinegar

2 tbsp sherry vinegar

4 tbsp clear honey

150ml (¼ pint) olive oil

6 boneless chicken breasts or
    12 boneless thighs, with skin

salt and ground black pepper

mashed potatoes to serve

1 Preheat the oven to 200°C (180°C fan oven) mark 6. Grate the zest and squeeze the juice of one lemon, then put to one side. Thinly slice the remaining lemon, then scatter the lemon slices and shallots or onions in a small roasting tin – it should be just large enough to hold the chicken comfortably in a single layer.

2 Whisk the lemon zest and juice, vinegars, honey and oil together in a bowl. Put the chicken into the roasting tin, season with salt and pepper and pour the lemon vinaigrette over it.

3 Roast in the oven, basting regularly, for about 35 minutes or until the chicken is golden and cooked through. Transfer the chicken to a serving dish and keep warm in a low oven. Put the roasting tin, with the juices, over a medium heat on the hob. Bring to the boil and bubble for 2–3 minutes until syrupy. Spoon over the chicken and serve with mashed potatoes.

GET AHEAD

To prepare ahead Complete the recipe to the end of step 2, then cool, cover and chill in the fridge for up to one day in a non-metallic dish. Transfer the chicken to a roasting tin before cooking.
To use Complete the recipe.

PER SERVING

353 calories

21g fat (of which 4g saturates)

10g carbohydrate

0.3g salt

gluten free • dairy free

Orange and Herb Chicken

Preparation Time 10 minutes   Cooking Time 20–30 minutes   Serves 4   **EASY**

125ml (4fl oz) orange juice

grated zest of 1 unwaxed orange

2 tbsp freshly chopped tarragon

2 tbsp freshly chopped flat-leafed
   parsley

1 tbsp olive oil

1 garlic clove, crushed

4 skinless chicken breasts, about 125g
   (4oz) each

4 small orange wedges

salt and ground black pepper

brown rice and watercress to serve

1 Preheat the oven to 200°C (180°C fan oven) mark 6. Whisk the orange juice, orange zest, herbs, oil and garlic together in a large bowl. Season with salt and pepper.

2 Slash the chicken breasts several times and put into a large ovenproof dish. Pour the marinade over them and top each chicken breast with an orange wedge.

3 Cook in the oven for 20–30 minutes until cooked through. Serve with brown rice and watercress.

HEALTHY TIP

This recipe is very low in fat – skinless chicken breast contains just 3g of fat per portion – making this an ideal dish for those on a low fat or low calorie diet. The orange juice adds vitamin C.

PER SERVING

180 calories

4g fat (of which 1g saturates)

5g carbohydrate

0.2g salt

gluten free • dairy free

Easy Thai Red Chicken Curry

Preparation Time 5 minutes   **Cooking Time** 20 minutes   **Serves 4**   **EASY**

1 tbsp vegetable oil

3 tbsp Thai red curry paste

4 boneless, skinless chicken breasts, about 600g (1lb 5oz) total weight, sliced

400ml can coconut milk

300ml (½ pint) hot chicken or vegetable stock

juice of 1 lime, plus lime halves to serve

200g pack mixed baby sweetcorn and mangetouts

2 tbsp freshly chopped coriander, plus sprigs to garnish

rice or rice noodles to serve

1 Heat the oil in a wok or large pan over a low heat. Add the curry paste and cook for 2 minutes or until fragrant.

2 Add the chicken and fry gently for about 10 minutes or until browned.

3 Add the coconut milk, hot stock, lime juice and sweetcorn to the pan and bring to the boil. Add the mangetouts, reduce the heat and simmer for 4–5 minutes until the chicken is cooked.

4 Stir in the chopped coriander, garnish with coriander sprigs and serve immediately with rice or noodles and lime halves to squeeze over.

HEALTHY TIP

Coconut milk is made from the pressed flesh of coconut. It contains around 18g (½oz) of fat per 100ml (3½fl oz), which is lower than coconut cream used in many Asian recipes (about 20–25g/¾–1oz –100ml/3½oz). You can cut the fat content of the dish further by using half-fat coconut milk (6–9g/¼oz fat/100ml/3½fl oz).

PER SERVING

248 calories

8g fat (of which 1g saturates)

16g carbohydrate

1g salt

dairy free

Thai Green Curry

Preparation Time 10 minutes   Cooking Time 15 minutes   Serves 6   **EASY**

2 tsp vegetable oil

1 green chilli, seeded and finely chopped
(see Cook's Tip, page 49)

4cm (1½in) piece fresh root ginger,
peeled and finely grated

1 lemongrass stalk, trimmed and cut
into three pieces

225g (8oz) brown-cap or oyster
mushrooms

1 tbsp Thai green curry paste

300ml (½ pint) coconut milk

150ml (¼ pint) chicken stock

1 tbsp Thai fish sauce

1 tsp light soy sauce

350g (12oz) boneless, skinless chicken
breasts, cut into bite-size pieces

350g (12oz) cooked peeled large
prawns

fresh coriander sprigs to garnish

Thai fragrant rice to serve

1 Heat the oil in a wok or large frying pan. Add the chilli, ginger, lemongrass and mushrooms and stir-fry for about 3 minutes or until the mushrooms begin to turn golden. Add the curry paste and fry for a further 1 minute.

2 Pour in the coconut milk, stock, fish sauce and soy sauce and bring to the boil. Stir in the chicken, then reduce the heat and simmer for about 8 minutes or until the chicken is cooked.

3 Add the prawns and cook for a further 1 minute. Garnish with coriander sprigs and serve immediately, with Thai fragrant rice.

PER SERVING

132 calories

2g fat (of which 0g saturates)

4g carbohydrate

1.4g salt

dairy free

Cod with Sweet Chilli Glaze

Preparation Time 10 minutes   Cooking Time 20 minutes   Serves 4   **EASY**

1 red chilli, seeded and finely chopped
   (see Cook's Tip, page 49)
2 tsp dark soy sauce
grated zest and juice of 1 lime
1/4 tsp ground allspice or 6 allspice
   berries, crushed
50g (2oz) light muscovado sugar
4 thick cod fillets, with skin, about 175g
   (6oz) each
finely sliced red chilli and finely sliced
   lime zest to garnish
lime wedges to serve

FOR THE SAFFRON MASH
900g (2lb) potatoes, roughly chopped
a pinch of saffron
50g (2oz) butter
salt and ground black pepper

1 To make the saffron mash,
   cook the potatoes in lightly salted
   boiling water until tender.
   Meanwhile, soak the saffron in
   2 tbsp boiling water. Drain the
   potatoes and mash with the butter,
   then beat in the saffron liquid.
   Season to taste with salt and pepper.

2 Meanwhile, preheat the grill
   or griddle pan until hot. Stir the
   chopped chilli, soy sauce, lime
   zest and juice, allspice and sugar
   together in a bowl.

3 Grill the cod for about 1 minute on
   the flesh side. Turn skin side up and
   grill for 1 minute. Spoon the chilli
   glaze over the fish and grill for a
   further 2–3 minutes until the skin is
   crisp and golden.

4 Garnish with finely sliced chilli and
   lime zest. Serve with the saffron
   mash and lime wedges.

TRY SOMETHING DIFFERENT
Use sea bass, gurnard, coley (saithe)
or pollack instead of the cod.

PER SERVING
193 calories
1g fat (of which trace saturates)
13g carbohydrate
0.7g salt
gluten free

Cod with Oriental Vegetables

Preparation Time 10 minutes, plus marinating   Cooking Time 6 minutes   Serves 4   **EASY**

4 thick cod fillets, 175g (6oz) each
grated zest of 1 lime
1 tbsp chilli oil
1 tbsp sesame oil
1 red chilli, seeded and chopped (see
    Cook's Tip, page 49)
2 garlic cloves, chopped
8 spring onions, trimmed and sliced
125g (4oz) shiitake mushrooms, sliced
225g (8oz) carrots, cut into strips
300g (11oz) pak choi, chopped
1 tbsp soy sauce
salt and ground black pepper
lime wedges to serve

1 Put the cod into a shallow non-metallic dish. Mix the lime zest with the chilli oil and rub over the fillets. Cover and leave in a cool place for 30 minutes.

2 Preheat the grill to medium-hot. Heat the sesame oil in a large frying pan. Add the chilli, garlic, spring onions, mushrooms and carrots and stir-fry for 2–3 minutes until the vegetables begin to soften. Add the pak choi and stir-fry for 1–2 minutes. Add the soy sauce and cook for a further minute. Season with salt and pepper.

3 Meanwhile, grill the cod fillets under the hot grill for 2–3 minutes on each side until the flesh has turned opaque and is firm to the touch.

4 Pile the stir-fried vegetables on top of the cod and serve immediately with lime wedges.

HEALTHY TIP

Cod contains less than 1g of fat per 100g (3½oz) and practically no saturated fat. It is a good source of protein, vitamin B6, niacin, vitamin B12 and potassium. The carrots provide high levels of betacarotene while the pak choi provides vitamin C.

TRY SOMETHING DIFFERENT

Replace the cod with any firm-fleshed fish: try salmon, coley (saithe), pollack or whiting.

PER SERVING

284 calories
9g fat (of which 1g saturates)
12g carbohydrate
1g salt
gluten free • dairy free

Chinese-style Haddock with Courgettes and Peas

Preparation Time 5 minutes   Cooking Time 10 minutes   Serves 4   **EASY**

2 tsp sunflower oil
1 small onion, finely chopped
1 green chilli, seeded and finely chopped
   (see Cook's Tip, page 49)
2 courgettes, thinly sliced
125g (4oz) frozen peas, thawed
350g (12oz) skinless haddock fillet, cut
   into bite-size pieces
2 tsp lemon juice
4 tbsp hoisin sauce
lime wedges to serve

1 Heat the oil in a large non-stick frying pan. Add the onion, chilli, courgettes and peas and stir-fry over a high heat for 5 minutes or until the onion and courgettes begin to soften.

2 Add the fish to the pan with the lemon juice, hoisin sauce and 150ml (¼ pint) water. Bring to the boil, then reduce the heat and simmer, uncovered, for 2–3 minutes until the fish is cooked through. Serve with lime wedges.

TRY SOMETHING DIFFERENT
There are plenty of alternatives to haddock: try sea bass, sea bream or gurnard.

PER SERVING
150 calories
3g fat (of which 1g saturates)
10g carbohydrate
0.7g salt
gluten free • dairy free

Smoked Salmon Salad with Mustard and Dill Dressing

Preparation Time 15 minutes, plus chilling   Serves 8   **EASY**

4 tbsp extra virgin olive oil

juice of 1 lemon

½ tsp golden caster sugar

2 tsp wholegrain mustard

4 tsp freshly chopped dill

FOR THE SALAD

1 small head of fennel

110g bag baby leaf salad

75g (3oz) wild rocket

400g (14oz) oak-smoked wild salmon

1 Pour the oil, lemon juice, sugar and mustard into a clean, lidded jar and season with salt and pepper. Seal, then shake to combine and chill for up to one day.

2 Using a sharp knife, trim and thinly slice the fennel. Wash the fennel, baby leaf salad and rocket, then dry in a salad spinner, or drain in a colander and spread out on a clean teatowel to remove excess moisture. (Once dried, the salad can be stored, covered, in the fridge for up to one day.)

3 To serve, place twists of salmon on each plate, then pile the salad leaves and fennel alongside and season with pepper. Add the dill to the dressing and shake well to mix. Drizzle the dressing over and around the salad leaves. Serve immediately.

COOK'S TIP

Keep the dressing and the salad separately chilled and covered in the fridge.

PER SERVING

163 calories

12g fat (of which 2g saturates)

1g carbohydrate

1g salt

Salmon with Roasted Vegetables

Preparation Time 10 minutes   **Cooking Time** 30 minutes   **Serves 4**   **EASY**

2 large leeks, cut into chunks
2 large courgettes, sliced
2 fennel bulbs, cut into chunks
125ml (4fl oz) hot vegetable stock
zest of ½ lemon
4 salmon fillets, 100g (3½oz) each
15g (½oz) pinenuts, toasted
salt and ground black pepper
lemon wedges to serve

1 Preheat the oven to 200°C (180°C fan oven) mark 6. Put the leeks into a roasting tin, then add the courgettes and fennel. Pour the hot stock over the vegetables, season well with salt and pepper and roast for 30 minutes or until tender.

2 Meanwhile, sprinkle the lemon zest over the salmon and season with salt and pepper. Put on a baking sheet lined with greaseproof paper and cook in the oven with the vegetables for the last 20 minutes of the cooking time.

3 Scatter the pinenuts over the roasted vegetables and mix well. Divide the vegetables among four plates and top each with a piece of salmon. Serve with lemon wedges.

HEALTHY TIP

Salmon is rich in omega-3 fats, which help reduce the risk of heart disease and stroke, as well as selenium. Fennel contains antioxidants that help combat certain cancers. It is a good source of fibre, vitamin C, folate, magnesium, calcium, iron and phosphorus, and also promotes healthy digestion.

PER SERVING

258 calories
15g fat (of which 2g saturates)
7g carbohydrate
0.1g salt
gluten free • dairy free

Mediterranean Salmon

Preparation Time 15 minutes, plus marinating **Cooking Time** 10–12 minutes **Serves** 12 **EASY**

12 × 125g (4oz) salmon fillets, skinned
5 tbsp Pesto (see Cook's Tip, page 71)
50g (2oz) sun-dried tomatoes, chopped
100g (3½oz) black olives
3 lemons
new potatoes and a green salad
  to serve

1 Mix the salmon, pesto, tomatoes and olives in a large bowl. Sprinkle with the zest of 1 lemon, then cover and chill for 30 minutes.

2 Preheat the oven to 200°C (180°C fan oven) mark 6. Arrange the salmon in a large ovenproof serving dish and spoon the tomato, olive and pesto marinade over it.

3 Cut each of the remaining lemons into six wedges and put around the salmon. Cook in the oven for 10–12 minutes until the fish flakes when pushed with a knife, then serve with new potatoes and salad.

GET AHEAD

To prepare ahead Complete the recipe to the end of step 1, then cover and chill for up to two days.
To use Complete the recipe.

PER SERVING

251 calories
18g fat (of which 3g saturates)
1g carbohydrate
0.8g salt
gluten free

Spicy Monkfish Stew

Preparation Time 10 minutes   Cooking Time 35 minutes   Serves 6   **EASY**

1 tbsp olive oil
1 onion, finely sliced
1 tbsp tom yum paste (see Cook's Tip)
450g (1lb) potatoes, cut into 2cm (¾in)
　　chunks
400g can chopped tomatoes in rich
　　tomato juice
600ml (1 pint) hot fish stock
450g (1lb) monkfish, cut into 2cm (¾in)
　　chunks
200g (7oz) ready-to-eat baby spinach
salt and ground black pepper

1 Heat the oil in a pan over a medium
heat. Add the onion and fry
for 5 minutes until golden.

2 Add the tom yum paste and
potatoes and stir-fry for 1 minute.
Add the tomatoes and hot stock,
season well with salt and pepper
and cover. Bring to the boil, then
reduce the heat and simmer,
partially covered, for 15 minutes or
until the potatoes are just tender.

3 Add the monkfish to the pan and
continue to simmer for 5–10
minutes until the fish is cooked.
Add the baby spinach leaves and
stir through until wilted.

4 Spoon the fish stew into warmed
bowls and serve immediately.

COOK'S TIP

Tom yum paste is a hot and spicy Thai
mixture used in soups and stews. It is
available from large supermarkets
and Asian food shops.

PER SERVING

142 calories
3g fat (of which 1g saturates)
16g carbohydrate
0.2g salt
dairy free

Fish Stew

Preparation Time 15 minutes   **Cooking Time** about 30 minutes   **Serves 4**   **EASY**

2 tbsp olive oil

1 onion, chopped

1 leek, trimmed and chopped

2 tsp smoked paprika

2 tbsp tomato purée

450g (1lb) cod or haddock, roughly chopped

125g (4oz) basmati rice

175ml (6fl oz) white wine

450ml (¾ pint) hot fish stock

200g (7oz) cooked and peeled king prawns

a large handful of spinach leaves

crusty bread to serve

1 Heat the oil in a large pan. Add the onion and leek and fry for 8–10 minutes until they start to soften. Add the smoked paprika and tomato purée and cook for 1–2 minutes.

2 Add the fish, rice, wine and hot stock. Bring to the boil, then cover the pan, reduce the heat and simmer for 10 minutes or until the fish is cooked through and the rice is tender. Add the prawns and cook for 1 minute or until heated through. Stir in the spinach until it wilts, then serve with chunks of bread.

HEALTHY TIP

This dish is packed with body-building protein. The onions and leeks are rich in powerful sulphur-containing compounds, including the phytochemical quercetin, which helps keep the heart healthy.

TRY SOMETHING DIFFERENT

There are lots of alternatives to cod and haddock: try sea bass, gurnard, coley (saithe) or pollack.

PER SERVING

280 calories

7g fat (of which 1g saturates)

34g carbohydrate

0.3g salt

gluten free • dairy free

Lemon Tuna

Preparation Time 15–20 minutes, plus marinating   **Cooking Time** 4–6 minutes   **Serves 8**   **EASY**

3 large lemons
2 garlic cloves, crushed
100ml (3½fl oz) extra virgin olive oil
900g (2lb) fresh tuna in one piece
3 tbsp freshly chopped flat-leafed
   parsley
ground black pepper
flatbread to serve

1 Finely grate the zest from one lemon and squeeze the juice from the grated lemon and one other lemon. Mix the zest and juice with the garlic and olive oil and season well with pepper.

2 Cut the tuna in half lengthways, then cut into strips about 2cm (¾in) thick. Lay the strips in a shallow dish, pour the marinade over them, then turn the fish to coat. Cover and leave to marinate for at least 30 minutes.

3 Preheat the barbecue or grill. Soak eight bamboo skewers in water for 20 minutes.

4 Fold the strips of tuna and thread on to the soaked skewers. Cut the remaining lemon into eight wedges and push one on to each skewer. Drizzle with any remaining marinade and sprinkle with the chopped parsley.

5 Lay the skewers on the barbecue or grill and cook for 2–3 minutes on each side. Serve immediately with warmed flatbread.

PER SERVING

180 calories
8g fat (of which 2g saturates)
trace carbohydrate
0.1g salt
gluten free • dairy free

Prawns in Yellow Bean Sauce

Preparation Time 10 minutes, plus standing   Cooking Time 5 minutes   Serves 4   **EASY**

250g pack medium egg noodles

1 tbsp stir-fry oil or sesame oil

1 garlic clove, sliced

1 tsp freshly grated ginger

1 bunch of spring onions, each stem cut into four lengthways

250g (9oz) frozen raw peeled tiger prawns, thawed

200g (7oz) pak choi, leaves separated and the white base cut into thick slices

160g jar Chinese yellow bean stir-fry sauce

1 Put the noodles into a bowl, pour 2 litres (3½ pints) boiling water over them and leave for 4 minutes. Drain and put to one side.

2 Heat the oil in a wok over a medium heat. Add the garlic and ginger and stir-fry for 30 seconds. Add the spring onions and prawns and cook for 2 minutes.

3 Add the chopped white part of the pak choi and the yellow bean sauce. Fill the empty sauce jar with boiling water and pour this into the wok too.

4 Add the noodles to the wok and continue to cook for 1 minute, tossing every now and then to heat through. Finally, stir in the green pak choi leaves and serve immediately.

HEALTHY TIP

Prawns are good sources of protein and zinc, while being low in fat. The egg noodles have a low GI (see page 12), which means they are digested more slowly, keeping you satisfied longer. The pak choi adds valuable vitamins A and C.

TRY SOMETHING DIFFERENT

Instead of prawns, use skinless chicken breast, cut into thin strips.

PER SERVING

394 calories

10g fat (of which 2g saturates)

59g carbohydrate

0.9g salt

dairy free

Meat-free Meals

Baked Eggs

Preparation Time 10 minutes   **Cooking Time** 15 minutes   **Serves 2**   **EASY**

2 tbsp olive oil
125g (4oz) mushrooms, chopped
225g (8oz) fresh spinach
2 medium eggs
2 tbsp single cream
salt and ground black pepper

1 Preheat the oven to 200°C (180°C fan oven) mark 6. Heat the oil in a large frying pan. Add the mushrooms and stir-fry for 30 seconds. Add the spinach and stir-fry until wilted. Season to taste, then divide the mixture between two shallow ovenproof dishes.

2 Carefully break an egg into the centre of each dish, then spoon 1 tbsp single cream over it.

3 Cook in the oven for about 12 minutes or until just set – the eggs will continue to cook a little once they're out of the oven. Grind a little more pepper over the top, if you like, and serve.

PER SERVING

238 calories
21g fat (of which 5g saturates)
2g carbohydrate
0.6g salt
vegetarian • gluten free

Red Onion Tarte Tatin

Preparation Time 15 minutes   **Cooking Time** 35–40 minutes, plus cooling   **Serves** 12   **EASY**

50g (2oz) butter

2 tbsp olive oil

1.1kg (2½lb) red onions, sliced into rounds

1 tbsp light muscovado sugar

175ml (6fl oz) white wine

4 tsp white wine vinegar

1 tbsp freshly chopped thyme, plus extra to garnish (optional)

450g (1lb) puff pastry

plain flour to dust

salt and ground black pepper

1 Lightly grease two 23cm (9in) non-stick sandwich tins with a little of the butter and put to one side.

2 Melt the remaining butter with the oil in a large non-stick frying pan. Add the onions and sugar and fry for 10–15 minutes until golden, keeping the onions in their rounds.

3 Preheat the oven to 220°C (200°C fan) mark 7. Add the wine, vinegar and thyme to the pan. Bring to the boil and let it bubble until the liquid has evaporated. Season with salt and pepper, then divide the mixture between the tins and leave to cool.

4 Halve the pastry. On a lightly floured surface, roll out each piece thinly into a round shape just larger than the sandwich tin. Put one pastry round over the onion mixture in each tin and tuck in the edges. Prick the pastry dough all over with a fork.

5 Cook the tarts for 15–20 minutes until the pastry is risen and golden. Remove from the oven and put a large warmed plate over the pastry. Turn over and shake gently to release the tart, then remove the tin. Scatter with thyme, if you like, and cut into wedges to serve.

GET AHEAD

To prepare ahead Complete the recipe to the end of step 4 up to one day in advance. Cover and keep in the fridge for up to 24 hours.

To use Complete the recipe.

PER SERVING

235 calories

15g fat (of which 3g saturates)

23g carbohydrate

0.4g salt

vegetarian

Tomato and Butter Bean Stew

Preparation Time 10 minutes   **Cooking Time** 50–55 minutes   **Serves** 4   **EASY**

2 tbsp olive oil
1 onion, finely sliced
2 garlic cloves, finely chopped
2 large leeks, trimmed and sliced
2 × 400g cans cherry tomatoes
2 × 400g cans no-added-sugar-or-salt
   butter beans, drained and rinsed
150ml (¼ pint) hot vegetable stock
1–2 tbsp balsamic vinegar
salt and ground black pepper

1 Preheat the oven to 180°C (160°C fan oven) mark 4. Heat the oil in a flameproof casserole over a medium heat. Add the onion and garlic and cook for 10 minutes or until golden and soft. Add the leeks, cover and cook for 5 minutes.

2 Add the tomatoes, beans and hot stock and season well with salt and pepper. Bring to the boil, then cover and cook in the oven for 35–40 minutes until the sauce has thickened. Remove from the oven, stir in the vinegar and spoon into warmed bowls.

HEALTHY TIP

Butter beans provide good amounts of protein, complex carbohydrate, iron and fibre; they have a low GI (see page 12), so tend to release their energy over a longer period of time keeping you feeling full longer. They are also high in potassium, which helps to regulate fluid balance in the body.

PER SERVING

214 calories
7g fat (of which 1g saturates)
29g carbohydrate
0.2g salt
vegetarian • dairy free

Leek and Broccoli Bake

Preparation Time 20 minutes   **Cooking Time** 45–55 minutes   **Serves** 4   **EASY**

2 tbsp olive oil
1 large red onion, cut into wedges
1 aubergine, chopped
2 leeks, trimmed and cut into chunks
1 broccoli head, cut into florets and
   stalks chopped
3 large flat mushrooms, chopped
2 × 400g cans cherry tomatoes
3 fresh rosemary sprigs, chopped
50g (2oz) Parmesan, freshly grated (see
   Cook's Tips, page 184)
salt and ground black pepper

1 Preheat the oven to 200°C (180°C fan oven) mark 6. Heat the oil in a large flameproof dish, add the onion, aubergine and leeks and cook for 10–12 minutes until golden and softened.

2 Add the broccoli, mushrooms, cherry tomatoes, half the rosemary and 300ml (½ pint) boiling water. Season with salt and pepper. Stir well, then cover and cook in the oven for 30 minutes.

3 Meanwhile, put the Parmesan into a bowl. Add the remaining rosemary and season with pepper. When the vegetables are cooked, remove the lid and sprinkle the Parmesan mixture on top. Cook, uncovered, in the oven for a further 5–10 minutes until the topping is golden.

TRY SOMETHING DIFFERENT
Use sliced courgettes instead
of aubergine.

PER SERVING
245 calories
13g fat (of which 4g saturates)
18g carbohydrate
0.4g salt
vegetarian • gluten free

Cheese and Vegetable Bake

Preparation Time 15 minutes   Cooking Time 15 minutes   Serves 4   **EASY**

250g (9oz) macaroni
1 cauliflower, cut into florets
2 leeks, trimmed and finely chopped
100g (3½oz) frozen peas
25g (1oz) wholemeal breadcrumbs
crusty bread to serve

FOR THE CHEESE SAUCE
15g (½oz) butter
15g (½oz) plain flour
200ml (7fl oz) skimmed milk
75g (3oz) Parmesan, grated (see
   Cook's Tips)
2 tsp Dijon mustard
salt and ground black pepper

1 Cook the macaroni in a large pan of boiling water for 6 minutes, adding the cauliflower and leeks for the last 4 minutes and the peas for the last 2 minutes.

2 Meanwhile, make the cheese sauce. Melt the butter in a pan and add the flour. Cook for 1–2 minutes, then take off the heat and gradually stir in the milk. Bring to the boil slowly, stirring until the sauce thickens. Stir in 50g (2oz) Parmesan and the mustard. Season to taste with salt and pepper.

3 Preheat the grill to medium. Drain the pasta and vegetables and put back into the pan. Add the cheese sauce and mix well. Spoon into a large shallow 2 litre (3½ pint) ovenproof dish and scatter the remaining Parmesan and the breadcrumbs over the top. Grill for 5 minutes or until golden and crisp. Serve hot with bread.

COOK'S TIPS

• **Microwave Cheese Sauce**
Put the butter, flour and milk into a large microwave-proof bowl and whisk together. Cook in a 900W microwave oven on full power for 4 minutes, whisking every minute, until the sauce has thickened. Stir in the cheese until it melts. Stir in the mustard and season to taste.
• Vegetarian cheeses: some vegetarians prefer to avoid cheeses that have been produced by the traditional method, because this uses animal-derived rennet. Most supermarkets and cheese shops now stock an excellent range of vegetarian cheeses, produced using vegetarian rennet, which comes from plants, such as thistle and mallow, that contain enzymes capable of curdling milk.

PER SERVING
471 calories
13g fat (of which 7g saturates)
67g carbohydrate
0.8g salt
vegetarian

Roasted Stuffed Peppers

Preparation Time 20 minutes   Cooking Time 45 minutes   Serves 8   **EASY**

40g (1½oz) butter
4 Romano peppers, halved, with stalks
    on and seeded
3 tbsp olive oil
350g (12oz) chestnut mushrooms,
    roughly chopped
4 tbsp finely chopped fresh chives
100g (3½oz) vegetarian feta cheese
50g (2oz) fresh white breadcrumbs
25g (1oz) freshly grated Parmesan (see
    Cook's Tips, page 184)
salt and ground black pepper

1 Preheat the oven to 180°C (160°C fan oven) mark 4. Use a little of the butter to grease a shallow ovenproof dish and put the peppers in it side by side, ready to be filled.

2 Heat the remaining butter and 1 tbsp oil in a pan. Add the mushrooms and fry until they're golden and there's no excess liquid left in the pan. Stir in the chives, then spoon the mixture into the pepper halves.

3 Crumble the feta over the mushrooms. Mix the breadcrumbs and Parmesan in a bowl, then sprinkle over the peppers.

4 Season with salt and pepper and drizzle with the remaining oil. Roast in the oven for 45 minutes or until golden and tender. Serve warm.

GET AHEAD

To prepare ahead Complete the recipe to the end of step 4, up to one day ahead. Cover and chill.
To use Reheat under the grill for 5 minutes.

PER SERVING

189 calories
14g fat (of which 6g saturates)
11g carbohydrate
0.9g salt
vegetarian

Beef Tomatoes with Bulgur

Preparation Time 10 minutes   **Cooking Time** 30–35 minutes   **Serves 4**   **EASY**

125g (4oz) bulgur wheat
20g (³/₄oz) flat-leafed parsley, finely
   chopped
75g (3oz) vegetarian feta cheese,
   chopped
1 courgette, chopped
50g (2oz) flaked almonds, toasted
4 large beef tomatoes
1 tbsp olive oil

1 Preheat the oven to 180°C (160°C fan oven) mark 4. Cook the bulgur according to the pack instructions. Chop the parsley, feta and courgette and stir into the bulgur with the almonds.

2 Chop the top off each tomato and scoop out the seeds. Put on to a baking sheet and spoon in the bulgur mixture. Drizzle with the oil and cook in the oven for 15–20 minutes until the cheese is starting to soften. Serve.

HEALTHY TIP

Tomatoes are full of betacarotene and vitamin C, both antioxidants with heart-protective properties. They also contain the antioxidant lycopene, which helps combat prostate cancer. It is more readily absorbed by the body when the tomatoes are cooked.

TRY SOMETHING DIFFERENT

Try quinoa instead of the bulgur wheat. Put the quinoa in a bowl of cold water and mix well, then soak for 2 minutes. Drain. Put into a pan with twice its volume of water and bring to the boil. Simmer for 20 minutes. Remove from the heat, cover and leave to stand for 10 minutes.

PER SERVING

245 calories
14g fat (of which 4g saturates)
21g carbohydrate
0.7g salt
vegetarian

Spicy Vegetable Kebabs

Preparation Time 30 minutes, plus marinating   **Cooking Time** 25 minutes   Serves 4   **EASY**

12 baby onions

12 new potatoes

12 button mushrooms

2 courgettes

2 garlic cloves, crushed

1 tsp each ground coriander and
   turmeric

½ tsp ground cumin

1 tbsp sun-dried tomato paste

1 tsp chilli sauce

juice of ½ lemon

4 tbsp olive oil

275g (10oz) smoked tofu, cut into
   2.5cm (1in) cubes

salt and ground black pepper

Yogurt Sauce (see Cook's Tip) and
   lemon wedges to serve

1 Blanch the baby onions in a pan of lightly salted boiling water for 3 minutes, then drain, refresh in cold water and peel away the skins. Put the potatoes into a pan of lightly salted cold water, bring to the boil and parboil for 8 minutes, then drain and refresh under cold water. Blanch the button mushrooms in boiling water for 1 minute, then drain and refresh under cold water. Cut each courgette into six chunky slices and blanch for 1 minute, then drain and refresh under cold water.

2 Mix the garlic, spices, tomato paste, chilli sauce, lemon juice, olive oil, salt and pepper together in a shallow dish. Add the well-drained vegetables and tofu and toss to coat. Cover and chill for several hours or overnight.

3 Preheat the barbecue or grill. Soak six wooden skewers in water for 20 minutes. Thread the vegetables and tofu on to the skewers. Cook the kebabs for 8–10 minutes until the vegetables are charred and tender, turning frequently and basting with the marinade. Serve with the yogurt sauce and lemon wedges.

COOK'S TIP

Yogurt Sauce

Mix 225g (8oz) Greek yogurt with 1 crushed garlic clove and 2 tbsp freshly chopped coriander. Season to taste with salt and pepper. Chill until ready to serve.

PER SERVING

247 calories

14g fat (of which 3g saturates)

22g carbohydrate

0.1g salt

vegetarian

Mediterranean Halloumi and Vegetable Kebabs

Preparation Time 15 minutes   **Cooking Time** 8–10 minutes   **Serves 4**   **EASY**

1 large courgette, cut into chunks

1 red pepper, seeded and cut into
    chunks

12 cherry tomatoes

125g (4oz) halloumi cheese, cubed

100g (3½oz) natural yogurt

1 tsp ground cumin

2 tbsp olive oil

squeeze of lemon

1 lemon, cut into eight wedges

couscous tossed with freshly chopped
    flat-leafed parsley to serve

1 Preheat the barbecue or grill. Soak eight wooden skewers in water for 20 minutes. Put the courgette into a large bowl with the red pepper, cherry tomatoes and halloumi cheese. Add the yogurt, cumin, oil and a squeeze of lemon and mix.

2 Push a lemon wedge on to each skewer, then divide the vegetables and cheese among the skewers. Grill the kebabs, turning regularly, for 8–10 minutes until the vegetables are tender and the halloumi is nicely charred. Serve with couscous.

HEALTHY TIP

These kebabs are packed with vitamins and minerals. Both the tomatoes and red peppers supply vitamin C and betacarotene, which assist the immune system. Halloumi cheese is a semi-hard cheese traditionally prepared from a mixture of sheep's and goat's milk. It contains 25g (1oz) fat per 100g (3½oz), which is lower than Cheddar cheese (35g/1¾oz per 100g/3½oz).

PER SERVING

164 calories

13g fat (of which 5g saturates)

7g carbohydrate

1.1g salt

gluten free

Stir-fried Vegetables with Crispy Crumb

Preparation Time 10 minutes   **Cooking Time** 15–20 minutes   **Serves 4**   **EASY**

1 thick slice wholemeal bread, crusts removed
2 tbsp olive oil
1 broccoli head, chopped into florets
1 large carrot, cut into thin strips
1 red pepper, cut into thin strips
4 anchovy fillets, chopped

1 Whiz the bread in a food processor to make breadcrumbs. Heat 1 tbsp oil in a large non-stick frying pan or wok. Add the breadcrumbs and stir-fry for about 4–5 minutes until crisp. Remove from the pan and put to one side on a piece of kitchen paper.

2 Heat the remaining oil in the frying pan until hot. Add the broccoli, carrot and pepper and stir-fry over a high heat for 4–5 minutes until they're starting to soften. Add the anchovies and continue to cook for a further 5 minutes until slightly softened. Serve the vegetables immediately, scattered with the breadcrumbs.

TRY SOMETHING DIFFERENT
Use other vegetables in season: try 400g (14oz) cauliflower florets instead of the broccoli.

PER SERVING
145 calories
8g fat (of which 1g saturates)
13g carbohydrate
0.5g salt
dairy free

Sesame and Cabbage Rolls

Preparation Time 30 minutes, plus soaking   Cooking Time about 15 minutes, plus cooling   Makes 12
A LITTLE EFFORT

50g (2oz) dried shiitake mushrooms

3 tbsp sesame oil

4 garlic cloves, crushed

4 tbsp sesame seeds

450g (1lb) cabbage, finely shredded

1 bunch of spring onions, chopped

225g can bamboo shoots, drained

3 tbsp soy sauce

1/2 tsp caster sugar

2 × 270g packs filo pastry

1 large egg, beaten

vegetable oil for deep-frying

Spiced Plum Sauce or Thai Chilli
    Dipping Sauce to serve (see
    Cook's Tips)

1 Put the mushrooms into a heatproof bowl and cover with boiling water. Soak for 20 minutes.

2 Heat the sesame oil in a wok or large frying pan. Add the garlic and sesame seeds and fry gently until golden brown. Add the cabbage and spring onions and fry, stirring, for 3 minutes.

3 Drain and slice the mushrooms. Add them to the pan with the bamboo shoots, soy sauce and sugar and stir until well mixed. Remove the pan from the heat and leave to cool.

4 Cut the filo pastry into 24 × 18cm (7in) squares. Keep the filo squares covered with a damp teatowel as you work. Place one square of filo pastry on the worksurface and cover with a second square. Place a heaped tablespoon of the cabbage mixture across the centre of the top square to within 2.5cm (1in) of the ends. Fold the 2.5cm (1in) ends of pastry over the filling. Brush one unfolded edge of the pastry with a little beaten egg, then roll up to make a thick parcel shape. Shape the remaining pastry and filling in the same way to make 12 parcels.

5 Heat a 5cm (2in) depth of vegetable oil in a deep-fryer or large heavy-based saucepan to 180°C (test by frying a small cube of bread: it should brown in 30 seconds). Fry the rolls in batches for about 3 minutes or until crisp and golden. Remove with a slotted spoon and drain on kitchen paper; keep them warm while you fry the remainder. Serve hot with a sauce for dipping.

PER ROLL

154 calories

13g fat (of which 2g saturates)

23g carbohydrate

0.7g salt

vegetarian • dairy free

COOK'S TIPS

• **Spiced Plum Sauce**
Slice 2 spring onions as thinly as possible. Put them in a small pan with 6 tbsp plum sauce, the juice of 1 lime, 1/2 tsp Chinese five-spice powder and 2 tbsp water. Heat gently for 2 minutes.

• **Thai Chilli Dipping Sauce**
Put 200ml (7fl oz) white wine vinegar and 6 tbsp caster sugar in a small pan, bring to the boil, then reduce the heat and simmer for 2 minutes. Add 1 finely chopped red chilli and 50g (2oz) each finely chopped cucumber, onion and pineapple.

Chilli Vegetable and Coconut Stir-fry

Preparation Time 25 minutes   **Cooking Time** about 10 minutes   **Serves 4**   **EASY**

2 tbsp sesame oil

2 green chillies, seeded and finely
  chopped (see Cook's Tip, page 49)

2.5cm (1in) piece fresh root ginger,
  peeled and finely grated

2 garlic cloves, crushed

1 tbsp Thai green curry paste

125g (4oz) carrots, cut into fine
  matchsticks

125g (4oz) baby sweetcorn, halved

125g (4oz) mangetouts, halved on
  the diagonal

2 large red peppers, seeded and finely
  sliced

2 small pak choi, quartered

4 spring onions, finely chopped

300ml (½ pint) coconut milk

2 tbsp peanut satay sauce

1 tbsp light soy sauce

1 tsp soft brown sugar

4 tbsp freshly chopped coriander, plus
  extra sprigs to garnish

ground black pepper

25g (1oz) roasted peanuts to garnish

rice or noodles to serve

1 Heat the oil in a wok or large non-stick frying pan over a medium heat. Add the chillies, ginger and garlic and stir-fry for 1 minute. Add the curry paste and fry for a further 30 seconds.

2 Add the carrots, sweetcorn, mangetouts and red peppers. Stir-fry over a high heat for 3–4 minutes, then add the pak choi and spring onions. Cook, stirring, for a further 1–2 minutes.

3 Pour in the coconut milk, satay sauce, soy sauce and sugar. Season with pepper, bring to the boil and cook for 1–2 minutes, then add the chopped coriander. Garnish with the peanuts and coriander sprigs and serve with rice or noodles.

COOK'S TIP

Check the ingredients in the Thai curry paste: some contain shrimp and are therefore not suitable for vegetarians.

PER SERVING

191 calories

11g fat (of which 2g saturates)

18g carbohydrate

1.3g salt

vegetarian • dairy free

Black-eye Bean Chilli

Preparation Time 10 minutes   Cooking Time 20 minutes   Serves 4   **EASY**

1 tbsp olive oil
1 onion, chopped
3 celery sticks, finely chopped
2 × 400g no-added-sugar-or-salt cans
    black-eye beans, drained and rinsed
2 × 400g cans chopped tomatoes
2 or 3 splashes of Tabasco sauce
3 tbsp freshly chopped coriander
4 warmed tortillas and soured cream
    to serve

1 Heat the oil in a frying pan. Add the onion and celery and cook for 10 minutes or until softened.

2 Add the beans, tomatoes and Tabasco to the pan. Bring to the boil, then reduce the heat and simmer for 10 minutes.

3 Just before serving, stir in the coriander. Spoon the chilli on to the warmed tortillas, roll up and serve with soured cream.

HEALTHY TIP

Black-eye beans are a good source of protein, soluble fibre, iron, zinc and B vitamins. The fibre increases satiety (so you feel satisfied longer) and helps lower blood cholesterol levels. Tomatoes add valuable vitamin C and betacarotene.

TRY SOMETHING DIFFERENT

Replace half the black-eye beans with red kidney beans.

PER SERVING

332 calories
4g fat (of which 1g saturates)
61g carbohydrate
0.7g salt
vegetarian

Chilli Bean Cake

Preparation Time 10 minutes   **Cooking Time** 20 minutes   **Serves 4**   **EASY**

3 tbsp olive oil

75g (3oz) wholemeal breadcrumbs

1 bunch of spring onions, finely chopped

1 orange pepper, seeded and chopped

1 small green chilli, seeded and finely
   chopped (see Cook's Tip, page 49)

1 garlic clove, crushed

1 tsp ground turmeric (optional)

400g can no-added-sugar-or-salt mixed
   beans, drained and rinsed

3 tbsp mayonnaise

a small handful of fresh basil, chopped

salt and ground black pepper

TO SERVE

soured cream

freshly chopped coriander

lime wedges (optional)

1 Heat 2 tbsp oil in a non-stick frying pan over a medium heat and fry the breadcrumbs until golden and beginning to crisp. Remove and put to one side.

2 Add the remaining oil to the pan and fry the spring onions until soft and golden. Add the orange pepper, chilli, garlic and turmeric, if using. Cook, stirring, for 5 minutes.

3 Tip in the beans, mayonnaise, two-thirds of the fried breadcrumbs and the basil. Season with salt and pepper, mash roughly with a fork, then press the mixture down to flatten and sprinkle with the remaining breadcrumbs. Fry the bean cake over a medium heat for 4–5 minutes until the base is golden. Remove from the heat, cut into wedges and serve with soured cream, coriander and the lime wedges, if you like.

PER SERVING

289 calories

17g fat (of which 3g saturates)

27g carbohydrate

0.5g salt

vegetarian

Mushroom and Bean Hotpot

Preparation Time 15 minutes   **Cooking Time** 30 minutes   **Serves 6** **EASY**

3 tbsp olive oil

700g (1½lb) chestnut mushrooms, roughly chopped

1 large onion, finely chopped

2 tbsp plain flour

2 tbsp mild curry paste (see Cook's Tip)

150ml (¼ pint) dry white wine

400g can chopped tomatoes

2 tbsp sun-dried tomato paste

2 × 400g cans mixed beans, drained and rinsed

3 tbsp mango chutney

3 tbsp roughly chopped fresh coriander and mint

1 Heat the oil in a large pan over a low heat. Add the mushrooms and onion and fry until the onion is soft and dark golden. Stir in the flour and curry paste and cook for 1–2 minutes.

2 Add the wine, tomatoes, sun-dried tomato paste and beans and bring to the boil, then reduce the heat and simmer gently for 30 minutes or until most of the liquid has reduced. Stir in the chutney and herbs before serving.

HEALTHY TIP

Beans are rich in protein, fibre and many vitamins and minerals. They have been linked with a reduced risk of cancers of the breast, prostate and colon, as well as heart disease and Type 2 diabetes.

COOK'S TIP

Check the ingredients in the curry paste: some may not be suitable for vegetarians.

PER SERVING

280 calories

10g fat (of which 1g saturates)

34g carbohydrate

1.3g salt

vegetarian • dairy free

Pumpkin with Chickpeas

Preparation Time 15 minutes   **Cooking Time** 25–30 minutes   **Serves 6**   **EASY**

900g (2lb) pumpkin or squash, such as
    butternut, crown prince or kabocha
    (see Cook's Tip), peeled, seeded and
    chopped into roughly 2cm (³⁄₄in)
    cubes
1 garlic clove, crushed
2 tbsp olive oil
2 × 400g cans chickpeas, drained
½ red onion, thinly sliced
1 large bunch coriander, roughly
    chopped
salt and ground black pepper
steamed spinach to serve

FOR THE TAHINI SAUCE

1 large garlic clove, crushed
3 tbsp tahini paste
juice of 1 lemon

1 Preheat the oven to 220°C (200°C
fan oven) mark 7, Toss the squash
or pumpkin in the garlic and oil and
season. Put into a roasting tin and
roast for 25 minutes or until soft.

2 Meanwhile, put the chickpeas into a
pan with 150ml (¼ pint) water over
a medium heat, to warm through.

3 To make the tahini sauce, put the
garlic into a bowl, add a pinch of
salt, then whisk in the tahini paste.
Add the lemon juice and 4–5 tbsp
cold water – enough to make a
consistency somewhere between
single and double cream – and
season to taste.

4 Drain the chickpeas, put into a large
bowl, then add the pumpkin, onion
and coriander. Pour on the tahini
sauce and toss carefully. Adjust the
seasoning and serve while warm,
with spinach.

COOK'S TIP

Kabocha is a Japanese variety of
winter squash and has a dull-coloured
deep green skin with whitish stripes.
Its flesh is a yellow-orange colour.

PER SERVING

228 calories
12g fat (of which 2g saturates)
22g carbohydrate
0.6g salt
**vegetarian • gluten free
dairy free**

Chickpea and Chilli Stir-fry

Preparation Time 10 minutes   Cooking Time 15–20 minutes   Serves 4   **EASY**

2 tbsp olive oil

1 tsp ground cumin

1 red onion, sliced

2 garlic cloves, finely chopped

1 red chilli, seeded and finely chopped
(see Cook's Tip, page 49)

2 × 400g cans chickpeas, drained and
rinsed

400g (14oz) cherry tomatoes

125g (4oz) baby spinach leaves

salt and ground black pepper

rice or pasta to serve

1 Heat the oil in a wok or large frying
pan. Add the cumin and fry for 1–2
minutes. Add the onion and stir-fry
for 5–7 minutes.

2 Add the garlic and chilli and
stir-fry for 2 minutes.

3 Add the chickpeas to the wok with
the tomatoes. Reduce the heat and
simmer until the chickpeas are hot.
Season with salt and pepper. Add
the spinach and cook for 1–2
minutes until the leaves have wilted.
Serve with rice or pasta.

HEALTHY TIP

Chickpeas are an excellent low-fat
source of protein and complex
carbohydrate. Being high in both
soluble and insoluble fibre and with a
low GI (see page 12), chickpeas can
help you to feel fuller for longer,
thereby helping to control appetite
and manage weight. Eaten regularly
they can also help to reduce the risk
of chronic diseases such as obesity,
diabetes, heart disease and also
certain cancers.

PER SERVING

258 calories

11g fat (of which 1g saturates)

30g carbohydrate

1g salt

vegetarian • dairy free

Lentil Chilli

Preparation Time 10 minutes   **Cooking Time** 30 minutes   **Serves 6**   **EASY**

oil-water spray (see Cook's Tip,
    page 92)
2 red onions, chopped
1½ tsp each ground coriander and
    ground cumin
½ tsp ground paprika
2 garlic cloves, crushed
2 sun-dried tomatoes, chopped
¼ tsp crushed dried chilli flakes
125ml (4fl oz) red wine
300ml (½ pint) hot vegetable stock
2 × 400g cans brown or green lentils,
    drained and rinsed
2 × 400g cans chopped tomatoes
sugar to taste
salt and ground black pepper
natural low-fat yogurt and rice
    to serve

1 Spray a pan with the oil-water spray
and cook the onions for 5 minutes
or until softened. Add the
coriander, cumin and paprika.
Combine the garlic, sun-dried
tomatoes, chilli, wine and hot stock
and add to the pan. Cover and
simmer for 5–7 minutes. Uncover
and simmer until the onions are
very tender and the liquid has
almost gone.

2 Stir in the lentils and tomatoes and
season with salt and pepper.
Simmer, uncovered, for 15 minutes
or until thick. Stir in sugar to taste.
Remove from the heat.

3 Ladle out a quarter of the mixture
and whiz in a food processor or
blender, then combine the puréed
and unpuréed portions. Serve with
yogurt and rice.

PER SERVING
195 calories
2g fat (of which trace saturates)
32g carbohydrate
0.1g salt
gluten free

Lentil Casserole

Preparation Time 20 minutes   **Cooking Time** 1 hour   **Serves 6**   **EASY**

2 tbsp olive oil

2 onions, sliced

4 carrots, sliced

3 leeks, trimmed and sliced

450g (1lb) button mushrooms

2 garlic cloves, crushed

2.5cm (1in) piece fresh root ginger,
  peeled and grated

1 tbsp ground coriander

225g (8oz) split red lentils, rinsed and
  drained

750ml (1¼ pints) hot vegetable stock

4 tbsp freshly chopped coriander

salt and ground black pepper

1 Preheat the oven to 180°C (160°C fan oven) mark 4. Heat the oil in a flameproof casserole. Add the onions, carrots and leeks and fry, stirring, for 5 minutes. Add the mushrooms, garlic, ginger and ground coriander and fry for a further 2–3 minutes.

2 Stir the lentils into the casserole with the hot stock. Season with salt and pepper and bring back to the boil. Cover and cook in the oven for 45–50 minutes or until the vegetables and lentils are tender. Stir in the chopped coriander before serving.

HEALTHY TIP

Lentils have a low GI (see page 12), meaning their carbohydrate is absorbed slowly, thus giving you sustained energy. They are a good source of protein, iron, zinc, B vitamins and fibre. Their high content of fibre increases the amount of friendly bacteria in the gut that aid digestion.

PER SERVING

239 calories

6g fat (of which 1g saturates)

36g carbohydrate

0.4g salt

vegetarian • gluten free

dairy free

Mixed Beans with Lemon Vinaigrette

Preparation Time 15 minutes   **Serves 6**   **EASY**

400g can mixed beans, drained and
    rinsed
400g can chickpeas, drained and rinsed
2 shallots, finely chopped
fresh mint sprigs and lemon zest to
    garnish

FOR THE VINAIGRETTE
2 tbsp lemon juice
2 tsp clear honey
8 tbsp extra virgin olive oil
3 tbsp freshly chopped mint
4 tbsp freshly chopped flat-leafed
    parsley
salt and ground black pepper

1 Put the beans and chickpeas into a
bowl and add the shallots.

2 To make the vinaigrette, whisk
together the lemon juice, honey and
salt and pepper to taste. Gradually
whisk in the oil and stir in the
chopped herbs. Just before serving,
pour the dressing over the bean
mixture and toss well.

3 Transfer the salad to a serving dish,
garnish with mint sprigs and lemon
zest and serve immediately.

GET AHEAD

To prepare ahead Complete the
recipe to the end of step 2 but don't
add the herbs to the vinaigrette.
Cover and chill for up to two days.
To use Remove from the fridge up
to 1 hour before serving, stir in the
herbs and complete the recipe.

PER SERVING
285 calories
19g fat (of which 3g saturates)
22g carbohydrate
1g salt
**vegetarian • gluten free
dairy free**

Veggie Pitta

Preparation Time 8 minutes   Serves 1   **EASY**

1 wholemeal pitta bread
1 tbsp hummus, plus extra to serve
   (optional)
15g (½oz) unsalted cashew nuts
2 closed-cup mushrooms, finely sliced
¼ cucumber, chopped
fresh watercress or mixed salad leaves
ground black pepper

1 Split the pitta bread and spread with
the hummus.

2 Fill the pitta with the cashew nuts,
mushrooms, cucumber and a
generous helping of fresh
watercress or salad leaves.
Serve with extra hummus, if you
like, and season with pepper.

HEALTHY TIP

Hummus is made from chickpeas,
which are packed with fibre, protein
and iron. They also contain fructo-
oligosaccharides, a type of soluble
fibre that boosts the friendly bacteria
in the gut and increases immunity.
The cashews add extra protein, iron
and zinc.

TRY SOMETHING DIFFERENT

Add a diced ripe avocado. It is rich in
omega fats and good for your skin.

PER SERVING

322 calories
11g fat (of which 2g saturates)
47g carbohydrate,
1.2g salt
vegetarian

Summer Couscous

Preparation Time 10 minutes   **Cooking Time** 20 minutes   **Serves 4**   **EASY**

175g (6oz) baby plum tomatoes, halved

2 small aubergines, thickly sliced

2 large yellow peppers, seeded and roughly chopped

2 red onions, cut into thin wedges

2 fat garlic cloves, crushed

5 tbsp olive oil

250g (9oz) couscous

400g can chopped tomatoes

2 tbsp harissa paste

25g (1oz) toasted pumpkin seeds (optional)

1 large bunch of coriander, roughly chopped

salt and ground black pepper

1 Preheat the oven to 230°C (210°C fan oven) mark 8. Put the vegetables and garlic into a large roasting tin, drizzle 3 tbsp oil over them and season with salt and pepper. Toss to coat. Roast for 20 minutes or until tender.

2 Meanwhile, put the couscous into a separate roasting tin and add 300ml (½ pint) cold water. Leave to soak for 5 minutes. Stir in the tomatoes and harissa and drizzle with the remaining oil. Put in the oven next to the vegetables for 4–5 minutes to warm through.

3 Stir the pumpkin seeds, if you like, and the coriander into the couscous and season. Add the vegetables and stir through.

PER SERVING

405 calories

21g fat (of which 3g saturates)

49g carbohydrate

0g salt

vegetarian • dairy free

Curried Tofu Burgers

Preparation Time 20 minutes   **Cooking Time** 6–8 minutes   **Serves 4**   **EASY**

I tbsp sunflower oil, plus extra
    to fry
I large carrot, finely grated
I large onion, finely grated
2 tsp coriander seeds, finely crushed
    (optional)
I garlic clove, crushed
I tsp curry paste (see Cook's Tip,
    page 195)
I tsp tomato purée
225g pack firm tofu
25g (1oz) fresh wholemeal breadcrumbs
25g (1oz) mixed nuts, finely chopped
plain flour to dust
salt and ground black pepper
rice and green vegetables to serve

1 Heat the oil in a large frying pan. Add the carrot and onion and fry for 3–4 minutes until the vegetables are softened, stirring all the time. Add the coriander seeds, if using, the garlic, curry paste and tomato purée. Increase the heat and cook for 2 minutes, stirring all the time.

2 Put the tofu into a bowl and mash with a potato masher. Stir in the vegetables, breadcrumbs and nuts and season with salt and pepper. Beat thoroughly until the mixture starts to stick together. With floured hands, shape the mixture into eight burgers.

3 Heat some oil in a frying pan and fry the burgers for 3–4 minutes on each side until golden brown. Alternatively, brush lightly with oil and cook under a hot grill for 3 minutes on each side or until golden brown. Drain on kitchen paper and serve hot, with rice and green vegetables.

PER SERVING

253 calories
18g fat (of which 3g saturates)
15g carbohydrate
0.2g salt
vegetarian • dairy free

Sweet Chilli Tofu Stir-fry

Preparation Time 5 minutes, plus marinating   **Cooking Time** 12 minutes   **Serves 4**   **EASY**

200g (7oz) firm tofu

4 tbsp sweet chilli sauce

2 tbsp light soy sauce

1 tbsp sesame seeds

2 tbsp toasted sesame oil

600g (1lb 5oz) ready-prepared mixed stir-fry vegetables, such as carrots, broccoli, mangetouts and bean sprouts

a handful of pea shoots or young salad leaves to garnish

rice to serve

1 Drain the tofu, pat it dry and cut it into large cubes. Put the tofu into a shallow container and pour 1 tbsp sweet chilli sauce and 1 tbsp light soy sauce over it. Cover and marinate for 10 minutes.

2 Meanwhile, toast the sesame seeds in a hot wok or large frying pan until golden. Tip on to a plate.

3 Put the wok or frying pan on to the heat and add 1 tbsp sesame oil. Add the marinated tofu and stir-fry for 5 minutes until golden. Remove and put to one side.

4 Heat the remaining 1 tbsp oil in the pan. Add the vegetables and stir-fry for 3–4 minutes until just tender. Stir in the cooked tofu.

5 Pour the remaining sweet chilli sauce and soy sauce into the pan, toss well and cook for a further minute until heated through. Sprinkle with the toasted sesame seeds and pea shoots or salad leaves, and serve immediately, with rice.

HEALTHY TIP

Tofu is an excellent low fat source of protein and calcium. It is made from soy beans, which contain phytoestrogens called isoflavones, helpful for controlling menopausal symptoms such as hot flushes. Studies have shown that isoflavones can help protect against cancers of the breast and prostrate.

PER SERVING

167 calories

11g fat (of which 2g saturates)

5g carbohydrate

1.6g salt

vegetarian • dairy free

Smoked Sesame Tofu

Preparation Time 20 minutes, plus marinating   **Cooking Time** 12 minutes   **Serves 4**   **EASY**

2 tbsp toasted sesame seeds

2 tbsp tamari (wheat-free Japanese soy sauce)

1 tsp light muscovado sugar

1 tsp rice wine vinegar

1 tbsp sesame oil

225g (8oz) smoked tofu, cubed

½ small white or green cabbage, shredded

2 carrots, peeled and cut into strips

200g (7oz) bean sprouts

4 roasted red peppers, roughly chopped

2 spring onions, shredded

brown rice to serve

1 Put the sesame seeds into a bowl, add the tamari, sugar, vinegar and ½ tbsp sesame oil. Mix together, then add the smoked tofu and stir to coat. Leave to marinate for 10 minutes.

2 Heat a large wok or non-stick frying pan. Add the marinated tofu, reserving the marinade, and fry for 5 minutes or until golden all over. Remove from the wok with a slotted spoon and put to one side.

3 Heat the remaining oil in the wok. Add the cabbage and carrots and stir-fry for 5 minutes. Stir in the bean sprouts, peppers, spring onions, cooked tofu and reserved marinade and cook for a further 2 minutes. Serve with brown rice.

PER SERVING

208 calories

11g fat (of which 2g saturates)

19g carbohydrate

1.4g salt

vegetarian • gluten free

dairy free

Thai Vegetable Curry

Preparation Time 10 minutes   **Cooking Time** 15 minutes   **Serves 4**   **EASY**

2–3 tbsp red Thai curry paste (see
   Cook's Tip, page 192)
2.5cm (1in) piece fresh root ginger,
   peeled and finely chopped
50g (2oz) cashew nuts
400ml can coconut milk
3 carrots, cut into thin batons
1 broccoli head, cut into florets
20g (¾ oz) fresh coriander, roughly
   chopped
zest and juice of 1 lime
2 large handfuls of spinach leaves
basmati rice to serve

1 Put the curry paste into a large pan,
   add the ginger and cashew nuts and
   stir-fry over a medium heat for
   about 2–3 minutes.

2 Add the coconut milk, cover and
   bring to the boil. Stir the carrots
   into the pan, then reduce the heat
   and simmer for 5 minutes. Add the
   broccoli florets and simmer for a
   further 5 minutes until tender.

3 Stir the coriander and lime zest into
   the pan with the spinach. Squeeze
   the lime juice over and serve with
   basmati rice.

TRY SOMETHING DIFFERENT
Replace carrots and/or broccoli with
alternative vegetables – try baby
sweetcorn, sugarsnap peas or
mangetouts and simmer for only
5 minutes until tender.

PER SERVING
200 calories
10g fat (of which 2g saturates)
19g carbohydrate
0.7g salt
**vegetarian • gluten free
dairy free**

Chickpea Curry

Preparation Time 20 minutes   Cooking Time 40–45 minutes   Serves 6 **EASY**

2 tbsp vegetable oil

2 onions, finely sliced

2 garlic cloves, crushed

1 tbsp ground coriander

1 tsp mild chilli powder

1 tbsp black mustard seeds

2 tbsp tamarind paste

2 tbsp sun-dried tomato paste

750g (1lb 10oz) new potatoes,
   quartered

400g can chopped tomatoes

1 litre (1¾pints) hot vegetable stock

250g (9oz) green beans, trimmed

2 × 400g cans chickpeas, drained and
   rinsed

2 tsp garam masala

salt and ground black pepper

basmati rice to serve

1 Heat the oil in a pan. Add the onions and fry for 10–15 minutes until golden – when they have a good colour they will add depth of flavour. Add the garlic, coriander, chilli, mustard seeds, tamarind paste and sun-dried tomato paste. Cook for 1–2 minutes until the aroma from the spices is released.

2 Add the potatoes and toss in the spices for 1–2 minutes. Add the tomatoes and hot stock and season with salt and pepper, then cover and bring to the boil. Reduce the heat and simmer, half covered, for 20 minutes or until the potatoes are just cooked.

3 Add the beans and chickpeas and continue to cook for 5 minutes or until the beans are tender and the chickpeas are warmed through. Stir in the garam masala and serve with basmati rice.

PER SERVING

291 calories

8g fat (of which 1g saturates)

46g carbohydrate

1.3g salt

vegetarian • gluten free

dairy free

Mauritian Vegetable Curry

Preparation Time 15 minutes   **Cooking Time** 30 minutes   **Serves 4**   **EASY**

3 tbsp vegetable oil
1 onion, finely sliced
4 garlic cloves, crushed
2.5cm (1in) piece fresh root ginger,
   peeled and grated
3 tbsp medium curry powder
6 fresh curry leaves
150g (5oz) potato, cut into 1cm
   (½in) cubes
125g (4oz) aubergine, cut into 2.5cm
   (1in) sticks, 5mm (¼in) wide

150g (5oz) carrots, cut into 5mm
   (¼in) dice
900ml (1½ pints) hot vegetable stock
a pinch of saffron threads
½ tsp salt
150g (5oz) green beans, trimmed
75g (3oz) frozen peas
ground black pepper
3 tbsp freshly chopped coriander
   to garnish
naan bread to serve

1 Heat the oil in a large heavy-based pan over a low heat. Add the onion and fry for 5–10 minutes until golden. Add the garlic, ginger, curry powder and curry leaves and fry for a further minute.

2 Add the potato and aubergine to the pan and fry, stirring, for 2 minutes. Add the carrots, hot stock, saffron and salt and season with plenty of pepper. Cover and cook for 10 minutes or until the vegetables are almost tender.

3 Add the beans and peas to the pan and cook for a further 4 minutes. Sprinkle with the chopped coriander and serve with naan bread.

COOK'S TIP

To prepare ahead Complete the recipe, without the garnish, and chill quickly. It will keep, in the fridge, for up to two days.
To use Put into a pan, cover and bring to the boil, then simmer for 10–15 minutes. Complete the recipe.

PER SERVING

184 calories
11g fat (of which 1g saturates)
18g carbohydrate
0.6g salt
vegetarian • dairy free

Aubergine and Lentil Curry

Preparation Time 10 minutes   **Cooking Time** 40–45 minutes   **Serves** 4   **EASY**

3 tbsp olive oil

2 aubergines, cut into 2.5cm
   (1in) chunks

1 onion, chopped

2 tbsp mild curry paste (see Cook's Tip,
   page 195)

3 × 400g cans chopped tomatoes

200ml (7fl oz) hot vegetable stock

150g (5oz) red lentils, rinsed

100g (3½oz) spinach leaves

25g (1oz) fresh coriander, roughly
   chopped, plus extra leaves to garnish

2 tbsp fat-free Greek yogurt

rice to serve

1 Heat 2 tbsp oil in a large pan over a
low heat. Add the aubergine chunks
and fry until golden. Remove from
the pan and put to one side.

2 Heat the remaining oil in the same
pan. Add the onion and fry for
about 8–10 minutes until soft. Add
the curry paste and stir-fry for a
further 2 minutes.

3 Add the tomatoes, hot stock, lentils
and reserved aubergines to the pan.
Bring to the boil, then reduce the
heat to a low simmer, half-cover
with a lid and simmer for
25 minutes or according to the
lentils' pack instructions.

4 At the end of cooking, stir the
spinach, coriander and yogurt
through the curry. Garnish with
extra coriander leaves and serve
with rice.

HEALTHY TIP

Aubergines are low in fat and have
many health benefits. They contain
flavonoids, which are potent
antioxidants that help block the
formation of harmful free radicals.
This helps protect cell membranes
from damage. Some studies suggest
aubergines may help reduce blood
cholesterol levels.

COOK'S TIP

Choose aubergines that are firm,
shiny and blemish-free, with a bright
green stem.

PER SERVING

335 calories
15g fat (of which 3g saturates)
39g carbohydrate
0.2g salt
vegetarian

Vegetables

Lemon and Orange Carrots

Preparation Time 10 minutes   **Cooking Time** 10–15 minutes   **Serves 8**   **EASY**

900g (2lb) carrots, cut into long batons
150ml (¼ pint) orange juice
juice of 2 lemons
150ml (¼ pint) dry white wine
50g (2oz) butter
3 tbsp light muscovado sugar
4 tbsp freshly chopped coriander to garnish

1 Put the carrots, orange and lemon juices, wine, butter and sugar into a pan. Cover and bring to the boil.

2 Remove the lid and cook for about 10 minutes or until almost all the liquid has evaporated. Serve sprinkled with the coriander.

FREEZING TIP

To freeze Cook the carrots for only 5 minutes, then cool and freeze with the remaining liquid.
To use Thaw for 5 hours, then reheat in a pan for 5–6 minutes, or cook on full power in a 900W microwave for 7–8 minutes.

PER SERVING

127 calories
6g fat (of which 3g saturates)
17g carbohydrate
0.2g salt
vegetarian • gluten free

Spinach with Tomatoes

Preparation Time 10 minutes   Cooking Time 15 minutes   Serves 6   **EASY**

50g (2oz) butter
2 garlic cloves, crushed
450g (1lb) baby plum tomatoes, halved
250g (9oz) baby spinach leaves
a large pinch of freshly grated nutmeg
salt and ground black pepper

1 Heat half the butter in a pan, add the garlic and cook until just soft. Add the tomatoes and cook for 4–5 minutes or until just beginning to soften.

2 Put the spinach and a little water into a clean pan, cover and cook for 2–3 minutes until just wilted. Drain well, chop roughly and stir into the tomatoes.

3 Add the remaining butter and heat through gently. Season well with salt and pepper, stir in the nutmeg and serve immediately.

HEALTHY TIP

Spinach contains the phytochemical lutein, which helps protect against age-related deterioration of vision, as well as carotenoids, which help reduce the risk of colon cancer. It also supplies high levels of vitamin C and vitamin A.

PER SERVING

85 calories
7g fat (of which 5g saturates)
3g carbohydrate
0.3g salt
vegetarian • gluten free

Spicy Roasted Roots

Preparation Time 25 minutes   **Cooking Time** about 1½ hours   **Serves 8**   **EASY**

3 carrots, sliced lengthways

3 parsnips, sliced lengthways

3 tbsp olive oil

1 butternut squash, chopped

2 red onions, cut into wedges

2 leeks, sliced

3 garlic cloves, roughly chopped

2 tbsp mild curry paste (see Cook's Tip, page 195)

salt and ground black pepper

1 Preheat the oven to 200°C (180°C fan oven) mark 6. Put the carrots and parsnips into a large roasting tin, drizzle with 1 tbsp oil and cook for 40 minutes.

2 Add the butternut squash, onions, leeks and garlic to the roasting tin. Season with salt and pepper, then drizzle with the remaining 2 tbsp oil.

3 Roast in the oven for 45 minutes until the vegetables are tender and golden. Stir in the curry paste and roast for a further 10 minutes. Serve immediately.

HEALTHY TIP

This dish is full of betacarotene – both carrots and butternut squash are rich sources of this nutrient, which strengthens the immune system and protects against colds and flu. Butternut squash also contains good amounts of vitamins C and E.

FREEZING TIP

To freeze Complete the recipe, then cool, wrap and freeze for up to one month.

To use Thaw overnight at room temperature, then reheat at 200°C (180°C fan oven) mark 6 for 20 minutes in an ovenproof dish with 200ml (7fl oz) hot vegetable stock.

PER SERVING

134 calories

8g fat (of which 1g saturates)

14g carbohydrate

0.1g salt

vegetarian • gluten free

dairy free

Charred Courgettes

Preparation Time 5 minutes   **Cooking Time** 10 minutes   **Serves 4**   **EASY**

4 courgettes, halved lengthways
olive oil to brush
coarse sea salt to sprinkle

1 Preheat the barbecue or a griddle pan. Score a criss-cross pattern on the fleshy side of the courgettes. Brush lightly with olive oil and sprinkle with sea salt.

2 Cook the courgettes on the barbecue or griddle for 10 minutes or until just tender, turning occasionally.

TRY SOMETHING DIFFERENT
• Mix the olive oil with a good pinch of dried chilli flakes and a small handful of fresly chopped rosemary leaves.
• Use a mixture of yellow and green courgettes, if you like.

PER SERVING
36 calories
2g fat (of which trace saturates)
2g carbohydrate
0g salt
vegetarian • gluten free dairy free

Braised Red Cabbage

Preparation Time 15 minutes   **Cooking Time** about 50 minutes   **Serves 6**   **EASY**

1 tbsp olive oil
1 red onion, halved and sliced
2 garlic cloves, crushed
1 large red cabbage, about 1kg (2¼lb), shredded
2 tbsp light muscovado sugar
2 tbsp red wine vinegar
8 juniper berries
¼ tsp ground allspice
300ml (½ pint) vegetable stock
2 pears, cored and sliced
salt and ground black pepper
fresh thyme sprigs to garnish

1 Heat the oil in a large pan. Add the onion and fry for 5 minutes. Add the remaining ingredients, except the pears, and season with salt and pepper. Bring to the boil, then reduce the heat, cover and simmer for 30 minutes.

2 Add the pears and cook for a further 15 minutes or until nearly all the liquid has evaporated and the cabbage is tender. Serve hot, garnished with thyme.

GET AHEAD

To prepare ahead Red cabbage improves if made a day ahead. Complete step 1, cover and chill.
To use Reheat the red cabbage gently, add the pears and complete the recipe.

PER SERVING

63 calories
1g fat (of which 0g saturates)
12g carbohydrate
0.9g salt
**vegetarian • gluten free
dairy free**

Baked Tomatoes and Fennel

Preparation Time 10 minutes   **Cooking Time** 1¼ hours   **Serves 6**   **EASY**

900g (2lb) fennel, trimmed and cut
    into quarters
75ml (2½fl oz) white wine
5 thyme sprigs
75ml (2½fl oz) olive oil
900g (2lb) ripe beef or plum tomatoes

1 Preheat the oven to 200°C (180°C fan oven) mark 6. Put the fennel into a roasting tin and pour the white wine over it. Snip the thyme sprigs over the fennel, drizzle with the oil and roast for 45 minutes.

2 Halve the tomatoes, add to the roasting tin and roast for a further 30 minutes or until tender, basting with the juices halfway through.

HEALTHY TIP

Tomatoes are rich in vitamin C, vitamin E and betacarotene. Roasting them in olive oil increases the absorption of the latter two nutrients. The fennel is a good source of cancer-fighting antioxidants, fibre, and numerous vitamins including vitamin C, folate and betacarotene.

COOK'S TIP

This is an ideal accompaniment to a vegetarian frittata.

PER SERVING

127 calories
9g fat (of which 1g saturates)
7g carbohydrate
0.1g salt
**vegetarian • gluten free
dairy free**

Spicy Squash Quarters

Preparation Time 10 minutes   **Cooking Time** 20–30 minutes   **Serves 8**   **EASY**

2 small butternut squash, quartered and
   seeds discarded
coarse sea salt to sprinkle
75g (3oz) butter, melted
4 tsp peppered steak seasoning
wild rocket to serve

1 Preheat the barbecue to medium-
   hot. Sprinkle the squash with sea
   salt, brush with butter and sprinkle
   the steak seasoning over.

2 Cook for 20–30 minutes until
   tender, turning occasionally. Serve
   hot, with wild rocket.

HEALTHY TIP

Butternut squash contains an
abundance of powerhouse nutrients
known as carotenoids, known to
protect against heart disease. In
particular, it boasts very high levels of
betacarotene, identified as a
deterrent against breast cancer and
age-related macular degeneration. It
is also rich in vitamin C and fibre.

TRY SOMETHING DIFFERENT

Instead of the steak seasoning, lightly
toast 2 tsp coriander seeds, roughly
crush and stir into the melted butter
before brushing on to the squash.
When cooked, toss with fresh
coriander leaves.

PER SERVING

97 calories
8g fat (of which 5g saturates)
4g carbohydrate
0.1g salt
vegetarian • gluten free

Roasted Ratatouille

Preparation Time 15 minutes   **Cooking Time** 1½ hours   **Serves 6**   **EASY**

400g (14oz) red peppers, seeded and
  roughly chopped
700g (1½lb) aubergines, stalk removed,
  cut into chunks
450g (1lb) onions, peeled and cut into
  wedges
4 or 5 garlic cloves, unpeeled and left
  whole
150ml (¼ pint) olive oil
1 tsp fennel seeds
200ml (7fl oz) passata
sea salt and ground black pepper
a few fresh thyme sprigs to garnish

1 Preheat the oven to 240°C (220°C
fan oven) mark 9. Put the peppers,
aubergine, onions, garlic, oil and
fennel seeds into a roasting tin.
Season with sea salt flakes and
pepper and toss together.

2 Transfer to the oven and cook for
30 minutes (tossing frequently
during cooking) or until the
vegetables are charred and
beginning to soften.

3 Stir the passata through the
vegetables and put the roasting tin
back in the oven for 50–60 minutes,
stirring occasionally. Garnish with
the thyme sprigs and serve.

TRY SOMETHING DIFFERENT

Replace half the aubergines with
400g (14oz) courgettes; use a mix of
green and red peppers; garnish with
fresh basil instead of thyme.

PER SERVING

224 calories
18g fat (of which 3g saturates)
14g carbohydrate
0g salt
**vegetarian • gluten free
dairy free**

Roasted Root Vegetables with Herbs

Preparation Time 15 minutes   Cooking Time 1 hour   Serves 4   **EASY**

1 large potato, cut into large chunks
1 large sweet potato, cut into large
   chunks
3 carrots, cut into large chunks
4 small parsnips, halved
1 small swede, cut into large chunks
3 tbsp olive oil
2 fresh rosemary and 2 fresh
   thyme sprigs
salt and ground black pepper

1 Preheat the oven to 200°C (180°C fan oven) mark 6. Put all the vegetables into a large roasting tin. Add the oil.

2 Use scissors to snip the herbs over the vegetables, then season with salt and pepper and toss everything together. Roast in the oven for 1 hour or until tender.

HEALTHY TIP

Both potatoes and sweet potatoes provide vitamin C but the latter is also an excellent source of beta-carotene, a powerful antioxidant linked with protection against cancer. Swede and parsnips add potassium, which helps regulate fluid balance and blood pressure.

TRY SOMETHING DIFFERENT

Use other combinations of vegetables: try celeriac instead of parsnips, fennel instead of swede, peeled shallots instead of carrots.

PER SERVING

251 calories
10g fat (of which 1g saturates)
39g carbohydrate
0.2g salt
vegetarian • dairy free

Sage-roasted Parsnips, Apples and Prunes

Preparation Time 20 minutes   **Cooking Time** 45–55 minutes   **Serves 8**   **EASY**

6–8 tbsp olive oil
1.8kg (4lb) parsnips, peeled, quartered and cored
6 apples, peeled, cored and quartered
16 ready-to-eat prunes
50g (2oz) butter
1–2 tbsp freshly chopped sage leaves
1–2 tbsp clear honey (optional)
salt and ground black pepper

1 Heat 3–4 tbsp oil in a large flameproof roasting tin over a medium heat. Add the parsnips in batches and fry until a rich golden brown all over. Remove from the tin and put to one side. Add 3–4 tbsp oil to the same tin. Fry the apples until golden brown. Remove from the tin and put to one side.

2 Preheat the oven to 200°C (180°C fan oven) mark 6. Put the parsnips back into the tin, season with salt and pepper and roast in the oven for 15 minutes.

3 Add the apples and roast for a further 10 minutes. Put the prunes in the tin and continue to roast for 5 minutes. At the end of this time, test the apples: if they're still firm, roast everything for a further 5–10 minutes until the apples are soft and fluffy.

4 Put the tin on the hob over a very low heat. Add the butter and sage, drizzle with honey if you like, and spoon into a hot serving dish.

GET AHEAD

To prepare ahead Fry the parsnips and apples, then cool, cover and chill for up to one day.
To use Complete the recipe.

PER SERVING

313 calories
16g fat (of which 5g saturates)
40g carbohydrate
0.2g salt
vegetarian • gluten free

Roasted Mediterranean Vegetables

Preparation Time 10 minutes   **Cooking Time** 35–40 minutes   **Serves** 4   **EASY**

4 plum tomatoes, halved
2 onions, quartered
4 red peppers, seeded and cut
  into strips
2 courgettes, cut into thick slices
4 garlic cloves, unpeeled
6 tbsp olive oil
1 tbsp freshly chopped thyme leaves
sea salt flakes and ground black pepper

1 Preheat the oven to 220°C (200°C fan oven) mark 7. Put the tomatoes into a large roasting tin with the onions, peppers, courgettes and garlic. Drizzle with the oil and sprinkle with thyme, sea salt flakes and black pepper.

2 Roast, turning occasionally, for 35–40 minutes until tender.

HEALTHY TIP

This dish is packed with vitamins. The tomatoes are rich in betacarotene and vitamin C as well as the phytochemical lycopene, linked to a reduced risk of prostate cancer. Studies indicate that people with low levels of lycopene in their bodies may be more likely to suffer from heart disease. The red peppers add high levels of vitamin C to the dish and the olive oil is rich in heart-healthy monounsaturated fats and vitamin E.

COOK'S TIP

• To make a nutritionally complete meal, sprinkle with toasted sesame seeds and serve with hummus.
• Use oregano instead of thyme.

PER SERVING

252 calories
18g fat (of which 3g saturates)
19g carbohydrate
0.4g salt
**vegetarian • gluten free
dairy free**

Sweet Roasted Fennel

Preparation Time 10 minutes   **Cooking Time** about 1 hour   **Serves 4**   **EASY**

700g (1½lb) fennel (about 3 bulbs)
3 tbsp olive oil
50g (2oz) butter, melted
1 lemon, halved
1 tsp caster sugar
2 large thyme sprigs
salt and ground black pepper

1 Preheat the oven to 200°C (180°C fan oven) mark 6. Trim and quarter the fennel and put into a large roasting tin.

2 Drizzle the fennel with the oil and melted butter and squeeze the lemon juice over. Add the lemon halves to the roasting tin. Sprinkle with sugar and season generously with salt and pepper. Add the thyme and cover with a damp piece of non-stick baking parchment.

3 Roast in the oven for 30 minutes, then remove the baking parchment and roast for a further 20–30 minutes or until lightly charred and tender.

HEALTHY TIP

Fennel contains betacarotene, folate, vitamin C, fibre, iron and potassium. It is packed with phytochemicals, including anethole, anisic acid, fenchone and limonine, which produce the unique flavour of the vegetable and help protect the body from certain cancers. Fennel is a good digestive aid, helping to reduce gas and bloating.

PER SERVING
192 calories
19g fat (of which 8g saturates)
4g carbohydrate
0.2g salt
vegetarian • gluten free

Roasted Rosemary Potatoes

Preparation Time 10 minutes   Cooking Time 20–25 minutes, plus cooling   Serves 8   **EASY**

750g (1lb 11oz) new potatoes, unpeeled
3 tbsp olive oil
8 rosemary stalks, each about 18cm
    (7in) long
salt and ground black pepper

1 Preheat the barbecue or grill. Cook the potatoes in a pan of lightly salted boiling water for 10 minutes or until nearly tender. Drain, cool a little, then toss in the oil. Season well. Strip most of the leaves from the rosemary stalks, leaving a few at the tip; put the stripped leaves to one side.

2 Thread the potatoes on to the rosemary stalks, place on the barbecue or grill and scatter with the leaves. Cook for 10–15 minutes, turning from time to time, until tender and lightly charred.

HEALTHY TIP

All types of potatoes are a useful source of vitamin C but new potatoes are richer in this nutrient than older ones. They are also a source of hydroxycinnamic acids, which have antioxidant properties, as well as fibre, iron and B vitamins. Roasting instead of boiling the potatoes helps retain the vitamins.

COOK'S TIP

Skewering the potatoes helps them to cook more quickly and makes them easier to handle on a barbecue. Using rosemary stalks adds a wonderful flavour.

PER SERVING

102 calories
4g fat (of which 1g saturates)
15g carbohydrate
trace salt
**vegetarian • gluten free
dairy free**

Roasted Parma Potatoes

Preparation Time 25 minutes   Cooking Time 45–50 minutes   Serves 4   **EASY**

about 50 fresh sage leaves

900g (2lb) new potatoes (around 25), scrubbed

200g (7oz) thinly sliced Parma ham, torn into strips

4 tbsp olive oil

salt and ground black pepper

1 Preheat the oven to 200°C (180°C fan oven) mark 6. Put two sage leaves on each potato and wrap a strip of Parma ham around. Repeat until all the potatoes are wrapped.

2 Put half the oil in an ovenproof dish. Add the potatoes, drizzle with the remaining oil and season well with salt and pepper. Roast for 45–50 minutes or until tender.

PER SERVING

201 calories

9g fat (of which 2g saturates)

24g carbohydrate

0.9g salt

gluten free • dairy free

Breads, Biscuits and Cakes

Oatmeal Soda Bread

Preparation Time 15 minutes   **Cooking Time** 25 minutes, plus cooling   **Makes** 1 loaf, cuts into about 10 slices   **EASY**

25g (1oz) butter, plus extra to grease
275g (10oz) plain wholemeal flour
175g (6oz) coarse oatmeal
2 tsp cream of tartar
1 tsp salt
about 300ml (½ pint) milk and
    water, mixed

1 Preheat the oven to 220°C (200°C fan oven) mark 7. Grease a 900g (2lb) loaf tin and baseline with baking parchment.

2 Mix together all the dry ingredients in a bowl. Rub in the butter.

3 Add the milk and water to bind to a soft dough. Spoon into the prepared tin.

4 Bake in the oven for 25 minutes or until golden brown and well risen. Turn out and leave to cool slightly on a wire rack. It is best eaten on the day of making.

HEALTHY TIP

This bread contains oatmeal, which is rich in betaglucan, a soluble fibre that helps lower levels of cholesterol in the bloodstream. It also helps make you feel full longer and controls blood sugar levels. Oats are also a good source of B vitamins and vitamin E.

PER SERVING

175 calories
4g fat (of which 1g saturates)
30g carbohydrate
0.5g salt
vegetarian

Corn Bread

Preparation Time 5 minutes   Cooking Time 25–30 minutes   Serves 8   **EASY**

oil to oil
125g (4oz) plain flour
175g (6oz) polenta or cornmeal
1 tbsp baking powder
1 tbsp caster sugar
½ tsp salt
300ml (½ pint) buttermilk, or equal
   quantities of natural yogurt and milk,
   mixed together
2 medium eggs
4 tbsp extra virgin olive oil
butter to serve

1 Preheat the oven to 200°C (180°C fan oven) mark 6. Generously oil a shallow 20.5cm (8in) square tin.

2 Put the flour into a large bowl, then add the polenta or cornmeal, the baking powder, sugar and salt. Make a well in the centre and pour in the buttermilk or yogurt and milk mixture. Add the eggs and oil, then stir together until evenly mixed.

3 Pour into the prepared tin and bake in the oven for 25–30 minutes until firm to the touch. Insert a skewer into the centre – if it comes out clean, the cornbread is done.

4 Leave the cornbread to rest in the tin for 5 minutes, then turn out and cut into chunky triangles. Serve warm with butter (see Cook's Tip).

HEALTHY TIP

Cornmeal is a good source of fibre, containing similar levels to wholemeal flour, as well as iron, important for making healthy red blood cells. Buttermilk has a similar nutritional profile to skimmed milk, containing good levels of protein and calcium yet is very low in fat.

COOK'S TIP

Serve warm with a bowl of soup for a substantial meal.

PER SERVING

229 calories
8g fat (of which 1g saturates)
33g carbohydrate
1.3g salt
vegetarian

Apricot and Hazelnut Bread

Preparation Time 25 minutes, plus rising   Cooking Time 30–35 minutes, plus cooling   Makes 2 loaves   **EASY**

75g (3oz) hazelnuts

450g (1lb) strong Granary bread flour, plus extra to dust

1 tsp salt

25g (1oz) unsalted butter, diced, plus extra to grease

75g (3oz) ready-to-eat dried apricots, chopped

2 tsp fast-action dried yeast

2 tbsp molasses

milk to glaze

1 Spread the hazelnuts on a baking sheet. Toast under a hot grill until golden brown, turning frequently. Put the hazelnuts in a clean teatowel and rub off the skins. Cool, then chop and put to one side.

2 Put the flour into a large bowl. Add the salt, then rub in the butter. Stir in the hazelnuts, apricots and yeast. Make a well in the middle and gradually work in the molasses and about 225ml (8fl oz) hand-hot water to form a soft dough, adding a little more water if the dough feels dry. Knead for 8–10 minutes until smooth, then transfer the dough to a greased bowl. Cover and leave to rise in a warm place for 1–1¼ hours or until doubled in size.

3 Punch the dough to knock back, then divide in half. Shape each portion into a small, flattish round and put on a well-floured baking sheet. Cover loosely and leave to rise for a further 30 minutes.

4 Preheat the oven to 220°C (200°C fan oven) mark 7 and put a large baking sheet on the top shelf to heat up.

5 Using a sharp knife, cut several slashes on each round, brush with a little milk and transfer to the heated baking sheet. Bake for 15 minutes, then reduce the oven temperature to 190°C (170°C fan oven) mark 5 and bake for a further 15–20 minutes until the bread is risen and sounds hollow when tapped underneath. Turn out of the tin on to a wire rack to cool.

TO STORE
Store in an airtight container. It will keep for up to two days.

TRY SOMETHING DIFFERENT
Replace the hazelnuts with walnuts or pecan nuts and use sultanas instead of apricots.

PER SERVING
94 calories
3g fat (of which 1g saturates)
14g carbohydrate
0g salt
vegetarian

Ginger and Fruit Teabread

Preparation Time 15 minutes, plus soaking   Cooking Time 1 hour, plus cooling   Cuts into 12 slices   **EASY**

125g (4oz) each dried apricots, apples and pitted prunes, chopped
300ml (½ pint) strong fruit tea
a little butter to grease
25g (1oz) preserved stem ginger in syrup, chopped
225g (8oz) wholemeal flour
2 tsp baking powder
125g (4oz) dark muscovado sugar
1 medium egg, beaten

1 Put the dried fruit into a large bowl, add the tea and leave to soak for 2 hours.

2 Preheat the oven to 180°C (160°C fan oven) mark 4. Grease a 900g (2lb) loaf tin and baseline with baking parchment.

3 Add the remaining ingredients to the soaked fruit and mix thoroughly. Spoon into the prepared tin and brush with 2 tbsp cold water. Bake for 1 hour or until cooked through.

4 Cool in the tin for 10–15 minutes, then turn out on to a wire rack to cool completely.

Banana and Chocolate Loaf

Preparation Time 20 minutes   Cooking Time 1 hour, plus cooling   Serves 5   **EASY**

butter to grease
175g (6oz) plain flour, sifted
2 tsp baking powder
½ tsp bicarbonate of soda
½ tsp salt
175g (6oz) light muscovado sugar
2 large eggs
3 medium ripe bananas, mashed
150g (5oz) natural yogurt
150g (5oz) butterscotch chocolate or
   milk chocolate, roughly chopped
100g (3½oz) pecan nuts, chopped
1–2 tbsp demerara sugar

1 Preheat the oven to 170°C (150°C fan oven) mark 3. Grease and line a 1.4kg (3lb) loaf tin.

2 Put the flour, baking powder, bicarbonate of soda and salt into a large bowl and mix together.

3 In a separate bowl, beat together the muscovado sugar and eggs with a hand-held electric whisk until pale and fluffy. Carefully stir in the bananas, yogurt, chocolate and 50g (2oz) pecan nuts, followed by the flour mixture.

4 Spoon the mixture into the prepared tin and sprinkle the remaining chopped pecan nuts and the demerara sugar over the surface. Bake for 1 hour or until a skewer inserted into the centre comes out clean. Leave to cool in the tin, then turn out and slice.

HEALTHY TIP

Bananas are an excellent source of energy-boosting (natural) sugars. They provide soluble fibre, which helps protect against bowel cancer and stabilise blood sugar levels, as well as potassium, magnesium and vitamin B6.

PER SERVING

221 calories
9g fat (of which 2g saturates)
34g carbohydrate
0.2g salt
vegetarian

Peanut and Raisin Cookies

Preparation Time 10 minutes   Cooking Time 15 minutes, plus cooling   Makes 30   **EASY**

125g (4oz) unsalted butter, softened,
    plus extra to grease
150g (5oz) caster sugar
1 medium egg
150g (5oz) plain flour, sifted
½ tsp baking powder
½ tsp salt
125g (4oz) crunchy peanut butter
175g (6oz) raisins

1 Preheat the oven to 190°C (170°C fan oven) mark 5 and grease two baking sheets. Beat together all the ingredients except the raisins, until well blended. Stir in the raisins.

2 Spoon large teaspoonfuls of the mixture, spaced well apart, on to the prepared baking sheets, leaving room for the mixture to spread.

3 Bake for about 15 minutes or until golden brown around the edges Leave to cool slightly, then transfer to a wire rack to cool completely.

TO STORE

Store in an airtight container. They will keep for up to three days.

TRY SOMETHING DIFFERENT

• **Chocolate Nut Cookies**
Omit the peanut butter and raisins and add 1 tsp vanilla extract. Stir in 175g (6oz) roughly chopped chocolate and 75g (3oz) roughly chopped walnuts.

• **Coconut Cherry Cookies**
Omit the peanut butter and raisins, reduce the sugar to 75g (3oz) and stir in 50g (2oz) desiccated coconut and 125g (4oz) rinsed, roughly chopped glacé cherries.

• **Oat and Cinnamon Cookies**
Omit the peanut butter and raisins and add 1 tsp vanilla extract. Stir in 1 tsp ground cinnamon and 75g (3oz) rolled oats.

PER COOKIE

111 calories
6g fat (of which 3g saturates)
14g carbohydrate
0.2g salt
vegetarian

Almond Macaroons

Preparation Time 10 minutes   Cooking Time 12–15 minutes, plus cooling   Makes 22   **EASY**

2 medium egg whites
125g (4oz) caster sugar
125g (4oz) ground almonds
¼ tsp almond extract
22 blanched almonds

1 Preheat the oven to 180°C (fan oven 160°C) mark 4. Line baking trays with baking parchment. Whisk the egg whites in a clean, grease-free bowl until stiff peaks form. Gradually whisk in the caster sugar, a little at a time, until thick and glossy. Gently stir in the ground almonds and almond extract.

2 Spoon teaspoonfuls of the mixture on to the prepared baking trays, spacing them slightly apart. Press an almond into the centre of each one and bake for 12–15 minutes until just golden and firm to the touch.

3 Leave on the baking sheets for 10 minutes, then transfer to wire racks to cool completely. On cooling, these biscuits have a soft, chewy centre; they harden up after a few days.

HEALTHY TIP

These cookies are relatively low in fat as they don't contain margarine or butter. Instead, they are made from almonds, which are a source of protein, fibre, vitamin E, calcium, iron, zinc and B-vitamin. Studies have shown that almonds help lower 'bad' cholesterol levels and heart disease risk, stave off hunger and also control the appetite.

TO STORE

Store in airtight containers. They will keep for up to one week.

PER MACAROON

86 calories
6g fat (of which 1g saturates)
7g carbohydrate
0g salt
vegetarian • gluten free
dairy free

Hazelnut and Chocolate Biscotti

Preparation Time 10 minutes   Cooking Time 35–40 minutes, plus cooling   Makes about 28   **EASY**

125g (4oz) plain flour, sifted, plus extra
 to dust
75g (3oz) golden caster sugar
¼ tsp baking powder
a pinch of cinnamon
a pinch of salt
1 large egg, beaten
1 tbsp milk
¼ tsp vanilla extract
25g (1oz) hazelnuts
25g (1oz) plain chocolate chips

1 Preheat the oven to 200°C (180°C fan oven) mark 6. Put the flour into a large bowl. Stir in the sugar, baking powder, cinnamon and salt. Make a well in the centre and, using a fork, stir in the beaten egg, milk, vanilla, hazelnuts and chocolate chips to form a sticky dough.

2 Turn out the dough on to a lightly floured worksurface and gently knead into a ball. Roll into a 28cm (11in) log shape. Put on a non-stick baking sheet and flatten slightly. Bake for 20–25 minutes until pale golden.

3 Reduce the oven temperature to 150°C (130°C fan oven) mark 2. Transfer the biscotti log on to a chopping board and slice diagonally with a bread knife at 1cm (½in) intervals. Arrange the slices on the baking sheet and put back into the oven for 15 minutes or until golden and dry. Transfer to a wire rack to cool completely.

COOK'S TIP

• To enjoy Italian-style, dunk in coffee or dessert wine.
• To make as gifts, divide the biscuits among four large squares of cellophane, then draw up the edges and tie with ribbon. Label the packages with storage information and an eat-by date.

TO STORE

Store in an airtight container. They will keep for up to one month.

PER BISCUIT

50 calories,
1g fat (of which trace saturates)
9g carbohydrate
0g salt
vegetarian

30-minute Fruit Cake

Preparation Time 15 minutes   **Cooking Time** 30 minutes, plus cooling   **Cuts into** 18 slices   **EASY**

125g (4oz) unsalted butter, softened
125g (4oz) light muscovado sugar
grated zest of 1 lemon
2 medium eggs
a few drops of vanilla extract
150g (5oz) self-raising flour, sifted
1 tsp baking powder
a little lemon juice, as needed
50g (2oz) glacé cherries, chopped
175g (6oz) mixed dried fruit
25g (1oz) desiccated coconut
25g (1oz) demerara sugar
50g (2oz) flaked almonds

1 Preheat the oven to 190°C (170°C fan oven) mark 5. Grease a 28 × 18cm (11 × 7in) shallow baking tin and baseline with baking parchment.

2 Beat the butter, muscovado sugar, lemon zest, eggs, vanilla extract, flour and baking powder together. Add a little lemon juice, if necessary, to form a soft, dropping consistency. Stir in the cherries, dried fruit and coconut.

3 Spoon the mixture into the prepared tin, level the surface and sprinkle with demerara sugar and almonds. Bake for 30 minutes or until golden.

4 Cool in the tin for a few minutes, then turn out on to a wire rack to cool completely.

HEALTHY TIP

This fruit-packed cake is a healthier choice than conventional cakes. It contains high levels of fibre, iron and antioxidant nutrients thanks to the dried fruit, while the almonds supply extra protein and vitamin E.

TO STORE

Store in an airtight container. It will keep for up to one week.

PER SLICE

180 calories
9g fat (of which 5g saturates)
24g carbohydrate
0.2g salt
vegetarian

Almond and Orange Torte

Preparation Time 30 minutes   Cooking Time 1 hour 50 minutes, plus cooling   Cuts into 12 wedges   **EASY**

oil to oil
flour to dust
1 medium orange
3 medium eggs
225g (8oz) golden caster sugar
250g (9oz) ground almonds
½ tsp baking powder
icing sugar to dust
crème fraîche to serve

1 Oil and line, then oil and flour a 20.5cm (8in) springform cake tin. Put the whole orange into a small pan and cover with water. Bring to the boil, then cover, reduce the heat and simmer for at least 1 hour or until tender (see Cook's Tip). Remove from the water and leave to cool

2 Cut the orange in half and remove the pips. Whiz the orange in a food processor or blender to make a smooth purée.

3 Preheat the oven to 180°C (160°C fan oven) mark 4. Put the eggs and caster sugar into a bowl and whisk together until thick and pale. Fold in the almonds, baking powder and orange purée. Pour the mixture into the prepared tin.

4 Bake for 40–50 minutes until a skewer inserted into the centre comes out clean. Leave to cool in the tin.

5 Release the clasp on the tin and remove the cake. Carefully peel off the lining paper and put the cake on a serving plate. Dust with icing sugar, then cut into 12 wedges. Serve with crème fraîche.

COOK'S TIP

To save time, you can microwave the orange. Put it into a small heatproof bowl, cover with 100ml (3½fl oz) water and cook in a 900W microwave oven on full power for 10–12 minutes until soft.

TO STORE

Store in an airtight container. It will keep for up to three days.

PER WEDGE

223 calories
13g fat (of which 1g saturates)
22g carbohydrate
0.1g salt
vegetarian

Cranberry and Apple Mince Pies

Preparation Time 45 minutes, plus chilling, plus mincemeat   Cooking Time 12–15 minutes, plus cooling
Makes 48   **A LITTLE EFFORT**

450g (1lb) Bramley apples, cored and
    chopped
225g (8oz) fresh cranberries, plus extra
    to decorate
125g (4oz) finely chopped candied peel
350g (12oz) each raisins, sultanas and
    currants
175g (6oz) each light and dark
    muscovado sugar
1 tbsp ground mixed spice
pinch of freshly grated nutmeg
grated zest and juice of 2 medium
    oranges
150ml (¼ pint) Calvados

FOR THE ALMOND PASTRY

225g (8oz) plain flour, plus extra to dust
50g (2oz) ground almonds
75g (3oz) golden icing sugar
175g (6oz) unsalted butter, chilled and
    diced
2 medium egg yolks

FOR THE SHORTBREAD
    TOPPING

75g (3oz) unsalted butter, softened
25g (1oz) golden caster sugar, plus extra
    to sprinkle
75g (3oz) plain flour
50g (2oz) ground almonds

1 To make the mincemeat, combine
all the ingredients in a large bowl.
Put into five 500ml (18fl oz)
sterilised jars, seal and label. Leave
to stand for at least 24 hours (or up
to three months).

2 To make the almond pastry, put the
flour, almonds, icing sugar and salt
into a food processor and whiz for
30 seconds. Add the butter and
whiz until the mixture resembles
fine crumbs. (Alternatively, rub the
butter into the flour in a large bowl
by hand or using a pastry cutter
until it resembles fine breadcrumbs.
Stir in the icing sugar and ground
almonds.) Add the egg yolks and
whiz, or stir with a fork, until the
mixture just comes together (if
it's a little dry, add 1–2 tsp cold
water). Knead lightly on a floured
worksurface. Wrap in clingfilm and
chill for 1 hour.

3 To make the topping, beat the
butter and sugar until light, then mix
in the flour and almonds to form a
dough. Wrap the dough and chill
for 15 minutes. Line four 12-hole
bun tins with paper cake cases.

4 On a lightly floured worksurface,
roll out the pastry to 3mm (⅛in)
thick. Stamp out rounds using a
7.5cm (3in) fluted cutter. Put in the
paper cases and prick the bases.
Chill for 10 minutes. Preheat the
oven to 190°C (170°C fan oven)
mark 5. Put 1 tbsp mincemeat into
each pastry case.

5 Roll out the topping to 3mm (⅛in)
thick. Using a small holly cutter, cut
and arrange two leaves on each pie.
Mark the leaves with veins.
Decorate each with two
cranberries. Sprinkle with caster
sugar. Bake in the oven for about
12–15 minutes or until golden. Cool
in the tins for 15 minutes, then cool
completely on a wire rack. Store
in an airtight container for up to
two days.

PER PIE

190 calories
6g fat (of which 3g saturates)
33g carbohydrate
0.1g salt
vegetarian

FREEZING TIP

To freeze Complete the recipe but do not bake. Freeze the unbaked pies in their
tins, covered with clingfilm. When frozen, remove from the tins and pack in an
airtight container for up to one month.
To use Bake the mince pies from frozen in the bun tins at 190°C (170°C fan oven)
mark 5 for 18–20 minutes until golden.

Bran and Apple Muffins

Preparation Time 20 minutes   Cooking Time 30 minutes, plus cooling   Makes 10   **EASY**

250ml (9fl oz) semi-skimmed milk
2 tbsp orange juice
50g (2oz) All Bran
9 ready-to-eat dried prunes
100g (3½oz) light muscovado sugar
2 medium egg whites
1 tbsp golden syrup
150g (5oz) plain flour, sifted
1 tsp baking powder
1 tsp ground cinnamon
1 eating apple, peeled and grated
demerara sugar to sprinkle

1 Preheat the oven to 190°C (170°C fan oven) mark 5. Line a bun tin or muffin tin with 10 paper muffin cases.

2 Mix the milk and orange juice with the All Bran in a bowl. Put to one side for 10 minutes.

3 Put the prunes into a food processor or blender with 100ml (3½fl oz) water and whiz for 2–3 minutes to make a purée, then add the muscovado sugar and whiz briefly to mix.

4 Put the egg whites into a clean, grease-free bowl and whisk until soft peaks form. Add the whites to the milk mixture with the golden syrup, flour, baking powder, cinnamon, grated apple and prune mixture. Fold all the ingredients together gently – don't over-mix or the muffins will be tough.

5 Spoon the mixture into the paper cases and bake for 30 minutes or until well risen and golden brown. Transfer to a wire rack to cool. Sprinkle with demerara sugar just before serving. These are best eaten on the day they are made.

HEALTHY TIP

These muffins are very low in fat and high in fibre. They contain no margarine or butter; instead they are made with prunes, which provide sweetness and a moist texture. Prunes are also a concentrated source of fibre and a number of antioxidant nutrients. All Bran in this recipe supplies high levels of fibre, as well as iron and B vitamins.

FREEZING TIP

To freeze Complete the recipe, but don't sprinkle with the sugar topping. Once the muffins are cold, pack, seal and freeze.
To use Thaw at cool room temperature. Sprinkle with the sugar to serve.

PER MUFFIN

137 calories
1g fat (of which trace saturates)
31g carbohydrate
0.3g salt
vegetarian

Cherry and Almond Muffins

Preparation Time 10 minutes   **Cooking Time** 25 minutes, plus cooling   **Makes** 12   **EASY**

225g (8oz) plain flour
1 tsp baking powder
a pinch of salt
75g (3oz) caster sugar
50g (2oz) ground almonds
350g (12oz) glacé cherries, roughly
   chopped
300ml (½ pint) milk
3 tbsp lemon juice
50ml (2fl oz) sunflower oil or melted
   butter
1 large egg
1 tsp almond extract
roughly crushed sugar cubes to
   decorate

1 Preheat the oven to 190°C (170°C fan oven) mark 5. Line a 12-hole bun tin or muffin tin with paper muffin cases.

2 Sift the flour, baking powder and salt together. Add the caster sugar and ground almonds, then stir in the chopped cherries.

3 Whisk the milk, lemon juice, oil or butter, the egg and almond extract together. Pour into the dry ingredients and stir until all the ingredients are just combined – the mixture should be lumpy. Do not over-mix or the muffins will be tough. Spoon the mixture equally into the paper cases and sprinkle with the crushed sugar cubes.

4 Bake for about 25 minutes or until golden and well risen.

5 Leave to cool in the tin for 5 minutes, then transfer to a wire rack to cool completely. These are best eaten on the day they are made.

FREEZING TIP

To freeze Complete the recipe. Once the muffins are cold, pack, seal and freeze.
To use Thaw at cool room temperature.

PER MUFFIN
230 calories
6g fat (of which 1g saturates)
42g carbohydrate
0.1g salt
vegetarian

Apple Shorties

Preparation Time 20 minutes   Cooking Time 30 minutes, plus cooling   Makes 16   **EASY**

75g (3oz) unsalted butter, softened, plus
  extra to grease
40g (1½oz) caster sugar
75g (3oz) plain flour, sifted
40g (1½oz) fine semolina
1 cooking apple, about 175g (6oz),
  peeled and grated
125g (4oz) sultanas
½ tsp mixed spice
2 tbsp light muscovado sugar
1 tsp lemon juice

1 Preheat the oven to 190°C (170°C fan oven) mark 5. Grease an 18cm (7in) square shallow cake tin.

2 Beat the butter, caster sugar, flour and semolina together in a bowl until the mixture is blended. Press the mixture into the prepared tin and level the surface. Bake in the oven for 15 minutes.

3 Meanwhile, mix the apple with the remaining ingredients. Spoon evenly over the shortbread and put back in the oven for a further 15 minutes.

4 Leave to cool in the tin for a few minutes, then cut into 16 squares. Leave to cool completely, then remove from the tin.

TO STORE
Store in an airtight container. They will keep for up to three days.

PER SQUARE
100 calories
4g fat (of which 3g saturates)
17g carbohydrate
0.1g salt
vegetarian

Cherry Chocolate Fudge Brownies

Preparation Time 20 minutes   Cooking Time 50 minutes, plus cooling and setting   Cuts into 12 brownies   **EASY**

150g (5oz) unsalted butter, plus extra
   to grease
200g (7oz) plain chocolate (at least 70%
   cocoa solids)
175g (6oz) caster sugar
2 tsp vanilla extract
5 medium eggs
175g (6oz) plain flour
¾ tsp baking powder
250g (9oz) glacé cherries, halved

FOR THE ICING
150g (5oz) plain chocolate (at least 70%
   cocoa solids)
2 tbsp Kirsch
4 tbsp double cream

1 Preheat the oven to 180°C (160°C fan oven) mark 4. Grease an 18cm (7in) square shallow cake tin and baseline with greaseproof paper. Put the butter and chocolate into a heatproof bowl set over a pan of gently simmering water, making sure the base of the bowl doesn't touch the water. Leave the chocolate to melt without stirring. Remove the bowl from the pan and stir until smooth. Leave to cool.

2 Whisk the sugar, vanilla extract and eggs until pale and thick. Stir the chocolate into the egg mixture. Sift the flour and baking powder together and lightly fold into the mixture with the cherries. Pour the mixture into the prepared tin and bake for 40 minutes or until just set. Leave to cool slightly in the tin before icing.

3 To make the icing, put the chocolate and Kirsch into a heatproof bowl set over a pan of gently simmering water, making sure the base of the bowl doesn't touch the water. Once melted, add the cream and 4 tbsp water and stir well. Pour over the brownie and leave to set for 1 hour. Cut into 12 individual brownies.

TO STORE
Store in an airtight container. They will keep for up to one week.

FREEZING TIP
To freeze Complete the recipe up to the end of step 2. Remove from the tin, wrap and freeze.
To use Thaw at cool room temperature for about 5 hours. Complete the recipe.

PER BROWNIE
462 calories
24g fat (of which 14g saturates)
59g carbohydrate
0.3g salt
vegetarian

Desserts and Puddings

Baked Apples

Preparation Time 5 minutes, plus soaking　**Cooking Time** 15–20 minutes　**Serves 6**　**EASY**

125g (4oz) hazelnuts
125g (4oz) sultanas
2 tbsp brandy
6 large Bramley apples, cored
4 tbsp soft brown sugar
100ml (3½fl oz) apple juice
plain low-fat yogurt to serve

1 Preheat the oven to 190°C (170°C fan oven) mark 5. Spread the hazelnuts over a baking sheet and toast under a hot grill until golden brown, turning them frequently. Put the hazelnuts in a clean teatowel and rub off the skins, then chop the nuts. Put to one side.

2 Soak the sultanas in the brandy and put to one side for 10 minutes. Using a small sharp knife, score around the middle of the apples to stop them from bursting, then stuff each apple with equal amounts of brandy-soaked sultanas. Put the apples in a roasting tin and sprinkle with the brown sugar and apple juice. Bake in the oven for 15–20 minutes until soft.

3 Serve the apples with the toasted hazelnuts and some yogurt.

HEALTHY TIP

Bramley apples are a good source of vitamin C, containing about twice as much as eating apples. This low fat dessert is also a good source of fibre while the hazelnuts provide useful amounts of vitamin E, iron and zinc.

PER SERVING

280 calories
13g fat (of which 1g saturates)
36g carbohydrate
0g salt
vegetarian • gluten free
dairy free

Apple and Blueberry Strudel

Preparation Time 15 minutes   **Cooking Time** 40 minutes   **Serves 6**   **EASY**

700g (1½lb) red apples, quartered,
    cored and thickly sliced
1 tbsp lemon juice
2 tbsp golden caster sugar
100g (3½oz) dried blueberries
1 tbsp olive oil
6 sheets of filo pastry, thawed
    if frozen
plain low-fat yogurt to serve

1 Preheat the oven to 190°C (170°C fan oven) mark 5. Put the apples into a bowl and mix with the lemon juice, 1 tbsp sugar and the blueberries.

2 Warm the oil. Lay three sheets of filo pastry side by side, overlapping the long edges. Brush with the oil. Cover with three more sheets of filo and brush again.

3 Tip the apple mixture on to the pastry and roll up from a long edge. Put on to a non-stick baking sheet. Brush with the remaining oil and sprinkle with the remaining caster sugar. Bake for 40 minutes or until the pastry is golden and the apples soft. Serve with yogurt

HEALTHY TIP

This dessert is low in fat as it is made with filo pastry (which contains virtually no fat) instead of shortcrust pastry (around 30g/1¼oz per 100g/3½oz). The blueberries are rich in anthocyanins – the pigment that gives berries their intense colour – which help prevent cancer and heart disease. Apples provide good levels of vitamin C and fibre.

PER SERVING

178 calories
2g fat (of which trace saturates)
40g carbohydrate
0g salt
vegetarian • dairy free

Baked Raspberry Meringue Pie

Preparation Time 15 minutes   **Cooking Time** 8 minutes   **Serves 8**   **EASY**

8 trifle sponges
450g (1lb) raspberries, lightly crushed
2–3 tbsp raspberry liqueur
3 medium egg whites
150g (5oz) golden caster sugar

1 Preheat the oven to 230°C (210°C fan oven) mark 8. Put the trifle sponges in the bottom of a 2 litre (3½ pint) ovenproof dish. Spread the raspberries on top and drizzle with the raspberry liqueur.

2 Whisk the egg whites in a clean, grease-free bowl until stiff peaks form. Gradually whisk in the sugar until the mixture is smooth and glossy. Spoon the meringue mixture over the raspberries and bake for 6–8 minutes until golden.

HEALTHY TIP

This dessert is very low in fat. Raspberries are one of the top fruit sources of fibre and vitamin C. They are high in anthocyanins, which are powerful antioxidants that help protect against cell damage, cancer and also heart disease. Blueberries contain a substance that helps the gut to stay clean and healthy, and, like cranberries, they are rich in antioxidants.

PER SERVING

176 calories
2g fat (of which 1g saturates)
37g carbohydrate
0.1g salt
vegetarian

Rhubarb and Raspberry Meringue

Preparation Time 15 minutes   **Cooking Time** 15–20 minutes   **Serves 4**   **A LITTLE EFFORT**

450g (1lb) rhubarb, cut into 2.5cm
(1in) pieces
75g (3oz) caster sugar
2.5cm (1in) piece preserved stem ginger
(optional), finely chopped
finely grated zest and juice of
1 orange
75g (3oz) frozen raspberries
1 large egg white

1 Preheat the oven to 180°C (160°C fan) mark 4. Place the rhubarb in a large pan with 25g (1oz) caster sugar, the chopped stem ginger, if using, and the orange zest. Cover and cook gently for 2–3 minutes, adding a little orange juice if necessary.

2 Add the raspberries. Spoon the mixture into four 150ml (5fl oz) ramekins or ovenproof teacups.

3 Whisk the egg white and remaining sugar together until foamy. Place the bowl over a pan of simmering water and continue to whisk for 5 minutes or until stiff and shiny.

4 Place a spoonful of meringue mixture on top of each ramekin and bake in the oven for 5–10 minutes until lightly golden.

PER SERVING

94 calories
trace fat
22g carbohydrate
0.1g salt
vegetarian • gluten free
dairy free

Almond Toffee Meringues

Preparation Time 35 minutes   **Cooking Time** 22–25 minutes, plus cooling and drying   **Makes 4**   **A LITTLE EFFORT**

oil to oil
25g (1oz) light muscovado sugar
100g (3½oz) egg whites (about
    3 medium eggs)
225g (8oz) caster sugar
25g (1oz) flaked almonds
lightly whipped cream to serve

**FOR THE MARINATED
    SUMMER FRUIT**
125ml (4fl oz) crème de cassis
juice of 1 orange
2 tbsp redcurrant jelly
200g (7oz) raspberries
4 nectarines, halved, stoned and sliced

1 To make the marinated fruit, put the crème de cassis, orange juice and redcurrant jelly into a small pan. Heat gently to melt, then bubble for 2–3 minutes until syrupy. Pour into a large bowl to cool. Add the raspberries and nectarines and stir gently. Cover and chill.

2 Preheat the oven to 170°C (150°C fan oven) mark 3 and preheat the grill. Lightly oil a baking sheet and sprinkle the muscovado sugar over it. Grill for 2–3 minutes until the sugar begins to bubble and caramelise. Cool for about 15 minutes, then break the sugar into a food processor and whiz to a coarse powder.

3 Put the egg whites and caster sugar into a large, clean bowl set over a pan of gently simmering water. Stir for about 10 minutes or until the sugar has dissolved and the egg white is warm. Remove from the heat and place on a teatowel. Beat with a hand-held electric whisk for at least 15 minutes or until cold and glossy and standing in stiff, shiny peaks when the whisk is lifted.

4 Cover two baking sheets with baking parchment. Fold half the powdered sugar into the meringue mixture. Spoon four oval mounds on to the baking sheets, leaving plenty of space between each. Sprinkle with flaked almonds and the remaining powdered sugar. Bake for 20 minutes, then turn off the heat and leave in the oven to dry out overnight. Serve the meringues with the marinated fruit and lightly whipped cream.

PER MERINGUE
458 calories
4g fat (of which trace saturates)
95g carbohydrate
0.2g salt
vegetarian • gluten free

COOK'S TIPS
• Make sure the bowl does not touch the hot water while you make the meringues.
• The flavour of the marinated fruit will be even better if you chill it overnight.
(If the syrup thickens during chilling, stir in 1–2 tbsp orange juice.)

Tropical Fruit Pots

Preparation Time 15 minutes   **Cooking Time** 5 minutes   **Serves 8   EASY**

400g can apricots in fruit juice

2 balls of preserved stem ginger in syrup, finely chopped, plus 2 tbsp syrup from the jar

½ tsp ground cinnamon

juice of 1 orange

3 oranges, cut into segments

1 mango, peeled, stoned and chopped

1 pineapple, peeled, core removed, and chopped

450g (1lb) coconut yogurt

3 tbsp lemon curd

3–4 tbsp light muscovado sugar

1 Drain the juice from the apricots into a pan and stir in the syrup from the ginger. Add the chopped preserved stem ginger, the cinnamon and orange juice. Put over a low heat and stir gently. Bring to the boil, then reduce the heat and simmer for 2–3 minutes to make a thick syrup.

2 Roughly chop the apricots and put into a bowl with the segmented oranges, the mango and pineapple. Pour the syrup over the fruit. Divide among eight 300ml (½ pint) glasses or dessert bowls.

3 Beat the yogurt and lemon curd together in a bowl until smooth. Spoon a generous dollop over the fruit and sprinkle with muscovado sugar. Chill if not serving immediately.

HEALTHY TIP

This dessert is brimming with beta-carotene, vitamin C and cancer-protective nutrients. Mango is a good source of the phytochemical beta-cryptoxanthin, which has antioxidant properties. Pineapple is a useful source of potassium and vitamin C.

GET AHEAD

To prepare ahead Complete the recipe to the end of step 2 up to 2 hours before you plan to eat – no need to chill.
To use Complete the recipe.

PER SERVING

192 calories

1g fat (of which trace saturates)

45g carbohydrate

0.1g salt

vegetarian • gluten free

Oranges with Caramel Sauce

Preparation Time 15 minutes **Cooking Time** 30–40 minutes **Serves 6** **EASY**

6 oranges
25g (1oz) butter
2 tbsp golden caster sugar
2 tbsp Grand Marnier
2 tbsp marmalade
grated zest and juice of 1 large orange
plain yogurt or crème fraîche to serve

1 Preheat the oven to 200°C (180°C fan oven) mark 6. Cut away the peel and pith from the oranges, then put them in a roasting tin just big enough to hold them.

2 Melt the butter in a pan and add the sugar, Grand Marnier, marmalade, orange zest and juice. Heat gently until the sugar dissolves. Pour the mixture over the oranges in the tin, then bake for 30–40 minutes until the oranges are caramelised. Serve warm with yogurt or crème fraîche.

HEALTHY TIP

Oranges are rich in vitamin C – one fruit supplies more than 100% of your daily vitamin C, which helps keep blood vessels healthy and defend the body against bacteria and viruses. They also contain bioflavanoids, which help lower blood cholesterol levels and protect your eyesight from age-related damage.

COOK'S TIP

Use thick-skinned oranges, such as navel oranges, as they are much easier to peel.

PER SERVING

139 calories
4g fat (of which 2g saturates)
24g carbohydrate
0.1g salt
vegetarian • gluten free

Strawberry Compôte

Preparation Time 15 minutes, plus chilling   **Cooking Time** 10 minutes, plus cooling   **Serves 4**   **EASY**

175g (6oz) raspberry conserve
juice of 1 orange
juice of 1 lemon
1 tsp rosewater
350g (12oz) strawberries, hulled and
   thickly sliced
150g (5oz) blueberries

1 Put the raspberry conserve into a pan with the orange and lemon juices. Add 75ml (2½fl oz) boiling water. Stir over a low heat to melt the conserve, then leave to cool.

2 Stir in the rosewater and taste – you may want to add a squeeze more lemon juice if it's too sweet. Put the strawberries and blueberries into a large serving bowl, then strain the raspberry conserve mixture over them. Cover and chill overnight. Remove the bowl from the fridge 30 minutes before serving.

HEALTHY TIP

Berries are densely packed with vitamins, antioxidants and other phytonutrients. They contain compounds called anthocyanins – the pigment that gives berries their intense colour, mops up damaging free radicals and helps prevent cancer and heart disease. They are also rich in vitamin C, which, together with the anthocyanins, helps strengthen blood capillaries and improve blood flow around the body.

PER SERVING

156 calories
0g fat
40g carbohydrate
0g salt
vegetarian • gluten free
dairy free

Summer Pudding

Preparation Time 10 minutes, plus overnight chilling   **Cooking Time** 10 minutes   **Serves 8**   **EASY**

800g (1lb 12oz) mixed summer berries, such as 250g (9oz) each redcurrants and blackcurrants and 300g (11oz) raspberries
125g (4oz) golden caster sugar
3 tbsp crème de cassis
9 thick slices slightly stale white bread, crusts removed
crème fraîche to serve

1 Put the redcurrants and blackcurrants into a medium pan. Add the sugar and cassis. Bring to a simmer and cook for 3–5 minutes until the sugar has dissolved. Add the raspberries and cook for 2 minutes. Once the fruit is cooked, taste it – there should be a good balance between tart and sweet.

2 Meanwhile, line a 1 litre (1¾ pint) bowl with clingfilm. Put the base of the bowl on one piece of bread and cut around it. Put the circle of bread in the base of the bowl.

3 Line the inside of the bowl with more slices of bread, slightly overlapping them to prevent any gaps. Spoon in the fruit, making sure the juice soaks into the bread. Keep back a few spoonfuls of the juice in case the bread is unevenly soaked when you turn out the pudding.

4 Cut the remaining bread to fit the top of the pudding neatly, using a sharp knife to trim any excess bread from around the edges. Wrap in clingfilm, weigh down with a saucer and a can and chill overnight.

5 To serve, unwrap the outer clingfilm, upturn the pudding on to a plate and remove the inner clingfilm. Drizzle with the reserved juice and serve with crème fraîche.

PER SERVING
173 calories
1g fat (of which trace saturates)
38g carbohydrate,
0.4g salt
vegetarian • dairy free

Exotic Fruit Salad

Preparation Time 10 minutes   **Serves 4**   **EASY**

2 oranges
1 mango, peeled, stoned and chopped
450g (1lb) peeled and diced fresh
    pineapple
200g (7oz) blueberries
½ Charentais melon, cubed
grated zest and juice of 1 lime

1 Using a sharp knife, peel the
  oranges, remove the pith and
  cut the flesh into segments.
  Put into a bowl.

2 Add the mango, pineapple,
  blueberries and melon to the
  bowl, then add the lime zest
  and juice. Gently mix together
  and serve immediately.

HEALTHY TIP

This dessert is packed with vitamins C
and betacarotene. Fresh pineapple
contains the enzyme bromelain,
which aids digestion and is beneficial
for inflammatory conditions such as
sinusitis and rheumatoid arthritis.

TRY SOMETHING DIFFERENT

• Use 2 papayas, peeled, seeded and
chopped, instead of the pineapple.
• Mix the seeds of 2 passion fruit
with the lime juice before adding to
the salad.

PER SERVING

187 calories
1g fat (of which 0g saturates)
47g carbohydrate
0.1g salt
**vegetarian • gluten free
dairy free**

Fruit Kebabs with Spiced Pear Dip

Preparation Time 20 minutes, plus soaking **Cooking Time** 8 minutes **Serves 6** **EASY**

3 large fresh figs, cut into quarters
1 large ripe mango, peeled, stoned and
    cut into cubes
1 baby pineapple or 2 thick slices,
    peeled and cut into cubes
1 tbsp clear honey

FOR THE SPICED PEAR DIP

150g (5oz) ready-to-eat dried pears,
    soaked in hot water for 30 minutes
juice of 1 orange
1 tsp finely chopped fresh root ginger
1/2 tsp vanilla extract
50g (2oz) very low-fat plain yogurt
1/2 tsp ground cinnamon, plus extra to
    dust
1 tsp clear honey
25g (1oz) hazelnuts, toasted (see page
    230) and roughly chopped

1 Soak six 20.5cm (8in) wooden skewers in water for 30 minutes. To make the dip, drain the pears and put into a food processor or blender with the orange juice, ginger, vanilla extract, yogurt, cinnamon and 50ml (2fl oz) water. Whiz until smooth. Spoon the dip into a bowl. Drizzle with the honey, sprinkle with the toasted hazelnuts and dust with a little ground cinnamon. Cover and put to one side in a cool place until ready to serve.

2 Preheat the grill to its highest setting. To make the kebabs, thread pieces of fruit on to the skewers, using at least two pieces of each type of fruit per skewer. Put the skewers on a foil-covered tray. Drizzle with honey and grill for about 4 minutes on each side, close to the heat, until lightly charred. Serve warm or at room temperature with the spiced pear dip.

GET AHEAD

To prepare ahead Make the dip as in step 1 and spoon the dip into a bowl. Cover and chill for up to two days. Thread the fruit on to the skewers as in step 2. Cover and chill for up to one day.
To use Drizzle the dip with clear honey, sprinkle with toasted nuts and dust with cinnamon. Allow the chilled kebabs to come to room temperature. Finally, complete step 2.

PER SERVING

122 calories
3g fat (of which trace saturates)
23g carbohydrate
0g salt
vegetarian • gluten free

Rice Pudding

Preparation Time 5 minutes   **Cooking Time** 1½ hours   **Serves 6**   **EASY**

butter to grease
125g (4oz) short-grain pudding rice
1.1 litres (2 pints) full-fat milk
4 tbsp golden caster sugar
grated zest of 1 small orange
2 tsp vanilla extract
whole nutmeg to grate

1 Preheat the oven to 180°C (160°C fan oven) mark 4. Lightly grease a 900ml (1½ pint) ovenproof dish. Add the pudding rice, milk, sugar, orange zest and vanilla extract and stir everything together. Grate a little nutmeg all over the top of the mixture.

2 Bake the pudding in the oven for 1½ hours or until the top is golden brown, then serve.

HEALTHY TIP

This comfort pud is low in fat and a good source of protein and calcium, needed for maintaining strong bones. You can use semi-skimmed milk to reduce the fat content further.

PER SERVING

235 calories
7g fat (of which 5g saturates)
35g carbohydrate
0.2g salt
vegetarian • gluten free

Mocha Soufflés

Preparation Time 15 minutes, plus cooling   **Cooking Time** 12 minutes   **Serves 6**   **EASY**

50g (2oz) plain chocolate (at least 70% cocoa solids), roughly chopped
1 tbsp cornflour
1 tbsp cocoa powder
1–1½ tsp instant coffee granules
4 tbsp golden caster sugar
150ml (¼ pint) skimmed milk
2 medium egg yolks
3 medium egg whites
icing sugar or cocoa powder to dust

1 Preheat the oven to 190°C (170°C fan oven) mark 5 and put a baking sheet inside to heat up.

2 Put the chocolate into a non-stick pan with the cornflour, cocoa powder, coffee granules, 1 tbsp caster sugar and the milk. Warm gently, stirring over a low heat, until the chocolate has melted. Increase the heat and cook, stirring continuously, until the mixture just thickens. Leave to cool a little, then stir in the egg yolks. Cover the surface with a piece of damp greaseproof paper and leave to cool.

3 Put the egg whites into a clean, grease-free bowl and whisk until soft peaks form. Gradually whisk in the remaining caster sugar, a spoonful at a time, until the meringue is stiff but not dry.

4 Stir one-third of the meringue into the cooled chocolate mixture to lighten it, then gently fold in the remainder, using a large metal spoon. Divide the mixture among six 150ml (¼ pint) ramekins or ovenproof tea or coffee cups. Stand them on the hot baking sheet and bake for about 12 minutes or until puffed up.

5 Dust the soufflés with a little icing sugar or cocoa powder and serve immediately.

PER SERVING
132 calories
5g fat (of which 2g saturates)
20g carbohydrate
0.2g salt
vegetarian

Chocolate and Prune Pudding

Preparation Time 10 minutes **Cooking Time** 30–40 minutes **Serves 6** **EASY**

600ml (1 pint) skimmed milk

50g (2oz) plain chocolate, broken into tiny pieces (at least 70% cocoa solids), or chocolate chips

2 large eggs

2 large egg yolks

40g (1½oz) light brown sugar

½ tsp cornflour

2 tbsp unsweetened cocoa powder, plus extra to dust

100g (3½oz) ready-to-eat prunes, chopped

1 Preheat the oven to 170°C (150°C fan oven) mark 3. Heat the milk to simmering point, then remove from the heat. Add the broken chocolate and stir until it has melted completely.

2 In a heatproof bowl, whisk together the eggs, egg yolks, sugar, cornflour and cocoa until smooth. Gradually pour in the hot chocolate milk, stirring until it is combined.

3 Put the prunes into the base of a serving dish or individual dishes, then strain in the milk mixture through a sieve. Put the dish(es) in a roasting tin and carefully fill the tin with boiling water so it comes halfway up the sides of the dish(es). Bake in the oven for about 30–40 minutes until just set.

4 Remove the dish(es) from the roasting tin and serve warm. Alternatively, leave to cool, then chill until ready to serve. Dust with cocoa before serving.

HEALTHY TIP

This dish is made with skimmed milk, which supplies high levels of protein and calcium but very little fat. Cocoa powder and plain chocolate are rich in flavanols, which may help lower blood pressure, blood cholesterol, and heart disease risk. They also contain useful amounts of magnesium and iron.

PER SERVING

195 calories

8g fat (of which 4g saturates)

24g carbohydrate

0.3g salt

vegetarian • gluten free

Dark Chocolate Soufflés

Preparation Time 20 minutes   **Cooking Time** 20 minutes, plus cooling   **Serves 6**   **EASY**

50g (2oz) plain chocolate (at least 70% cocoa solids), broken into pieces

2 tbsp cornflour

1 tbsp cocoa powder

1 tsp instant coffee granules

4 tbsp golden caster sugar

150ml (¼ pint) skimmed milk

2 medium eggs, separated, plus
   1 egg white

1 Preheat the oven to 190°C (170°C fan oven) mark 5 and put a baking sheet inside to heat up. Put the chocolate into a pan with the cornflour, cocoa powder, coffee, 1 tbsp sugar and the milk. Warm gently to melt the chocolate. Increase the heat and stir until the mixture thickens. Leave to cool a little, then stir in the egg yolks. Cover with a piece of damp greaseproof paper.

2 Whisk the egg whites in a clean, grease-free bowl until soft peaks form. Gradually whisk in the remaining sugar until the mixture is stiff.

3 Stir one-third of the egg whites into the chocolate mixture. Fold in the remaining whites and divide among six 150ml (¼ pint) ramekins. Put the ramekins on a baking sheet and bake for 12 minutes or until well risen. Serve immediately.

TRY SOMETHING DIFFERENT

Use flavoured plain chocolate for an unusual twist, such as ginger, mint or even chilli.

PER SERVING

134 calories

4g fat (of which 2g saturates)

22g carbohydrate

0.1g salt

vegetarian • gluten free

Chocolate Cherry Roll

Preparation Time 30 minutes   **Cooking Time** 30 minutes, plus cooling   **Serves 8**   **A LITTLE EFFORT**

4 tbsp cocoa powder, plus extra
  to dust
100ml (3½fl oz) milk, plus 3 tbsp extra
5 medium eggs, separated
125g (4oz) golden caster sugar
1–2 tbsp cherry jam
400g can pitted cherries, drained
  and chopped
icing sugar to dust

1 Preheat the oven to 180°C (160°C fan oven) mark 4. Line a 30.5 × 20.5cm (12 × 8in) Swiss roll tin with baking parchment. Mix the cocoa and 3 tbsp milk together in a bowl. Heat 100ml (3½fl oz) milk in a pan until almost boiling, then add to the bowl, stirring. Leave to cool for 10 minutes.

2 Whisk the egg whites in a clean grease-free bowl until soft peaks form. In a separate bowl, whisk together the egg yolks and caster sugar until pale and thick. Gradually whisk in the cooled milk, then fold in the egg whites. Spoon the mixture into the prepared tin and smooth the surface. Bake in the oven for 25 minutes or until just firm.

3 Turn out on to a board lined with baking parchment and peel off the lining parchment. Cover with a damp teatowel.

4 Spread the jam over the sponge and top with the cherries. Roll up from the shortest end, dust with cocoa and icing sugar, then cut into slices and serve.

TRY SOMETHING DIFFERENT
You can add whipped cream to the roll, but you will need to cool it first. To do this, turn out the sponge on to baking parchment. Do not remove the lining paper but roll the sponge around it while still warm. Leave to cool, unroll and peel off the paper. Spread with the jam and fruit, then the cream, and re-roll.

PER SERVING
185 calories
5g fat (of which 2g saturates)
30g carbohydrate
0.3g salt
vegetarian • gluten free

Elderflower and Fruit Jelly

Preparation Time 15 minutes, plus chilling   **Cooking Time** 10 minutes, plus cooling   **Serves 6** **EASY**

2–3 tbsp elderflower cordial

200g (7oz) caster sugar

4 gelatine leaves (see Cook's Tips)

150g (5oz) raspberries

150g (5oz) seedless grapes, halved

1 Put the elderflower cordial into a large pan and add 750ml (1¼ pints) water and the sugar. Heat gently, stirring to dissolve the sugar.

2 Soak the gelatine leaves in cold water for 5 minutes. Lift out the gelatine, squeeze out the excess water, then add to the liquid in the pan. Stir to dissolve, then strain into a jug.

3 Divide the raspberries and grapes among six 200ml (7fl oz) glass dishes. Pour the liquid over the fruit, then cool and chill for at least 4 hours or overnight.

COOK'S TIPS

• Gelatine is available in leaf and powdered forms. Both must be soaked in liquid to soften before being dissolved in a warm liquid. Always add dissolved gelatine to a mixture that is warm or at room temperature – if added to a cold liquid, it will set in fine threads and spoil the final texture of the dish.

• Gelatine is derived from meat bones, but there are also several vegetarian alternatives, such as agar agar and gelazone.

PER SERVING

189 calories

0g fat,

42g carbohydrate

0g salt

gluten free • dairy free

Lemon Sorbet

Preparation Time 10 minutes, plus chilling and freezing   **Cooking Time** 15 minutes, plus cooling   **Serves 4   EASY**

3 juicy lemons
125g (4oz) golden caster sugar
1 large egg white

1 Finely pare the lemon zest, using a zester, then squeeze the juice. Put the zest into a pan with the sugar and 350ml (12fl oz) water and heat gently until the sugar has dissolved. Increase the heat and boil for 10 minutes. Leave to cool.

2 Stir the lemon juice into the cooled sugar syrup. Cover and chill in the fridge for 30 minutes.

3 Strain the syrup through a fine sieve into a bowl. In another bowl, beat the egg white until just frothy, then whisk into the lemon mixture.

4 For best results, freeze in an ice-cream maker. (Alternatively, pour into a shallow freezerproof container and freeze until almost frozen; mash well with a fork and freeze until solid.) Transfer the sorbet to the fridge 30 minutes before serving to soften slightly.

HEALTHY TIP

This dessert contains virtually no fat so is a good option if you are on a low fat diet. The lemon juice is rich in vitamin C, as well as phytochemicals called limonoids and limonene, which have recognised cancer-fighting actions.

TRY SOMETHING DIFFERENT

• **Orange Sorbet**
Replace two of the lemons with oranges.
• **Lime Sorbet**
Replace two of the lemons with four limes.

PER SERVING

130 calories
0g fat
33g carbohydrate
0g salt
**vegetarian • gluten free
dairy free**

Chocolate Cinnamon Sorbet

Preparation Time 5 minutes, plus chilling and freezing   **Cooking Time** 15 minutes   **Serves 8**   **EASY**

200g (7oz) golden granulated sugar
50g (2oz) unsweetened cocoa powder
1 tsp instant espresso coffee powder
1 cinnamon stick
8 tsp crème de cacao (chocolate
    liqueur) to serve (optional)

1 Put the sugar into a large pan and add the cocoa powder, coffee and cinnamon stick with 600ml (1 pint) water. Bring to the boil, stirring until the sugar has completely dissolved. Boil for 5 minutes, then remove from the heat. Leave to cool. Discard the cinnamon stick, then chill in the fridge.

2 If you have an ice-cream maker, put the mixture into it and churn for about 30 minutes until firm. (Alternatively, pour into a shallow freezerproof container and freeze until almost frozen; mash well with a fork and freeze for at least 1 hour or until solid.)

3 To serve, scoop the sorbet into individual cups and, if you like, drizzle 1 tsp chocolate liqueur over each portion. Serve immediately.

PER SERVING
118 calories
1g fat (of which 1g saturates)
27g carbohydrate
0.2g salt
vegetarian • gluten free
dairy free

Frozen Yogurt Sorbet

Preparation Time 15 minutes, plus freezing **Serves 8** **EASY**

450g (1lb) frozen mixed fruit, thawed,
plus extra to serve
100g (3½oz) clear honey
3 medium egg whites
450g (1lb) low-fat Greek yogurt

1 Line a 750ml (1¼ pint) loaf tin with clingfilm. Whiz the thawed fruit in a food processor or blender to make a purée. Strain through a fine nylon sieve into a bowl, pressing all the juice through with the back of a spoon. Stir the honey into the juice.

2 Put the egg whites into a clean, grease-free bowl and whisk until soft peaks form, then fold into the fruit with the yogurt. Pour the mixture into the prepared tin and freeze for 4 hours. Stir to break up the ice crystals, then freeze again for 4 hours. Stir again, then freeze for a further 4 hours or until firm.

3 Transfer the sorbet to the fridge 20 minutes before serving. Turn out on to a serving plate and remove the clingfilm. Slice and serve with a spoonful of thawed fruit.

HEALTHY TIP

This is a low fat dessert that is also a good source of protein and calcium. Greek yogurt contains 10% fat but low fat varieties containing just 2% fat and fat-free varieties are also available. Frozen mixed fruit contains similar levels of vitamin C as fresh fruit.

COOK'S TIP

Use any selection of frozen mixed fruit. Summer berries and forest fruits work well.

PER SERVING

120 calories
6g fat (of which 3g saturates)
14g carbohydrate
0.2g salt
vegetarian • gluten free

Instant Banana Ice Cream

Preparation Time 5 minutes, plus freezing   **Serves 4**   **EASY**

6 ripe bananas, about 700g (1½lb),
   peeled, cut into thin slices and frozen
   (see Cook's Tip)
1–2 tbsp virtually fat-free fromage frais
1–2 tbsp orange juice
1 tsp vanilla extract
splash of rum or Cointreau (optional)
a few drops of lime juice to taste

1 Leave the frozen banana slices to stand at room temperature for 2–3 minutes. Put the still frozen pieces in a food processor or blender with 1 tbsp fromage frais, 1 tbsp orange juice, the vanilla extract and the liqueur, if using.

2 Whiz until smooth, scraping down the sides of the bowl and adding more fromage frais and orange juice as necessary to give a creamy consistency. Add lime juice to taste and serve at once or turn into a freezerproof container and freeze for up to one month.

COOK'S TIP
To freeze bananas, peel them and slice thinly, then put the banana slices on a large non-stick baking tray and put into the freezer for 30 minutes or until frozen. Transfer to a plastic bag and store in the freezer until needed.

PER SERVING
173 calories
1g fat (of which 0g saturates)
42g carbohydrate
0g salt
vegetarian • gluten free

Zabaglione

Preparation Time 5 minutes   **Cooking Time** 20 minutes   **Serves 4**   **EASY**

4 medium egg yolks
100g (3½oz) caster sugar
100ml (3½fl oz) sweet Marsala wine

1 Heat a pan of water to boiling point. Put the egg yolks and sugar into a heatproof bowl large enough to rest over the pan without its base touching the water. With the bowl in place, reduce the heat so that the water is just simmering.

2 Using a hand-held electric whisk, whisk the yolks and sugar for 15 minutes until pale, thick and foaming. With the bowl still over the heat, gradually pour in the Marsala, whisking all the time.

3 Pour the zabaglione into four glasses or small coffee cups and serve immediately.

PER SERVING

193 calories
6g fat (of which 2g saturates)
28g carbohydrate
0g salt
vegetarian • gluten free
dairy free

Cinnamon Pancakes

Preparation Time 5 minutes, plus standing   **Cooking Time** 20 minutes   **Serves 6**   **EASY**

150g (5oz) plain flour
½ tsp ground cinnamon
1 medium egg
300ml (½ pint) skimmed milk
olive oil to fry
fruit compote or sugar and Greek
  yogurt to serve

1 Whisk the flour, cinnamon, egg and milk together in a large bowl to make a smooth batter. Leave to stand for 20 minutes.

2 Heat a heavy-based frying pan over a medium heat. When the pan is really hot, add 1 tsp oil, pour in a ladleful of batter and tilt the pan to coat the base with an even layer. Cook for 1 minute or until golden. Flip over and cook for 1 minute. Repeat with the remaining batter, adding more oil if necessary, to make six pancakes. Serve with a fruit compote or a sprinkling of sugar, and a dollop of yogurt.

TRY SOMETHING DIFFERENT
Serve with sliced bananas and vanilla ice cream instead of the fruit compote and Greek yogurt.

PER SERVING
141 calories
5g fat (of which 1g saturates)
20g carbohydrate
0.1g salt
vegetarian

Vitality Drinks

Banana Vitality Shake

Preparation Time 10 minutes   **Serves** 2, makes 600ml (1 pint)   **EASY**

25g (1oz) whole shelled almonds
1 large ripe banana
150ml (¼ pint) low-fat milk
150ml (¼ pint) low-fat plain yogurt
8g sachet powdered egg white
2 tsp wheatgerm
1–2 tsp maple syrup
a pinch of freshly grated nutmeg

1 Grind the almonds in a spice grinder or food processor – the mixture needs to be very fine to get a good blend.

2 Peel and roughly chop the banana, then put into a blender with the ground almonds. Add the milk, yogurt, powdered egg white and wheatgerm to the blender and whiz for a few seconds until smooth.

3 Add maple syrup to taste, then pour into two glasses and serve immediately, sprinkled with nutmeg.

HEALTHY TIP

A good source of protein, calcium, carbohydrates and B vitamins, this shake makes a highly nutritious supplement for regular exercisers. Almonds add healthy monounsaturated fats as well as vitamin E and iron.

PER SERVING

246 calories
9g fat (of which 1g saturates)
32g carbohydrate
0.4g salt
vegetarian

Mega Vitamin C Tonic

Preparation Time 10 minutes   **Serves** 1, makes 200ml (7fl oz)   **EASY**

1 large orange
1 lemon
1 lime
½ pink grapefruit
1–2 tsp clear honey
crushed ice
slices of citrus fruit to decorate

1 Using a sharp knife, cut off the peel from all the citrus fruit, removing as much of the white pith as possible. Chop the flesh roughly, discarding any pips, and put into a blender.

2 Add the honey to taste and whiz for a few seconds until smooth.

3 Pour over crushed ice in a glass and decorate with citrus fruit to serve.

PER SERVING

144 calories
trace fat
35g carbohydrate
0g salt
**vegetarian • gluten free
dairy free**

Busy Bee's Comforter

Preparation Time 5 minutes   Serves 1, makes 200ml (7fl oz)   **EASY**

2 lemons

150ml (¼ pint) full fat plain or soya yogurt, at room temperature

1–2 tsp thick honey

2–3 tsp bee pollen grains or equivalent in capsule form (see Healthy Tip)

1 Using a sharp knife, cut off the peel from one lemon, removing as much of the white pith as possible. Chop the flesh roughly, discarding any pips, and put into a blender. Squeeze the juice from the remaining lemon and add to the blender.

2 Spoon in the yogurt and whiz until smooth. Taste and sweeten with honey as necessary. Stir in the bee pollen, then pour into a glass and serve immediately.

HEALTHY TIP

This drink is a good source of protein and calcium. It contains honey, which is a source of slow-releasing sugars and a powerful antibacterial and anti-viral ingredient.

COOK'S TIP

Not suitable for those with an allergy to pollen, such as hayfever sufferers.

TRY SOMETHING DIFFERENT

Use oranges instead of lemons.

PER SERVING

130 calories
2g fat (of which 1g saturates),
24g carbohydrate
0.3g salt
vegetarian • gluten free

Strawberry and Camomile Calmer

Preparation Time 5 minutes, plus infusing and cooling   **Serves 2, Makes 600ml (1 pint)**   **EASY**

2 camomile teabags
5cm (2in) piece cinnamon stick
175g (6oz) strawberries
150ml (¼ pint) freshly pressed apple
   juice or 2 large dessert apples, juiced

1 Put the teabags and cinnamon stick into a small heatproof jug and pour in 150ml (¼ pint) boiling water. Leave to infuse for 5 minutes, then discard the bags and cinnamon stick. Leave to cool.

2 When ready to serve, remove the hulls from the strawberries, then wash and pat the fruit dry with kitchen paper. Put into a blender.

3 Pour in the apple juice and cold camomile tea. Whiz for a few seconds until smooth. Pour into two tall glasses and serve.

TRY SOMETHING DIFFERENT
Camomile tea bags are very convenient and easy to use, but freshly dried flowers will give a stronger flavour.

PER SERVING
52 calories
trace fat
13g carbohydrate
0g salt
vegetarian • gluten free
dairy free

Green Tea Pick-me-up

Preparation Time 10 minutes, plus infusing and cooling   Serves 1, makes 300ml (½ pint)   **EASY**

1 tsp, or 1 teabag, Japanese green tea
1 ripe kiwi fruit
8 fresh lychees
a few ice cubes

1 Put the tea or teabag into a heatproof jug and pour in 200ml (7fl oz) boiling water. Leave to infuse for 3 minutes, then strain to remove the tea leaves, or discard the teabag. Leave to cool.

2 When ready to serve, peel and roughly chop the kiwi fruit. Put into a blender. Peel the lychees, then cut in half and remove the stones.

3 Add to the blender with the cold tea. Whiz until smooth, then pour over ice in a glass to serve.

HEALTHY TIP

Green tea is a powerhouse of polyphenols, which help counteract cancer-causing agents and lower the risk of heart disease. It may also help lower blood pressure and blood cholesterol. Kiwi fruit and lychees both add vitamin C.

TRY SOMETHING DIFFERENT

For extra zing, add a 5cm (2in) piece fresh root ginger, peeled and chopped, to the blender in step 2.

PER SERVING

99 calories
trace fat
24g carbohydrate
0g salt
vegetarian • gluten free
dairy free

Raspberry Rascal Booster

Preparation Time 5 minutes   **Serves** I, makes 300ml (¹/₂ pint) **EASY**

225g (8oz) raspberries, thawed if frozen,
   juices reserved
I medium orange
2 tsp thick honey

I If using fresh raspberries, remove
   the hulls, then wash and pat the
   fruit dry with kitchen paper. Put
   two raspberries to one side for
   decoration and put the rest into a
   blender. If the fruit has been frozen,
   add the juices as well.

2 Peel the orange, removing as much
   of the white pith as possible. Chop
   the flesh roughly, discarding any
   pips, and put into blender. Add the
   honey. Whiz until smooth, then
   pour into a glass, decorate with the
   raspberries and serve immediately.

HEALTHY TIP

This drink is bursting with vitamin C
and anthocyanins, which help
strengthen blood vessels and boost
your immune system.

COOK'S TIP

If you find this smoothie too thick,
water it down a little.

PER SERVING

I47 calories
Ig fat (of which trace saturates)
33g carbohydrate
0g salt
vegetarian • gluten free
dairy free

Wheatgrass Salad

Preparation Time 10 minutes   **Serves** 1, makes 200ml (7fl oz)   **EASY**

25g (1oz) fresh parsley
25g (1oz) fresh coriander
75g (3oz) watercress
75g (3oz) cucumber
5cm (2in) round wheatgrass (see
 Cook's Tip)

1 Wash and shake dry the herbs and watercress, then put into a blender.

2 Wash and pat the cucumber dry with kitchen paper. Peel if you like, then roughly chop and put into the blender.

3 Wash and shake the wheatgrass dry, then juice in a slow-turning or wheatgrass juicer. Add the juice to the cucumber and herbs. Whiz for a few seconds until well blended, then serve immediately, topped up with chilled water, if you like.

HEALTHY TIP

Wheatgrass is a concentrated source of vitamins A and C, calcium, potassium, zinc, magnesium and iron. The watercress, parsley and coriander also add folate and iron.

COOK'S TIP

Wheatgrass deteriorates quickly, so to ensure that you are getting the freshest drink possible it should be juiced once everything else has been prepared. You can buy wheatgrass from a health-food shop; it is sold sprouting, in cartons like mustard and cress. Using scissors, snip the wheatgrass as close to the base as possible and measure it tightly bunched in 'rounds' like spaghetti – a 5cm (2in) round will yield about 50ml (2fl oz) juice.

PER SERVING

43 calories
2g fat (of which trace saturates)
3g carbohydrate
0.1g salt
**vegetarian • gluten free
dairy free**

Creamy Dairy-free Banana

Preparation Time 5 minutes   Serves 1, makes 400ml (14fl oz)   **EASY**

1 large ripe banana
125g (4oz) silken tofu, well chilled (see
   Cook's Tip)
175ml (6fl oz) unsweetened soya milk,
   well chilled
2 tsp thick honey
a few drops of vanilla extract

1 Peel the banana and slice thickly.
   Put into a blender.

2 Drain the tofu, mash lightly with a
   fork and add to the blender.

3 Pour in the milk and add the honey
   with a few drops of vanilla extract.
   Whiz for a few seconds until thick
   and smooth. Pour into a large glass
   and serve.

COOK'S TIP
Silken tofu is very smooth and is the
best for blending in drinks. It is
available fresh or vacuum-packed in
cartons. Firmer types can be used but
give a grainier texture when blended.

PER SERVING
238 calories
8g fat (of which 1g saturates)
25g carbohydrate
0.2g salt
**vegetarian • gluten free
dairy free**

Apricot and Orange Smoothie

Preparation Time 5 minutes, plus chilling   **Serves 2, makes about 450ml (³/4 pint)**   **EASY**

400g (14oz) canned apricots in natural
   Juice
150g (5oz) apricot yogurt
200–250ml (7–9fl oz) unsweetened
   orange juice

1 Put the apricots, yogurt and orange
   juice into a blender or food
   processor and whiz for 1 minute
   or until smooth.

2 Chill well, then pour into two
   glasses and serve.

PER SERVING

172 calories
1g fat (of which trace saturates)
39g carbohydrate
0.2g salt
vegetarian • gluten free

Fruity Carrot with Ginger

Preparation Time 10 minutes **Serves 2, makes 400ml (14fl oz)** **EASY**

2 medium oranges
1cm (½ in) piece fresh root ginger,
    peeled and roughly chopped
150ml (¼ pint) freshly pressed apple
    juice or 2 dessert apples, juiced
150ml (¼ pint) freshly pressed carrot
    juice or 3 medium carrots, 250g
    (9oz), juiced
mint leaves to decorate

1 Using a sharp knife, cut a slice of
orange and put to one side for the
decoration. Cut off the peel from
the oranges, removing as much of
the white pith as possible. Chop the
flesh roughly, discarding any pips,
and put into a blender. Add the
chopped ginger.

2 Pour in the apple and carrot juice
and blend until smooth. Divide
between two glasses, decorate with
quartered orange slices and a mint
leaf and serve.

HEALTHY TIP

This drink is full of vitamin C and
betacarotene, making it a great
immunity-boosting supplement.
Fresh ginger is good for calming an
upset stomach and providing relief
from bloating and gas.

PER SERVING

128 calories
1g fat (of which trace saturates)
30g carbohydrate
0.1g salt
vegetarian • gluten free
dairy free

Apple Crush

Preparation Time 5 minutes, plus freezing   **Serves** 1, makes 300ml (½ pint)   **EASY**

175g (6oz) strawberries
150ml (¼ pint) freshly pressed apple
    juice or 2 dessert apples, juiced
strawberry leaves or mint leaves to
    decorate

1 Remove the hulls from the
strawberries, then wash and pat the
fruit dry with kitchen paper. Put on
a tray and freeze for 40 minutes or
until firm.

2 When ready to serve, put the
frozen strawberries into a blender
and pour in the juice. Blend until
smooth and slushy. Pile into a
serving glass and decorate.

TRY SOMETHING DIFFERENT
Use raspberries instead of
strawberries.

PER SERVING
100 calories
trace fat
24g carbohydrate
0g salt
**vegetarian • gluten free
dairy free**

Mango and Oat Smoothie

Preparation Time 5 minutes   **Serves 2**   **EASY**

150g (5oz) natural yogurt
1 small mango, peeled, stoned and
    chopped
2 tbsp oats
4 ice cubes

Put the yogurt into a blender. Put a little chopped mango to one side for the decoration, if you like, and add the remaining mango, oats and ice cubes to the yogurt. Whiz until smooth. Serve immediately, decorated with chopped mango.

HEALTHY TIP

This oaty drink will help satisfy hunger for relatively few calories. The fibre in oats helps stabilise blood sugar levels, lower cholesterol and control the appetite. Mangoes add lots of betacarotene.

TRY SOMETHING DIFFERENT

Instead of mango, use 2 nectarines or peaches, or 175g (6oz) soft seasonal fruits such as raspberries, strawberries or blueberries.

PER SERVING

145 calories
2g fat (of which 1g saturates)
27g carbohydrate
0.2g salt
vegetarian

Summer Berry Smoothie

Preparation Time 10 minutes   **Serves 6, Makes 900ml (1½ pints)**   **EASY**

2 large ripe bananas, about 450g (1lb)
150g (5oz) plain yogurt
500g (1lb 2oz) fresh or frozen summer
   berries

1 Peel and chop the bananas, then put into a blender. Add the yogurt and 150ml (¼ pint) water, then whiz until smooth. Add the berries and whiz to a purée.

2 Strain the mixture through a fine nylon sieve into a large jug, using the back of a ladle to press it through the sieve. Pour into six glasses and serve.

TRY SOMETHING DIFFERENT
Six ripe apricots or 16 ready-to-eat dried apricots or 400g (14oz) canned apricots in natural juice can be used instead of the berries.

PER SERVING
108 calories
1g fat (of which trace saturates)
24g carbohydrate
0.1g salt
vegetarian • gluten free

Cranberry Cooler

Preparation Time 2 minutes   Serves 1   **EASY**

75ml (3fl oz) cranberry juice
ice cubes
lemonade
slice of lemon (optional)

I Pour the cranberry juice into a tall glass half-filled with ice. Top up with lemonade, mix together quickly and finish with a slice of lemon, if you like. Serve.

Index

CONVERSION TABLES

TEMPERATURE

°C	FAN OVEN	GAS MARK	°C	FAN OVEN	GAS MARK
110	90	¼	190	170	5
130	110	½	200	180	6
140	120	1	220	200	7
150	130	2	230	210	8
170	150	3	240	220	9
180	160	4			

LIQUIDS

METRIC	IMPERIAL	METRIC	IMPERIAL
5ml	1 tsp	200ml	7fl oz
15ml	1 tbsp	250ml	9fl oz
25ml	1fl oz	300ml	½ pint
50ml	2fl oz	500ml	18fl oz
100ml	3½fl oz	600ml	1 pint
125ml	4fl oz	900ml	1½ pints
150ml	5fl oz/¼ pint	1 litre	1¾ pints
175ml	6fl oz		

MEASURES

METRIC	IMPERIAL	METRIC	IMPERIAL
5mm	¼in	10cm	4in
1cm	½in	15cm	6in
2cm	¾in	18cm	7in
2.5cm	1in	20.5cm	8in
3cm	1¼in	23cm	9in
4cm	1½in	25.5cm	10in
5cm	2in	28cm	11in
7.5cm	3in	30.5cm	12in